3 4028 08054 3870
HARRIS COUNTY PUBLIC LIBRARY

J 930 Hat
Hattstein, Markus
Prehistory, first empires,
and the ancient world :
from the Stone Age to 900
$46.60
ocn779874145
11/21/2012

D1613789

WITHDRAWN

PREHISTORY, FIRST EMPIRES, AND THE ANCIENT WORLD

FROM THE STONE AGE TO 900 CE

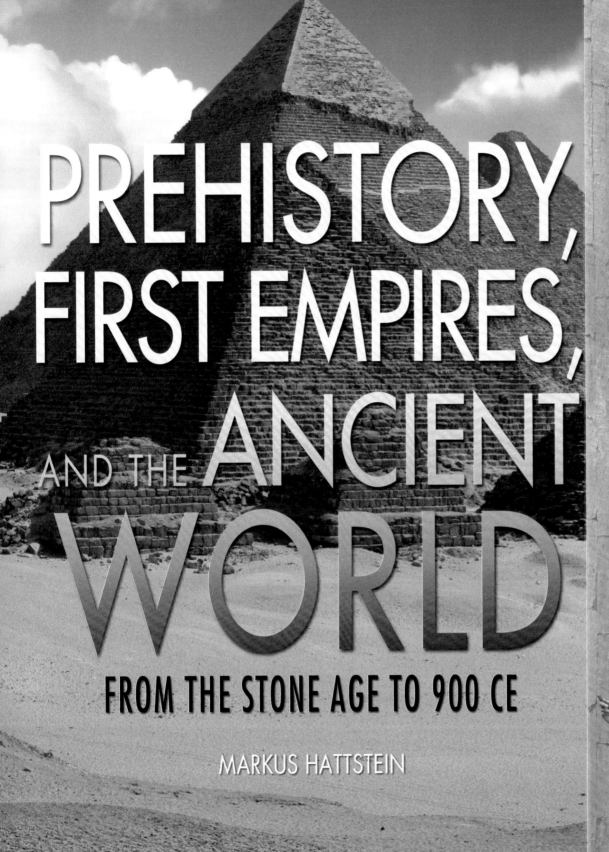

PREHISTORY, FIRST EMPIRES, AND THE ANCIENT WORLD

FROM THE STONE AGE TO 900 CE

MARKUS HATTSTEIN

ROSEN
PUBLISHING®

New York

This edition first published in 2013 by:

The Rosen Publishing Group, Inc.
29 East 21st Street
New York, NY 10010

Additional end matter copyright © 2013 by The Rosen Publishing Group, Inc.

All rights reserved. No part of this book may be reproduced, stored in a retrieval system or transmitted, in any form or by any means, without the prior written consent of the publisher.

Library of Congress Cataloging-in-Publication Data

Hattstein, Markus.
Prehistory, first empires, and the ancient world: from the Stone Age to 900 CE/Markus Hattstein.
     p. cm.—(Witness to history: a visual chronicle of the world)
Includes bibliographical references and index.
ISBN 978-1-4488-7222-0 (library binding)
1. Civilization, Ancient—Juvenile literature. 2. Civilization, Classical—Juvenile literature. I. Title.
CB311.H336 2013
930—dc23

2012010465

Manufactured in the United States of America

CPSIA Compliance Information: Batch #S12YA: For further information, contact Rosen Publishing, New York, New York, at 1-800-237-9932.

Copyright © 2005 Peter Delius Verlag, Berlin
Publisher: Peter Delius

All images from akg-images Berlin/London/Paris and from dpa Deutsche Presse Agentur, Hamburg. For detailed copyright information, please see *The Contemporary World: From 1945 to the 21st Century.*

The publishers would like to express their special gratitude to the team at akg-images Berlin/London/Paris who have made their incredible picture archive accessible and thus the extraordinary illustrations of this book possible.

Contents

The first art by humankind: Cave drawings from the Stone Age **p. 13**

The Sumerians: A high civilization develops in Mesopotamia **p. 26**

The "Tower of Babel": Myth-like cross-cultural significance **p. 33**

The Egyptian pyramids: Grave monuments of the early pharaohs **p. 35**

Imbued with mystery and timeless beauty: the Egyptian queen Nefertiti **p. 37**

The Parthenon temple on the Acropolis: A grand oeuvre of classical Greek architecture representing the power of the Athenian *polis* **p. 79**

One of the great commanders of Rome: Gaius Julius Caesar **p. 106**

The Great Wall of China: Legacy of the first emperors of China **p. 138**

Augustus, the first Roman emperor **p. 108**

Prehistory

until ca. 4000 BCE

When compared to the history of humankind, let alone that of the Earth, the inquiry into the development, roots and relations of humans is very young indeed. We recognize the dawn of recorded history as starting around 4,000 BCE, before which, we call "prehistory." The first empires rose from around 7000 BCE to 200 CE. What historians view as the Ancient World existed from around 2,500 BCE to 900 CE.

Until as recently as the 18th century, the biblical story of human creation—"So God created man in his own image, in the image of God he created him; male and female he created them."—was accepted as an incontestable truth in many parts of the world. Then, however, natural scientists—Charles Darwin the most celebrated among them—appeared. They doubted the special status attributed to humans by the Bible and viewed their development within the context of a theory of evolution. The theory has since been supported and modified by the discovery of skeletal remains, primitive tools, and the remnants of ancient settlements. Their classification, dating, and evaluation using modern technologies has made possible an increasingly accurate perception of human origins.

Reconstruction of a hunting scene from the Old Stone Age, ca. 25,000–30,000 BCE. For the Cro-Magnon man, the mammoth was a desirable prey as use could be made of the meat, hide, and teeth.

THE STONE AGE: THE BEGINNING OF MANKIND

1 Evolution from ape to *Homo sapiens*

FROM THE BEGINNINGS TO CA. 4000 BCE

Even today, no definitive answers to the questions about the origins of mankind have been found. In 1871, Charles Darwin challenged the answers given by the biblical story of creation with his theory of evolution. The evolution theory suggested that man had ❶ descended from anthropoids. Africa, site of the earliest hominoid discoveries, is considered to be "the cradle of mankind." The evolution of today's *Homo sapiens* can be traced by the trail of skeletal remains, tools, and the remnants of settlements—such as cave paintings—that have been left throughout the ages.

■ It All Began in Africa

With the development of the theory of evolution and the corroborating identification and classification of hominoid finds since the mid-19th century, the hypothesis of an African origin for humans is generally accepted today.

The ❷ story of man's origins and evolution was the subject of fierce controversy throughout the 19th century. There were two schools of thought. According to the creationist doctrine of the monotheistic religions, man had been created by God, after which he did not evolve. In opposition to this stood Charles Darwin's theo-

2 Evolution from *Australopithecus anamensis* (blue) to *Homo habilis*, *Homo rudolfensis*, *Homo erectus*, and archaic *Homo sapiens* to *Homo neanderthalensis* and *Homo sapiens sapiens*.

ry of evolution, which stated that life was ❸, ❹, ❺, ❻ continually evolving and emphasized the connection between human origins and the animal kingdom, specifically primates. Darwin's theory proposed a progressive refining of the intellectual, social, and creative abilities of early man. He illustrated this theory with reference to the increasing use of tools and man's lifestyle shift from hunter-gatherer to farmer and animal breeder.

Simultaneously the 19th century saw the beginning of a systematic notation and classification of hominoid fossils and stone

The Divisions of the Prehistoric Periods

Prehistory is divided into the Old Stone Age or Paleolithic period, the New Stone Age or Neolithic period, the Bronze Age, and the Iron Age:

Early or Lower Paleolithic: ca. 2.5 million BCE–250,000 BCE
Middle Paleolithic: ca. 250,000–30,000 BCE
Late or Upper Paleolithic: ca. 30,000–10,000 BCE
Neolithic Period: ca. 10,000/8000–4000/1800 BCE
Bronze Age: ca. 4000–700 BCE (Middle East), ca. 1800–800 BCE (Europe)
Iron Age: from ca. 1100/800 BCE

Mankind's prehistory occurred over the Quaternary period of geologic time:
Early Pleistocene: ca. 1.8 million–800,000 BCE
Middle Pleistocene: ca. 800,000–127,000 BCE
Late Pleistocene: ca. 127,000–10,000 BCE
Holocene (post–Ice Age): ca. 10,000 BCE to the present

Paleolithic scraper

tools. Of particular concern was the determination of the age of the fossils; however, accurately dating the finds only became reliable with the discovery of the radiocarbon dating method in 1947

by Professor Willard F. Libby of the University of Chicago.

As the oldest hominoids were found in East Africa, a theory proposing Africa as the "cradle of mankind" emerged. This hypothesis was substantiated by the discovery of the "Taung Baby," a 2.2-million-year-old *Australopithecus africanus* in 1924.

From left: (3) *Australopithecus anamensis* (ca. 4.2 million BCE), (4) *Australopithecus afarensis* (ca. 4–3 million BCE), (5) *Australopithecus africanus* (ca. 2.8–2 million BCE), and (6) *Homo erectus* (ca. 1.9 million– 200,000 BCE), reconstructions.

ca. 6 million years ago	*Orrorin tugenensis*	ca. 4.2–3.9 million years ago	*Australopithecus*
ca. 5.5–4 million years ago	*Ardipithecus ramidus*	ca. 4–3 million years ago	*Australopithecus afarensis*

■ Early Hominoids

According to the most recent discoveries, man's beginnings can be traced back more than six million years. Through a succession of progressive stages, the earliest hominoids developed increasingly greater skills. Slowly man began to leave his African "cradle."

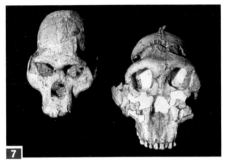

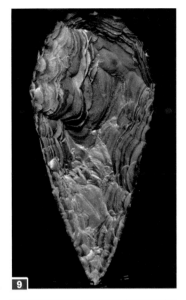

left: Skulls of *Australopithecus africanus* and *Australopithecus boisei*
right: Skull of an Australopithecus with added lower jaw

Following Darwin's theory, paleontologists looked for a "missing link" between man and his nearest relative in the animal world, the chimpanzee. Since then, many hominoid species have been discovered, not all of which are direct ancestors of the modern *Homo sapiens*.

For a long time, the *Ardipithecus ramidus*, which lived 5.5–4 million years ago in present-day Ethiopia, was considered the earliest hominoid. In 2000, however, *Orrorin tugenensis* ("millennium man") was found. It lived about six million years ago in Kenya. The next stage after the Ardipithecus was the ❼, ❽ Australopithecus, which lived 3.7–1.3 million years ago and was already using primitive pebble tools. The *Australopithecus afarensis* became famous through "Lucy," whose skeletal remains were found in 1974.

The next stage of development was the *Homo* genus. *Homo habilis*, which lived 1.5–2.3 million years ago, had a larger brain and ate a broader diet than did previous hominoids. The new diet included meat and animal fats—until then the hominoid diet had been purely vegetarian. *Homo habilis* was the first hominoid to leave the forest and ⓫ hunt in the savannas. He is credited with the earliest hewn stone tools, which were probably used to break open bones to get at the marrow.

Homo ergaster (*Homo erectus*), which lived approximately 1.8–1 million BCE, settled throughout the African continent and was the first hominoid that resembled modern man in size and proportions. He walked erect only, stored food supplies, and made stone artifacts. About 1.6 million years ago, he made the first completely reworked ❾, ❿ hand axe that also functioned as a pick. *Homo ergaster* was also the first hominid to

top and above: Flint hand axes, worked tools, Paleolithic period

travel beyond Africa, gradually populating the nearer parts of Asia and Europe.

"Lucy"

No hominoid discovery has elicited such a sensation as the almost complete, 43-inch-high (109-cm-high) skeleton of a female Australopithecus afarensis found in the Afar region of northeastern Ethiopia in 1974. She was named "Lucy" after a Beatles song that had been playing in the research camp. The press promptly named her the "missing link." She belongs to man's phylogenetic line and possesses all the anatomical prerequisites for walking erect. Her bones and teeth provided valuable information about her lifestyle.

Australopithecines hunting on the plains, Paleolithic period

ca. 2.8–2 million years ago	*Australopithecus africanus*		ca. 1.9 million–200,000 years ago	*Homo erectus*
	ca. 2.3–1.5 million years ago	*Homo habilis*	ca. 1.6 million years ago	First flint axe tool

■ Territorial Expansion

Spreading out of Africa, early man initially settled in Asia and Europe, and then in Australia and the Americas. Due to the climate, it was primarily the robust Ice Age hunters—represented by the Neanderthal and the Cro-Magnon man—who were able to establish themselves in Europe.

Neanderthal fossils

It was long believed that early man did not leave his African homeland until ca. 1.4 million years ago. However, in the 1990s, a 1.7–1.8 million-year-old hominoid skull was found in Georgia in western Asia.

The oldest *Homo erectus* fossils have been found in Asia; "Java man," named after the island where the first example was discovered, is today dated to 1.7 mil-

Skull of "Peking man," Middle Pleistocene period

lion years BCE, while ❷ "Peking man," found in China, is dated to 600,000–200,000 BCE. By that time, *Homo erectus* was probably already using fire and possibly a form of human speech. *Homo erectus* was also the first hominid

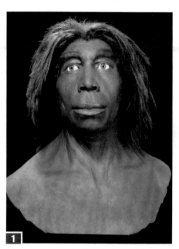

Homo heidelbergensis hunting

to live in Europe, which was at that time characterized by extreme ice ages. The European form of *Homo erectus* is named ❸ *Homo heidelbergensis* after a find near Heidelberg in 1907. They are thought to have lived 400,000–800,000 years ago.

The Late Pleistocene era (127,000–10,000 BCE) was the age of the Neanderthal. This new hominid, considered to be either a side branch of *Homo sapiens* or a separate subspecies, came about through a series of evolutionary stages and died out about 30,000 years ago. Since the first finding of a Neanderthal skullcap in 1856, this has become the best known example of primitive man. ❶, ❹ Neanderthals were stocky Ice Age hunters with the greatest skull volume of all hominoids known to date. Their wide nose and large nasal cavity were well suited to the cold climate.

Around 40,000 years ago, modern *Homo sapiens*, in the form of the Cro-Magnon man, finally migrated out of Africa to Europe. This direct ancestor of today's man inhabited modern-day Israel as early as 100,000 BCE ("Proto-Cro-Magnon"). They were taller, more slender and had more stamina than the Neanderthals, but the two coexisted in parallel in Europe for about 10,000 years. Many theories concerning their coexistence and the causes of the Neanderthal's displacement have been suggested. It

Homo neanderthalensis (ca. 150,000–30,000 BCE), sculpted reconstruction of a Neanderthal

is generally assumed that there was interaction and a mutual influence between the two hominid genera, but interbreeding of the two is considered highly unlikely.

At least 60,000 years ago, although possibly much earlier, early man settled the Australian subcontinent by way of New Guinea. The first hominids did not reach the Americas, however, until just 11,500 years ago. Ice Age hunters came to the continent via

Following the classification in 1863 of a partial skull found in a cave in the Neander Valley near Düsseldorf in 1856, one of man's early relatives became known as the Neanderthal. Researchers later determined that previously unclassifiable bones discovered in Engis, Belgium, in 1829–1830 and again at Kalpe (Gibraltar) in 1848 belonged to this hominid. The Kalpe skull is much better preserved than the skullcap that was finally identified, and the Neanderthal should perhaps have been named the "Kalpe."

above: Skull found at Kalpe

Siberia and Alaska. The oldest finds discovered in America are worked stone arrowheads and spear points. These, known as "Clovis points," are thought to stem from the Clovis culture.

Neanderthals hunting cave bears

■ Campsites and the Use of Tools

The extent of man's development can be gauged by the tools and hunting weapons he used. Another important indicator of this progress is the evidence of dwelling places that housed ever larger groups in increasingly permanent shelter.

Alongside skeletal remains, stone artifacts are the best preserved witnesses of the early period of man's existence. The hominids of the Lower Paleolithic made use of materials readily available to them. The first ❻ stone tools were fashioned by striking one stone with another or with a stick to chip flakes off it, shaping the stone into a tool such as a ❺ hand axe. Alternatively, flakes were used to scrape or ❽ chisel the stone into shape. In the Middle Paleolithic, the demands of the hunt necessitated improvements

5

Various stages in the production of the stone axe, worked in the Neolithic period

6   Neolithic axe and hammer

in hand weapons and precisely worked blade points. This resulted in the "thin blade technology"— long, narrow blades of stone or horn used as spear points or harpoons.

Early man used caves for shelter, though possibly not before the discovery of fire in the Lower Paleolithic period, as the caves were often inhabited by cave bears and wild cats. Initially the caves were probably used only in the cold seasons, but some ❼,❾ larger caves might have been lived in year-round as early as the end of the Lower Paleolithic period.

During the Paleolithic, early people first made their homes in the open—often near rivers or lakes—where they probably built mud huts with leaf roofs. Later dwellings were dug out of the ground. Tent-like constructions made with skins stretched over wooden posts or mammoth tusks began to appear during the Upper Paleolithic period. The dwelling sites of the groups probably changed with the seasons as the groups migrated, but there were also long-term habitation sites such as that uncovered at Willendorf, Austria. The living area was lined with stone slabs and animal skins. Evidence of houses and permanent settlements first appears during the Neolithic period.

Mysterious Pierced Staffs

Among the finds associated with Cro-Magnon man are elaborately decorated bone or horn staffs. All of them are pierced. They were first assumed to be cult status symbols and described as "staffs of office." Now it is accepted that they were implements for straightening the stone or bone points set in spear shafts. Cro-Magnons also used spear throwers or atlatls—staffs with a hook on one end; spears were placed against the hook. These increased throwing distance and striking force of the spears.

right: Pierced staffs by Cro-Magnon man

8   Flint daggers

7

Cave life in the Paleolithic period

9

Animal herds depicted in cave painting, France, Lower Paleolithic

■ Fire and the Hunt

The transition from forager to hunter broadened man's diet. In addition, it demanded teamwork; it required an evolution of man's social abilities to enable coordination within an effective hunting group. With the taming of fire, man learned to harness a force of nature. This and associated social changes are considered to be decisive in the development of modern man.

Flintstone found at the Messel excavation site, Kalkriese, Germany

The earliest hominoids were probably vegetarians who gathered plants and fruits and unearthed roots and tubers with digging instruments. The expansion of the diet to include meat, which accompanied the move to hunting—although the early ❹ hunters were definitely scavengers as well—was paralleled by a huge development in social intelligence. The hunt required collective effort, skill, strategy, and caution. It required communication within a group and possibly the definition of territories through agreements with other groups. One hunting strategy used by early man was the battue, in which the animals were driven into ravines or off cliffs. The essential knowledge of the ❸ prey and its habits also undoubtedly led to the early hunters' first awareness of their superiority over the other animals.

The most important ❷ weapon in the Lower and Middle Paleolithic was the pointed wooden spear or lance, which initially was thrust and later thrown. The bow and arrow did not appear until the Neolithic period. Shortly afterward the dog was domesticated to assist in the hunt.

The preferred prey was the aurochs (or wisent) and red deer in

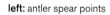

4 Base of hunting group ca. 10,000 BCE, reconstruction sketch after finds

Hunting Techniques

The use of wooden spears for hunting is evidenced by the many animal skeletons that have been found pierced by lances and spears. Near Hannover, Germany, for example, 400,000-year-old horse skeletons were found with three-foot-long lances embedded in their sides. Hunting scenes showing animals shot with spears and arrows are popular subjects of cave paintings. In the wisent hunt in Europe and the bison hunt in prehistoric America, individual animals would be isolated and then hunted. Nets into which animals were driven were also used in the battue for wild horses, red deer, and reindeer.

Mammoth hunt by Cro-Magnon hunting group

left: antler spear points   **right:** Bison sculpture, bone, both Lower Paleolithic

Europe, reindeer and moose in the northern lands, and antelope in Africa. Early man also hunted pachyderms such as the mammoth, forest elephant, and woolly rhinoceros. Cave bears, which played a special role in their cults, were also hunted. These animals became extinct during the transition to the Neolithic period.

The use of fire, verifiable in numerous places as early as the Lower Paleolithic, is seen by many researchers as the truly decisive step in the evolution of modern man. At first, early man probably made use of prairie fire and fire resulting from lighting, until he learned how to create it with ❶

flint stone and control it himself. Thus, he took control of a force of nature for his own protection and as a weapon. He also used it for cooking and roasting his food. Furthermore, it was probably the discovery of fire that made it possible for him to use caves as dwelling places.

Many theories about the division of labor between the sexes during this stage of human evolution have been proposed. Theories have suggested that this may have been the point at which the distinction between the male as hunter, and the female as gatherer and custodian of the fire and children, was first made.

ca. 2.3–1.5 million years ago | Transition to the hunt   **ca. 1.8–1 million years ago** | Development of communication into speech

ca. 2.2 million–130,000 years ago | Wooden spear used as hunting weapon

■ Language and Burial of the Dead

Mankind's progress also involved the evolution of mental and intellectual abilities. The learning and use of a symbolic language, together with the development of the early death cults, are considered milestones in this respect.

A "psychological revolution" took place hand in hand with the technical and social development of early man. The formation of social groups made it necessary for individuals to express their conscious concerns and feelings

6

7

top: Megalith graves, reconstruction drawing
above: Dolmens (megaliths) in Evora, Portugal

as well as to recognize differences. It is assumed that a basic awareness of the self and others and a capacity for simple speech were present from *Homo ergaster* onward.

Language serves as a way of transmitting thoughts, using

sounds and words to denote meanings (ideas). Thus, language would have required an ability to conceptualize the ideas communicated through words and symbols. Symbols are characters that—unlike pictographs—do not need to resemble the things they symbolize. These symbols are associated with certain agreed-upon (conventional) meanings, which are then learned by the members of the group.

The use of language therefore implies the parallel development of all these faculties between themselves and others. However, due to the lack of written evidence, only indirect conclusions as to the exact nature and extent of this development are possible.

A higher degree of intellectual abstraction was also a prerequisite for the burial of the dead by early man. With knowledge of the burial rites comes the supposition of an awareness of the mortality of man.

The special burial of human skulls and lower jawbones was

practiced as early as the Lower Paleolithic period, particularly by the groups inhabiting present-day China. Middle Paleolithic cave dwellers certainly seem to have performed burial rites. This is evidenced by the ❽ human skeletons found arranged in a way that suggests the dead were buried lying on their backs or squatting, with stone tools as burial objects. The skeletons, and particularly the skulls, were frequently covered with ❺, ❻, ❼ stone slabs. It is unclear whether this was to

8

Skeleton excavated from middle Paleolithic burial site, Les Eyzies, France

protect the dead or to protect the living from the spirits of the dead. ❿ Special treatment of the skull has been noted almost everywhere, often with the brain having been removed through holes bored in the rear of the skull.

In Upper Paleolithic times, the bodies of the dead and especially the skulls were generally sprinkled with ocher, a red pigment, and buried in separate stone encasements. Precious ❾ jewelry and finely worked, unused ⓫ stone implements have been found as burial objects inside the skeletons. Teeth with holes bored into them have also been found inside the graves and were probably worn as pendants.

5

Tumuli (burial mounds) made of stone slabs with stone engravings, France

Burial Rites and Skull Holes

During the Upper Paleolithic, the dead were buried in graves dug especially for this purpose. These were often in the middle of the dwelling area or near a fire site. Presumably the dead were buried there only after the group had moved on.

The circular holes in the back of many skulls are a greater riddle. Probably the brains of the deceased were removed through these holes. However, some skulls have been found in which the cranial bones had partially healed or grown back at the edges, suggesting that the person lived for some time after "trepanation" was performed.

Skeleton of a Neolithic woman buried in a sitting position, found in Backaskog, Sweden

9

10

11

left: Zoomorphic mask; **middle:** human skull with ivory inlay;
right: burial objects from a grave of the Globular Amphora culture, near Berlin

■ Religion and Cults

A series of prehistoric finds indicates the existence of ritual cults and sacrificial ceremonies. Opinions diverge widely as to whether a form of religion had already developed. It is generally assumed, however, that there was a link between the primitive cults, hunting mysticism, and the preparation of food.

Among the indications of man's psychological evolution, a fundamental one is the emergence of the belief in a transcendental power to whom sacrifices must be made.

Another is the consciousness of a special relationship between man and animal, hunter and prey (animalism), and man and his en-

"Venus of Willendorf," statuette, Upper Paleolithic period

Female idol, Neolithic period

vironment. It is widely accepted that the earliest "religions" or cults were associated with hunting. One of the oldest cult rituals, evidenced since the end of the Lower Paleolithic period, was the ceremonial sacrifice of animals. Examples of this include female reindeer that were submerged in lakes and moors with stones and wooden stakes in their open breast cavities. The buried skeletal remains of animals, especially mammoths, draped with jewelry have also been unearthed.

The cave dwellers of the Middle Paleolithic decorated and reworked the skulls of cave bears and buried them or stood them up behind stone walls. This practice has led to the supposition that a particular cave bear cult existed.

Parallel to the shaman concepts of Siberian hunting tribes, some researchers interpret the decoration and special treatment of animal bones as either a "compensation ritual" for the killing of the animal or an expression of early man's belief that through the burial, the prey would "arise anew." Others theorize that the early humans were sacrificing a portion of the kill to a hunting god or animal totem. Related to this are the representations of half-human creatures, such as the "Sorcerer of ❶, ❹ Trois-Frères," which have been the subject of particularly controversial interpretations.

Cult rituals may also have developed around the dividing up of the kill among the group and the preparation of food around the

Rock drawing of a human figure, possibly a shamanistic dancer

hearth. Possible evidence of this are the many ❷, ❸ female statuettes with voluptuous forms that have been found around hearths dating back to the Upper Paleolithic. These probably symbolize either fertility or a mother deity.

Another controversial subject is the religious or cult interpretation of the art of early man. The representations of game and hunting themes found in cave paintings may have been intended to invoke success in the hunt or protection against dangerous game.

The "Sorcerer of Trois-Frères"

No cave painting has provoked as many different attempts at interpretation as the famous "Sorcerer of Trois-Frères." The name itself is rejected by many researchers. The sorcerer is one of three hybrid creatures discovered on a cave wall in 1916. The painting depicts all three creatures with animal heads and front limbs. The rear part of the body, however, is human. Some researchers, referring to shaman practices in other cultures, see this figure as a "medicine man" dressed in animal skins and an animal mask. They suggest he might be performing a mystical hunting dance as a supplication for the successful outcome of the hunt. Other researchers doubt this theory and see him simply as an imaginative cross between man and animal, which testifies to the creativity of early man.

The "Sorcerer of Trois-Frères," cave painting, ca. 14,000 BCE

Shaman from the cave at Trois-Frères in French Pyrenees, Paleolithic period

ca. 2.3–1.5 million years ago | First animal sacrifices and cult rituals   ca. 3000 BCE | First family and clan cave graves

ca. 3000 BCE | Development of high religions

■ The Art of Early Man

The best known examples of the diverse and impressive artwork of early man are cave paintings. Predominant motifs include game animals and representations of people. Prehistoric art forms—including stone engraving, carvings, and figurines—are diverse in style and allow for a variety of interpretations.

6

Horse, bone carving, Middle Paleolithic

7

Fish, bone carving, Middle Paleolithic

❺ Cave paintings and ❾ wall engravings first appeared during the Upper Paleolithic period. The caves of France and northern Spain are particularly rich in art. For a long time, it was believed that motivation for these artworks originated from observation of the cracks and fissures on cave walls, which inspired early man to create first geometric designs and then drawings. However, the painted looping lines have been shown to be no older than the developed picture motifs. Thus from the start the artists must have been aware of the possibility of representing their environment in images.

Generally, it is assumed that the cave paintings did not primarily serve an aesthetic purpose, nor were they the work of one gifted individual but rather represented the world of the group. The dominant theme of the cave paintings is game animals, all depicted in profile and in motion. The rare human figures appear abstract by comparison. The figures are always standing alone and are not uniform in style. Realistic pictographic representations can be seen alongside stark abstractions of human and animal images with overly emphasized details. Another special subject in the caves is the ❽ human handprint.

Even more numerous than the paintings are the cave and rock engravings that occasionally overlap and portray themes similar to the paintings. Engravings are also found on stone, antler horn, and animal bone.

In addition to paintings, sculptured pieces were also produced in the Upper Paleolithic. Many ❻,❼ small sculptures made of limestone, soapstone, bone, and antler horn—as well as baked-clay figurines—have been found. The smaller ones were probably worn as pendants. The statuettes most often depict ❿ females and are considered to have been fertility symbols. The figures vary from coarse cone shapes to ones with well-detailed facial features.

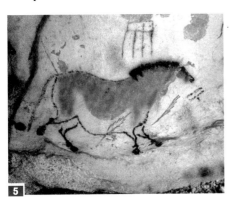

5

Horse, cave painting at Lascaux in France, Lower Paleolithic

Painting Techniques in the Upper Paleolithic

Cave drawing in Altamira, Spain

Upper Paleolithic cave paintings can be found in Western Europe, particularly in France and Spain, the Urals, and Siberia. Cave artists used various iron ochers dissolved in water for coloration. Egg whites, fat, plant juice, and blood created shades from red to yellow and brown (visible in paintings of the wisent of Altamira, Spain, for example) were used in the paintings. Black tones were achieved with animal charcoal or manganese.

Handprints in the caves usually appear in black or red. In some cases, the artist's hand was painted with a liquid color and then pressed against the cave wall (a positive print); in others, the hand was placed on the wall and paint was sprayed around it so that when the hand was removed a negative handprint remained.

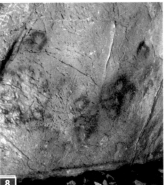

8

Handprint, cave wall

10

Statue, mammoth bone, Paleolithic

9

Fighting ibex, cave wall engraving, Le Roc de Sers in France, Lower Paleolithic

■ The "Neolithic Revolution"

During the Neolithic period, a rapid progression of human culture took place—primarily due to the introduction of agriculture and animal domestication. The new sedentary lifestyle demanded new technologies and shaped the beginnings of the modern form of settlement.

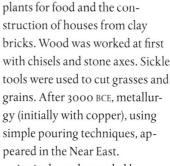

The Neolithic period saw a rapid development in many aspects of human culture, characterized by ❺ man's attempts to establish independence from the vagaries of the environment in which he lived. This process was made possible primarily by the broadening of the diet, which was linked to agriculture and the domestication of animals and occurred as a result of sedentary life in ❸, ❹ houses and communities. The hunt continued to play a role in providing nutrition, yet the supply of food was no longer completely dependent on the success of the hunt as there were now alternative food sources.

There was a parallel technological revolution. The introduction of fired ❶, ❷ ceramic vessels, initially used for storing food supplies, defined whole cultural communities, such as the Middle European "Linear Ceramic Culture." Advances also included the use of rotating grindstones and mortars for the processing of plants for food and the construction of houses from clay bricks. Wood was worked at first with chisels and stone axes. Sickle tools were used to cut grasses and grains. After 3000 BCE, metallurgy (initially with copper), using simple pouring techniques, appeared in the Near East.

Agriculture demanded long-term planning as well as knowledge of climatic periods and seasonal cycles. The cultivation of fertile alluvial land began, particularly in Mesopotamia and along the Nile. Goats, sheep, pigs, and later cattle were domesticated for man's use.

New cults also formed around plants and grains. Many Neolithic houses had their own cult niche where offerings such as grain, fruits, and animal remains have been found. The surviving clay, stone, and metal statuettes are thought to be votive offerings, as many have raised arms or open hands in an attitude of supplication. Some represent God.

1 Painted vase and pottery stemming from Neolithic cultures

View of Stone Age house interior

Most Neolithic settlements had separate cult edifices. In the Near East, there were early temple complexes. The transition to advanced civilizations began even before 3000 BCE in these regions with the development of script or hieroglyphics and of religious monarchies.

2 Ceramics stemming from the Funnel Beaker Culture

4 Early Stone Age family in a hut

The "Linear Ceramic Culture"

The oldest culture of the Paleolithic period in Central and Southern Europe is known as the Linear Ceramic Culture. It stretched from eastern France to Hungary in the fifth millenium BCE. The people lived in closed settlements with nave houses and pursued agriculture and animal husbandry.

The culture was named after the ribbon-like decorations typically used on their pottery. These decorations were made up of solid lines and dashes. The Linear Ceramic Culture tribes buried their dead positioned toward the sun, on their side, and with legs drawn up in a sleep-like pose. Some researchers infer from this that they had the concept of an afterlife. Skeletal remains have also been found in a supine position with outstretched arms, reminiscent of certain types of statuettes.

5 Reconstruction of Similaun man "Ötzi" found in the Similaun glacier, Italy

■ The Tell Cultures

Modern village and city cultures developed from the Tell (Arabic for "hill") settlements of the Near East. These give evidence of a social differentiation between the inhabitants as well as an organized economic life. These communities, identifiable mostly through their characteristic pottery, demonstrate a fluid transition to early advanced civilizations.

The peoples of the earliest known village-like hill communities in the Near East are called Tell Cultures. As a rule, new settlements were built on top of older ones. However, it is possible to date cultural peaks and distinctive features

6

Stamp, Late Paleolithic period

decorated its ceramics with axes or crosses.

Given the importance of ceramics in determining social and cultural development, a division is made between the "Aceramic Neolithic" (ca. 8000–6500 BCE) and the "Ceramic Neolithic" after about 6500 BCE.

The Tell Cultures displayed varied building styles—both round and angular—and pottery forms. The discovery of ❻ seals and counting markers indicates an early organization and control of economic life and trade, as well as sophisticated property-ownership relations, which paved the

way for more advanced civilizations and societies.

The Obed Culture in southern Babylon and Ur (ca. 5000–4000 BCE) possessed ❼ houses divided

7

Model of a building with animal skulls on the roof, Neolithic period

into rooms ("middle room houses"), early pottery wheels, seals, stamps, and cult and administrative buildings. It is believed that a cult and administration elite had emerged within the community—a sign of an advanced early civilization. These people dug a system of complex and strategically placed irrigation canals, and signs of a communication net-

8

Maternal goddess, statue, Anatolia, Neolithic period

by excavating deep shafts through the layers. ❽ Çatal Hüyük in Anatolia proved to be a particularly rich site for excavation. Many settlements were enclosed by protective stone walls, which testifies to competition between the sedentary agricultural communities and roaming nomad peoples.

Often the different cultures can be distinguished by their charac-teristic pottery forms or ceramic decorations: The Syrian ❾, ❿ Tell Halaf Culture, for example, which dominated the Mesopotamian area in the fifth and fourth millenium BCE,

Çatal Hüyük

The large city-like complexes in Anatolia of the early Neolithic period are a treasure trove for archaeologists because of their size and the variety of artifacts found. The clay brick houses possess central rooms that are usually decorated with painted figures, relief figures, and bull heads on the walls. The houses are so close together that the inhabitants had to enter them through a hole in the roof. Clay platforms are found along the walls under which the skeletal remains of the dead were buried. It is therefore assumed that some of the rooms were used for ancestor-worship. Numerous small sculpted figures indicate the worship of two pairs of deities and sacred animals. The inhabitants used wood and stone vessels but no pottery.

work and paths linking the communities have been found. The transition to the metropolitan civilizations of Mesopotamia began with the emergence of urban cultures in the Uruk period around 4000 BCE.

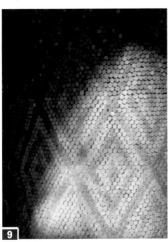

9

Detail from altar, castle of Guzana, Tell Halaf ruins, Syria, from ca. 800 BCE

10

Hill of ruins of Tell Mardich in Syria: Partial view of the excavation area, showing what was probably a palace during the Bronze Age

First Empires

ca. 7000 BCE—200 CE

The Middle East was the cradle of mankind's first advanced civilizations. In Egypt and the Fertile Crescent, which extends in an arc from the north of the Arabian Peninsula east through Palestine to Mesopotamia, the first state structures emerged in parallel with the further development of animal husbandry, agriculture, trade, and writing. The first great empires, such as those of the Egyptian pharaohs, the Babylonians, the Assyrians, and the Persians, evolved at the beginning of the third millennium BCE, out of small communities usually clustered around a city. Similar development also occurred on the Indian subcontinent and in China, where quite distinct early advanced civilizations took shape as well.

The golden mask of Tutankhamun, a jewel of ancient Egyptian artwork, showing the pharaoh in a ceremonial robe decorated with the heraldic animals, the vulture and cobra, ca. 1340 BCE

1 Bedouin shepherd with sheep in Jordan

2 Cattle herd at a river in Khuzistan, Iran

3 Camel and rider, ca. 700 BCE

THE FIRST GREAT CIVILIZATIONS

Long before Greek and Roman antiquity laid the foundations for Western culture, high civilizations were emerging in the Orient, particularly in the fertile "land between the rivers"—Mesopotamia. One of the most important preconditions for the development of such advanced cultures was the development of agriculture and livestock breeding, as both of these demanded increasing in-vestment in organizational structures. The early history of the Ancient Orient was also shaped by the immigration and settlement of ❶ nomad peoples. The relationship between the nomads and the settled peoples was long regarded in terms of certain tribes conquering the lands of others. However, the immigration of small tribes often occurred over the course of centuries and was more of an infiltration. A mutual permeation of culture and religion took place, but so did conflicts over natural resources such as grazing land and water for irrigation.

The transition from small-animal husbandry to ❷ livestock breeding contributed significantly to the settling of nomadic tribes in the Near East.

5 Engraving of carpenter, Babylon, second–third c. BCE

Cattle—which were incorporated into religion as ❹ cult symbols for strength and fertility—were used as draft animals as well as farm and pasture animals. The donkey and particularly the ❸ camel were also domesticated for riding and as pack animals. The camel became the main form of transportation in the caravan trade, while horses were used primarily in warfare.

Wheat and barley were the main crops cultivated. The invention of the field plow, cleverly devised ❻ irrigation systems, and dams and canals to protect against floods all increased efficiency and production within the settlements. The other important task of the growing communities was defense against outside enemies who were competing for resources.

The increasing number and complexity of tasks led to social differentiation between farmers, ❺, ❶ craftsmen, warriors, and administrators. In addition, there were ❼ priests who performed religious rites and also attempted to determine the favorable times for sowing and harvest through calculations, prophecies, and astrology.

Sumerian bull's head

Administration and Religion in the Ancient Orient

Early communities eventually developed into strictly hierarchical class-based societies. The officials, as administrative specialists, held a key position. They controlled the municipal trade and agrarian production. Central ❽ grain silos were usually placed in religious structures, and for this reason it is assumed that the state's property and administration was also concentrated

6 Cultivation of grain on artificially irrigated fields

7 Statue of a priest

8 Ruins of a grain silo

9 Byblos, ruins of the obelisk temple

10 Trade record in cuneiform script, ca. second c. BCE

here (that is, a "temple economy"). The ruler, a king or city prince, had a special role. He was the initiator of communal work projects as well as the head of administrative and religious activities. He administered the land in the name of the gods and acted as their earthly representative.

⓬ Religion in Mesopotamia was very complex and, as a result of the steady arrival and settlement of nomadic peoples, new elements were constantly added, and others changed over time, thus testifying to its integrative capacity. Various local heroes, such as Gilgamesh of Uruk (ca. 2700–2600 BCE), or city tutelary deities, such as Marduk in Babylon, rose to prominence in the pantheon of the gods with the support of the community. For example, Marduk was declared chief god under Hammurapi of Babylon (1792–1750 BCE). The Achaemenid ruler Cyrus the Great accepted the acclamation of the Marduk priesthood in Babylon and thereby renewed the Babylonian Kingdom. After his victory over Darius III in the battle at Gaugamela, Alexander the

11 Statuette of a baker, ninth–eighth century BCE

Great paid tribute to the city god Marduk in 331 BCE. His rule thereby acquired an element of divine legitimacy. In this way the conqueror made himself the successor of the Babylonian kings.

The Significance and Development of Writing

The change in the cultural development of man that resulted from the invention of writing cannot be overestimated. The earliest known script has been found on small clay tablets that were used in **⓾** commercial transactions. Early Sumerian cuneiform writing developed out of pictographs in which—as in Egyptian **⓭** hieroglyphics—the pictograph resembled the object it was meant to represent. It was a complicated system that was mastered only by specially trained scribes who therefore had a powerful position within the social hierarchy.

Pictographs differed from the earlier symbols and paintings by cavemen because they relied on the systematic coherency of the writing, rather than oral tradition, for the transmission of meaning. The desire to sim-

plify writing led from pictographs to cuneiform script. Characters expressing a sound or a group of sounds replaced the object symbols—and word-phonetic spelling developed. At first a syllabary script emerged in which a character represented a single syllable or combined syllables. Around 2500 BCE, the Akkadians adopted Sumerian syllable writing, which already existed in cuneiform, and expanded it with their own characters. Later, the Elamites, Hurrites, Hittites, Urartians, and other peoples adopted this writing system, and by 1400 BCE, it was in use as the common script for international trade.

The most abstract step in the development of writing was the creation of an alphabetic script assigning characters to sounds. With this method, an unlimited number of combinations can be formed with a small number of phonetic characters. The first scripts composed purely of phonetic characters were developed in the Canaanite metropolises of Ugarit (ca. 1400 BCE) and **⓽** Byblos (ca. 1000 BCE), with alphabets of 30 and 22 letters, respectively. Like all Semitic script, the alphabets of the Canaanites and their successors, the Phoenicians—which became the foundation for Israelite, Syrian, Arabic, and Greek alphabets—had no vowels.

The Greek alphabet was the first to include vowel characters, but it otherwise adopted the form and order of the letters from previous alphabets, as well as their use as numeric symbols. The oldest Greek texts are also written, like the old Semitic texts, from right to left.

12 Sacrificial procession for the goddess Inanna with a bull and other sacrifices, stone vase from Uruk

13 Egyptian hieroglyphics in a mural in the tomb of Haremhab, in the Valley of the Kings in Western Thebes, Egypt

MIGRATION OF PEOPLES 3000–1200 BCE

While urban culture was emerging in the Near East, mass ❷ migrations began to take place in Asia. In some cases, these continued for well over a thousand years—lasting longer than the migrations of late antiquity. From 3000 BCE onward, Semitic peoples from the south and Indo-European peoples from the north migrated into Mesopotamia. At the beginning of the first millennium BCE, the appearance of these seagoing and equestrian peoples triggered great turmoil.

Nomad woman herding sheep in Ararat, the Caucasus

■ Semitic and Indo-European Peoples

In approximately 3000 BCE, a shift of power took place in the Near East as the result of the immigration of Semitic and Indo-European tribes into the area.

Out of Arabia, Semitic tribes pushed in several waves into the area of the "Fertile Crescent"— that crucial swath of land reaching from Mesopotamia over the coasts of the Eastern Mediterranean and into Egypt. Around 2400 BCE the Semitic Akkadians subjugated the Sumerian city-states and created an empire. The Canaanites settled in Palestine and founded city-states, as did the Amorites in Syria. The Amorites also established the first dynasty of Babylon and ruled the old Babylonian Empire. In the 13th century BCE the Aramaeans, Semitic ancestors of the Israelites, appeared on the scene. They won control from the Assyrians in Syria and Palestine (in the kingdoms of David and Solomon, for example), increasing their influence in Mesopotamia after 1100 BCE. The Aramaic Chaldeans ultimately defeated the Assyrians and founded the Neo-Babylonian Kingdom (625–539 BCE).

Paralleling this Semitic migration, Iranian Indo-European peoples moved through the ❶ Caucasus into Mesopotamia, beginning with the Gutian invasion in 2150 BCE that dissolved the Akkadian empire. The Hurrites made up the upper class in the Mitanni kingdom (16th–14th century BCE; which was eventually conquered by the Hittites, an Indo-European tribe that settled in Asia Minor around 2000 BCE. The Kassites, who had moved down from Iran, ruled Mesopotamia from about 1530 to 1160 BCE.

The various "peoples" and "tribes" were never clearly defined or distinguishable units. It is as-sumed that the Hyksos, for exam-ple, who invaded Egypt in 1650 BCE, were composed of both Semitic peoples and Indo-European Hurrites. But even the divisions "Semitic" and "Indo-European" are based on the script and languages used by these groups and give little information as to the ethnic composition or indeed precise geographical origins of the tribes they are ascribed to. The Persians and the Medes were not part of this first migration but belong to a later wave of Indo-European migration into the region that occurred in the second century.

The story of the biblical patriarch Abraham

Abraham's story (Genesis 11:10–25:11) mirrors the migration of the Aramaic nomads: In the second half of the second millennium BCE, Abraham led his tribe out of Mesopotamia at God's behest and into Palestine, where they settled despite the resistance of the previous inhabitants. In the traditional Islamic version, he led them to Mecca, where he constructed the Ka'aba and founded the pilgrimage tradition.

above: "Abraham's Exodus," copperplate engraving, 17th century CE
left: Abraham's well in Beersheba, Israel

Semitic nomads, Egyptian painting, 19th century BCE

ca. 2400 BCE	Beginning of the Akkadian Empire		1650 BCE	Invasion of Egypt by the Hyksos
from 3000 BCE	Immigration of Semitic and Indo-European tribes	from 2150 BCE	Reign of the Gutians in Akkad	from 1400 BCE	Persians settle in Iran

The Sea Peoples and Equestrian Peoples

Around 1200 BCE, the Eastern Mediterranean area experienced great changes. Neither high civilizations, such as the Hittite empire, nor civilizations like the Mycenaeans, Minoans, or Canaanites were a match for the advance of the sea and equestrian peoples.

3 Seaborne procession, Minoan mural, 16th century BCE

The term "sea peoples," which appears in Egyptian and Hittite sources from around 1300 BCE onward, refers collectively to diverse foreign tribes. Controversy still exists as to their origins. Speculation has traced them to Illyria (to-day's Croatia and Slovenia) but also to Asia Minor and the Aegean area.

The **❹** seagoing people at first spread fear among the settled trading tribes, until they—like the Philistines—permanently settled. The Philistines conquered the coastal region of Palestine and Syria and destroyed the Canaanite city-states. This facilitated the immigration of the Israelites.

The migratory movements of the Greeks, Thracians, Phrygians, and Lydians fit into this pattern of sea peoples' migrations. The Greeks coming out of the Balkans and invading present-day Greece destroyed the cultures of the Mycenaeans and **❸** Minoans. The Hittite empire also went under with the onslaught of the seagoing tribes. The Thracians, Phrygians, and Lydians penetrated Asia Minor from the north; the Greeks and other seafaring peoples fell upon Asia Minor's coasts. The Etruscans also seem to be descended from a seafaring tribe as suggested by the Aeneas

saga, which is linked to the founding of Rome.

The most significant equestrian tribes of the period were the Indo-European Cimmerians and **❺** Scythians, who advanced out of the Eurasian steppes and into Asia Minor and Iran in the south, as well as modern Germany and Italy to the west. The Cimmerians, who had been expelled by the Scythians, destroyed the Kingdom of Urartu in alliance with the Assyrians. They were then pushed into Asia Minor, where they defeated the Phrygians only to be annihilated by the Lydians. Up until 100 BCE, the Scythians occupied the area of present-day Ukraine, but they were then absorbed by other nomadic

4 Prisoners of the sea peoples who have been tied together by the hair

5 Scythian riders, tapestry, fourth/fifth century BCE

and equestrian peoples such as the **❻** Sarmatians.

The Atlantis legend

Some researchers link the Atlantis legend to the emergence of the seafaring peoples. According to this theory, a great natural disaster set off the migratory movements. Today, archaeologists suspect the epicenter of this disaster was the island of Santorini (Thera) in the Aegean. Here, in the 17th century BCE, a volcanic eruption caused a large part of the island to sink into the sea. Underwater earthquakes and the fallout of ash affected the whole region and might have forced the inhabitants to flee in a long-term migration.

above: Reconstruction of Atlantis following the specifications of Plato

6 Sarmatian horse soldiers in armor on armored horses, Pillar of Troy, Rome, 113 BCE

THE EARLY STATES OF MESOPOTAMIA

CA. 3000–539 BCE

In contrast to the desert of the Arabian Peninsula to the south and the rugged mountain ranges to the north, Mesopotamia ("land between the rivers"), situated between the Tigris and Euphrates, provided fertile land for cultivation. Early inhabitants, therefore, called their home ❶ Sumer ("cultivated land"). One of the earliest civilization of the Near East developed here. Complex societies flourished and were later organized into city-states like Uruk. Over time, great empires developed who managed to extend their power well beyond the two rivers.

1 The bust of a Sumerian lady of the court at Ur wearing headgear and other jewelry, 300 BCE

◼ The City-States of Sumer

The advancement of hydraulic engineering led to the formation of the city-states, which were distinguished by functioning administrations.

2 Cylinder seal, second century BCE, and modern molding

The first communal settlements grew along the Tigris and Euphrates rivers in response to the development of organized irrigation systems. These settlements merged about 3000 BCE to form irrigation and flood control provinces. Around 2800–2400 BCE—the Early Dynastic period—centrally controlled city-states arose and competed with each other for political and economic dominance of the region. The most significant of these were Ur, Uruk, Umma, Lagash, Adab, Nippur, and Kish—whose rulers are known to us through the surviving "kings lists."

Tombs with valuable ❸, ❻ burial objects testify to the high standard of living of the upper social level of the city-states, as well as the ❹ hierarchical nature of these societies, which were dominated by princes, kings, priests, and state officials.

In addition to agriculture as the main economic engine, the mass production of pottery is apparent in archaeological finds. Minerals and raw material initially served as payment for the labor. Later, ❷ cylinder seals provided a useful instrument for commercial control and the verification of the delivery of goods. Seals and counter markers served a well-organized food storage system and also property allocation by officials.

Some cities had seaports that later filled with sand as the water level dropped in the Persian Gulf. Through sea and land trade routes, the Sumerian culture expanded into northern Mesopotamia and northern Syria.

3 A Sumerian helmet made of gold from an Ur king's tomb (third century BCE)

Seafaring

In 1977 adventurer Thor Heyerdahl proved that the ancient Sumerians were capable of constructing seaworthy ships by sailing a reed boat replicated from the specifications of an original Sumerian boat.

above: Heyerdahl's reconstruction of a reed boat
right: Sumerian vessel showing a depiction of a reed boat

4 A mosaic from Ur, depicting groups of differing social status within the hierarchy

Uruk

One of the most powerful Sumerian city-states was Uruk in southern Mesopotamia.

From its founding around 4000 BCE until about 2000 BCE ❼ Uruk was an important trading center. In the center of the city stood many great public buildings that probably served as meeting places and religious buildings. Later these were built upon to create the chief shrine Eanna for the city's goddess ❽. The oldest known written tablets, presumably concerned with commerce management, are from this period. At the time there were approximately 20,000 people living in Uruk and a further 15,000—20,000 in the immediate area. Depictions on

The Construction of the City Wall by Gilgamesh

"[The hero Gilgamesh] built the wall of Uruk-Haven …
Look at its wall, which gleams like [copper?] …
Go up on the wall of Uruk and walk around,
examine its foundation, inspect its brickwork thoroughly.
Is not [even the core of] the brick structure made of kiln-fired brick?"

(Gilgamesh epic, first tablet)

cylinder seals testify to armed conflicts with neighboring peoples and the punishment of prisoners.

The city was completely reconstructed between 3100 and 2900 BCE. A terrace was raised in the city center, upon which the main temple was built. The terraced temple became the predecessor of later temple towers of the Babylonians, the ziggurats. Writing also evolved, with pictographs transforming into cuneiform.

Uruk is thought to have been the home of the ❺, ❻ legendary ruler Gilgamesh, the hero of the most important ancient Sumerian epic.Gilgamesh is said to have ruled sometime between 2700 and 2600 BCE and is counted

among the kings of the first dynasty of Uruk (ca. 2700–2350 BCE). Besides numerous heroic deeds, Gilgamesh is credited with the construction of Uruk's six-mile-long (9.7 km) protective city wall.

5

Statue of Gilgamesh with a lion, from an Assyrian palace, eighth century BCE

The epic, handed down in a number of ancient Near Eastern languages and in various versions from the third to the first millennia BCE, in some passages shows parallels to the Old Testament story of Noah and also to the saga of Hercules.

6

"Tree of Life" sculpture, third c. BCE

7 A vase from Uruk decorated with animal depictions, ca. 3000 BCE

8

9

above: Gilgamesh in battle with two bulls and a lion; modern molding of a cylinder seal from the third century BCE
left: Facade of a temple of Inanna in Uruk, 15th/14th century BCE

■ Lagash and Umma

The history of the Sumerian city-state Lagash in southern Mesopotamia, which competed fiercely with neighboring Umma, is well documented. The rivalry between the city's princes and the priesthood are typical of the political conditions in the Sumerian city-states. Under the reign of Gudea the city enjoyed a period of great prosperity.

King Eannatum of the first dynasty of Lagash (ca. 2494–2342 BCE) succeeded in temporarily subjugating Umma. The famous ❶, ❺ "Vulture Stele" depicts the vanquished enemy in a net cast by the city god Ningirsu. Internally Eannatum fought the influence of the priest caste, which won the battle by helping the usurper Lugalanda to power. Social tensions lay behind the ascension to the throne of Urukagina, who promptly canceled the debts of the poorer classes and cut back the income of the priests. With the help of these disgruntled clergymen, Lugalzaggesi of Umma then conquered Lagash some-

where around 2250 BCE. He also controlled the cities of Uruk and Adab, and thus declared himself "king of Uruk and of the Land of Sumer." His plans to unite Mesopotamia brought Lugalzaggesi into conflict with the powerful ruler of Akkad, Sargon I, who defeated him before going on to realize the project himself. Lagash experienced its final period of prosperity during the 20 year reign of ❸ Gudea. His rule is associated less with military adventures than with the building of systematic irrigation works and temples of worship.

3 Statue of Gudea of Lagash, 2141–2122 BCE

1 Vultures pick at the bodies of vanquished enemies; detail from the "Vulture Stele," ca. 2454 BCE

2 Valley in Luristan, southwest Iran

■ Proto-Elam and Elam

Concurrently with Sumer, another early high culture emerged in the ❷ southwest of present-day Iran. The Elam kingdom produced the oldest known interstate treaty.

This little-known culture, identifiable only by a form of script used around 2900 BCE, is referred to as Proto-Elam. Out of it rose the later kingdom of Elam, perhaps as early as 2700 BCE. Around 2300 BCE, the Akkadians occupied the empire until Elam regained its independence in 2240 through an interstate treaty—the oldest surviving in the world. Several royal dynasties followed, with a supreme monarch—resident in the capital Susa—ruling over several vassal kings. ❹ Women generally played a larger role in Elamitic society than in neighboring Sumer and Akkad. The wife, and often the sister, of the king was a prominent figure. Upon his death, she married his successor. Occasionally successors in the female line predominated.

In the history of Elam, periods of rule by foreign powers alter-

nated with times of Elamite expansion. Around 2004 BCE the Elamites destroyed Ur. Six hundred years later Elam came under the rule of the old Babylonian Empire. Then in 1155 BCE, the Elamites expelled the Kassites from Babylon, ruling until 1100 when Nebuchadressar I of the second dynasty of Isin pushed the Elamites back out of Babylon and pillaged their capital ❻ Susa. Only in 646 BCE was Elam finally destroyed by the Assyrians. The area then fell to the Persians and became the central province of the vast empire forged by the powerful Achaemenid dynasty.

4 Women spinning, eighth c. BCE

5 King Eannatum of Lagash leads his army in the battle against the city Umma, fallen enemies lying on the floor; extract from the "Vulture Stele," ca. 2454 BCE

| 2494–2342 BCE | First dynasty of Lagash | 2334–2279 BCE | Sargon I of Akkad | ca. 2300 BCE | Akkad occupies Elam |
| 2454–2425 BCE | King Eannatum | ca. 2340–2360 BCE | Lugalzaggesi of Umma | 2230–2130 BCE | Rule of the Gutians |

6 Reconstructed fortification of Susa, Iran

7 Bronze head of an Akkadian ruler, presumably Sargon of Akkad, 2334–2279 BCE

The Kingdom of Akkad and the 3rd Dynasty of Ur

The Kingdom of Akkad (ca. 2334–2154 BCE) was the first large territorial state in Mesopotamia.

❼ Sargon of Agade founded the Kingdom of Akkad in 2334 BCE. He also founded the new capital city of Akkad, which gave the kingdom its name. Sargon, which comes from the Akkadian title of Sharrukenu ("legitimate king"), conquered Kish. He broke Uruk's domination of Sumer and extended his kingdom to the Mediterranean, Lebanon, and Asia Minor in numerous ❽, ❾ military campaigns, ruling over many city-states and territories. With his royal title of "King of the Four Corners of Earth," Sargon made perhaps the first claim to world dominance. Domestically, he trained administrators— the "sons of the palace"—and was the first monarch to maintain a standing army. The decline of the Akkadian kingdom began around 2250 BCE. The Guti, a mountain people from Iran, then gained dominance over Mesopotamia between 2230 and 2130. Subsequently, the kings Ur-Nammu and Shulgi of the third dynasty of Ur (ca. 2112–2004 BCE) ruled the most important cities of Sumer and a large part of the Kingdom of Akkad, pronouncing themselves the "Kings of Sumer and Akkad."

The third dynasty of Ur strictly supervised the economy. Huge numbers of laborers and craftsmen were employed in the service of the state in the "grand households," which included the great temples and palaces. The chancelleries produced documentation which bears witness to complex administrative processes. A standardized form was established for the high temples—multistoried structures with a central flight of steps—called ziggurats. This form was used for the religious edifices erected by and for the kings. The dynasty ended in 2004 BCE with the destruction of Ur by the invading Elamites. However, the administrative structures survived and were adopted and integrated by the new rulers who established themselves in the dynasty's place.

8 Stele celebrating the victory of an Akkadian king, ca. 2200 BCE

Sargon of Akkad

"To Sargon, the king of the land, Enlil gave no enemy from the upper to the lower sea. . . . Sargon, the king of the land, restored Kish, their city he gave them as their abode . . . to Sargon, the king, Enlil allowed no enemy to form. 5400 warriors daily eat their meal before him."
(Text from the Tablet of the Sargon)

9 Procession of Akkadian prisoners, ca. 2340–2320 BCE

The Old Assyrian and Middle Assyrian Kingdoms (ca. 1800–1047 BCE)

The Assyrian kingdom developed in the north of Mesopotamia at the beginning of the second millennium BCE. Due to their superior methods of warfare, the Assyrians were feared by neighboring peoples.

The city of Ashur was a hub of Mesopotamian trade with Syria, Anatolia, and Iran. Its rulers laid claims to an empire as early as the time of ❷ Shamshi-Adad I and briefly assumed independence (Old Assyrian Kingdom, ca. 1800–1375 BCE) before coming under the sovereignty of the Hurrites of Mitanni.

Assyria became an independent state under the "great kings" of the Middle Assyrian Kingdom (1375–1047 BCE). In the middle of the 14th century BCE, Ashur-uballit I (1365–1330 BCE) broke from Mitanni and forged close ties with Egypt and Babylon. Adadnirari I (ca. 1305–1275 BCE) extended the kingdom at Babylonia's expense and was

2 Clay tablet bearing the signature of the Assyrian king Shamshi-Adad I, 1813–1781 BCE

known by the title "King of All." Assyria's transformation into an expansive military power with a well-trained ❸ army began in the 13th century under rulers Shalmaneser I (1274–1245 BCE) and Tukulti-Ninurta I (ca. 1294–1208 BCE). Tukulti-Ninurta I immortalized his deeds in his *Tukulti-Ninurta Epic*, which then became the model for the personal aggrandizement of Assyrian rulers. According to the Assyrian religion, the

state god Ashur had destined his people, over whose welfare the ❹ genies watched, for world dominance. The Assyrians subjugated their neighbors in a series of devastating military ❶ campaigns, often conducted with great brutality. The inhabitants of the conquered territories were ❺ deported in the tens of thousands into other parts of the Assyrian Empire, where they were used as forced labor. Revolts of the subjugated regions were considered a crime against the "divine world order" and were crushed with cruel punitive expeditions.

Tiglath-pileser I (ca. 1115–1077 BCE) extended the empire into northern Syria and Asia Minor. After occupying the Phoenician trading cities, he levied tribute on them. Alongside these military conquests he also promoted scientific research, particularly with regard to zoology, and oversaw the compilation of a great library and encouraged cultural developments. After his death, the expansion of the Middle Assyrian Kingdom came to an end. Pressure from the Aramaean tribes seeking to break into the fertile lands of Mesopotamia, and a revived Babylonian kingdom, ushered in a period of Assyrian decline. The ancient capital of Ashur was later abandoned in favor of Nineveh, a new capital on the banks of the upper River Tigris.

1 An Assyrian fighter kills his enemy, ninth century BCE

The Assyrian Method of Fighting

"Impetuous they are, full of rage, as the storm god transformed, / They plunge into the tangle of battle, naked to the waist, / They test the ribbons; they tear the robes from their bodies, / They tie their hair, the swords they let dance in circles / Jumping about, naked weapons in hand, / The wild warriors, the lords of war, / They stormed ahead, as if lions would seize them."

(from Tukulti-Ninurta Epic)

5 Prisoners of war being carried away into slavery in the Assyrian empire, women and children riding on a wagon drawn by oxen; stone relief, seventh c. BCE

3 Assyrian spear-carrier, eighth c. BCE

4 Winged genie, ninth century BCE

ca. 1800–1372 BCE	Old Assyrian Kingdom	883–612 BCE	Neo-Assyrian Empire	858–824 BCE	Shalmanesar III	745–724 BCE	Tiglath-pileser III
1813–1781 BCE	Shamshi-Adad I 1375–1047 BCE	Middle Assyrian Kingdom		883–859 BCE	Ashurnasirpal II	810–806 BCE	Regent Queen Sammu-ramat

The Neo-Assyrian Empire (883-612 BCE)

During the period of the Neo-Assyrian Empire (883–612 BCE), the military power of the Assyrians expanded through Palestine and Israel, and into Egypt.

Assyria experienced a renewed period of expansion under King Ashurnasirpal II (883–859 BCE). Annual military campaigns were waged in order to break the resistance of neighboring kingdoms, and the conquests were followed by brutal mass executions.

Succeeding Ashurnasirpal, Queen Sammu-ramat, also known

provincial governors, and the growing power of Urartu threatened the empire. These dangers were averted after Tiglath-pileser III seized power in 745 BCE and set about refashioning the Kingdom and overseeing renewed military success. He advanced into Gaza in the west, conquered Babylon in the south, and triumphed over

the empire's subjects. His successor, Shalmaneser V, went on to conquer Samaria in 722 BCE and subjugated Israel, as it had ceased to pay ❻ tribute.

In 721 BCE a new dynasty was founded by ❼, ❾ Sargon II. His son Sennacherib (704–681 BCE) destroyed Babylon in 689 and had his capital, ❽ Nineveh, magnificently enlarged by an army of forced laborers. Both Esarhaddon and Ashurbanipal sought to conquer Egypt, but were unable to maintain control due to the great distances involved, as well as domestic intrigues originating with their own relatives. In 646 the Elamites were conclusively defeated and, together with the last small Hittite states, absorbed by the new Assyrian Empire during the seventh century BCE.

Ashurbanipal was a great art collector, and in Nineveh he built the largest cuneiform library of antiquity, holding copies of almost all the significant works of the ancient Near East. The empire declined under his successors, until finally—weakened by Scythians' attacks —it fell to the conquests of the Medes and the Babylonians.

6

Emissaries from King Jehu of Israel bring tributes, ninth century BCE

7 Sargon II (721–705 BCE) with a high dignitary, perhaps Crown Prince Sennacherib

8

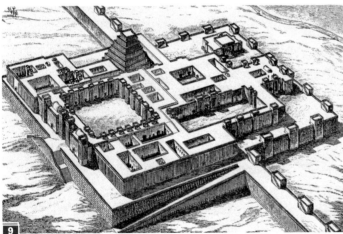

9

top: The king's palace at Nineveh, artist's reconstruction
above: The palace and temple area of Sargon II at Khorsabad (Dur Sharrukin), Iraq, artist's reconstruction

as Semiramis, conducted the empire's affairs very successfully. She first acted as regent for her son, Adadnirari III (810–783 BCE), and then continued to exert a significant influence over the throne even after he came of age. A succession of weak kings, rebellious

the ruler of Urartu. In addition to reviving Assyrian military fortunes, Tiglath-pileser proved a capable administrator, strengthening the empire by reordering the provinces and standardizing laws. His economic planning involved the forced relocation of

Queen Semiramis of Assyria

Queen Sammuramat (Semiramis) of Assyria, who reigned as regent after the death of her husband, is cloaked in legend. She allegedly had innumerable lovers and distinguished herself as a ruler and military commander. She is also credited with the construction of the "Hanging Gardens" of Babylon.

above: *Semiramis Puts Down an Uprising in Babylon*, painting by Matteo Rosselli, 17th century CE.

721 BCE	Conquest of Palestine	689 BCE	Destruction of Babylon	668–627 BCE	Ashurbanipal	614–612 BCE	Conquest of Assyria
721–705 BCE	Sargon II	704–681 BCE	Sennacherib	680–669 BCE	Asarhaddon	ca. 653 BCE	Subjugation of Elam

■ The Ancient Kingdom of Babylon

The city of Babylon in the heart of Mesopotamia rose to become the new dominant power in the region during the second millennium BCE.

Following the fall of the third dynasty of Ur, the old Babylonian Empire was the dominant power in Mesopotamia. The 1st dynasty of Babylon was descended from the Semitic Amorites. Their most famous member was King Hammurapi, who is best known for his ❶ Code of Hammurapi, considered to be the first detailed legal code of antiquity. It presents a collection of cases in 282 provisions for all of the areas of law then recognized. The punishments prescribed for the crimes accorded with the principle of "an eye for an eye, a tooth for a tooth" and went from whipping and maiming to death by impaling, burning, or drowning. Hammurapi, who called himself "the shepherd of the people," described in the foreword of his code how the Babylonian chief deity Marduk had charged him with introducing law and justice to his people.

Soon after Hammurapi's death, the ancient kingdom of Babylon came under pressure from external enemies such as the Hittites, who rose to prominence after 1650 BCE. From about 1531 to 1155, the Kassites ruled Babylon; after 1155, it was under the control of the Elamites and the second dynasty of the city of Isin (ca. 1157–1026 BCE). A prominent representative of this dynasty was Nebuchadressar I, who repulsed the Elamites and Assyrians in successful campaigns.

Eventually Babylon, which had already been weakened by invading Aramaean tribes, came under the rule of the Assyrian Empire.

> **From the epilogue of the Code of Hammurapi**
>
> *I Hammurapi … have not withdrawn myself from the men, whom Bel gave to me, the rule over whom Marduk gave to me, I was not negligent, but I made them a peaceful abiding-place. I expounded all great difficulties, I made the light shine upon them.*

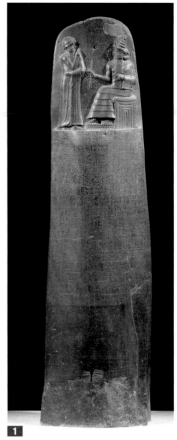

1
Hammurapi's law column, with the king in front of a deity, ca. 1700 BCE

■ The Neo-Babylonian Kingdom of the Chaldeans   625–539 BCE

The greed for power and the luxury of the Neo-Babylonian Kingdom served as the Old Testament model for the depths of iniquity.

The Chaldeans, one of the Semitic tribes of Aramaeans, moved into southern Mesopotamia in about 850 BCE and rose up against Babylon's Assyrian rulers. Eventually they prevailed. Nabopolassar (625–605 BCE) founded the Neo-Babylonian Kingdom and defeated the Assyrians in 612 BCE by capturing and destroying Nineveh on the east bank of the Tigris. Nabopolassar's son Nebuchadressar, known in the Bible as ❷ Nebuchadnezzar II (605–562 BCE), dedicated himself primarily to ❸ constructing imposing buildings. In the temple district of Babylon, he had a ❺ processional passage and the Ishtar Gate built and decorated with colored relief tiles. The passage led to a massive central ❹ ziggurat, which may have inspired the ❻ "Tower of Babel." His palace's ❾ hanging gardens became one of the Seven Wonders of the Ancient World. Babylon was also a world center for the sciences, above all of

2
Seal with the name and title of Nebuchadressar II, 604–562 BCE

3
Reconstruction sketch of Babylon under Nebuchadressar II

4
Model of the ziggurat of Babylon built under Nebuchadressar II

1792–1750 BCE	Hammurapi	1125–1104 BCE	Nebuchadressar I	635–539 BCE	Neo-Babylonian Kingdom
ca. 1894–1595 BCE	Old Babylonian Empire	ca. 1531–1155 BCE	Kassite period	8th century BCE	Revolt of the Chaldaeans

Festive procession in Babylon; still from the film *The Fall of Babylon*, 1916

Tower Building at Babel by Pieter Bruegel the Elder, 16th century CE

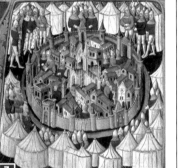

Nebuchadnessar Besieges Jerusalem, illumination from a medieval Bible translation, 14th century CE

Belshazzar's Fall

In Biblical tradition (Daniel 5), Belshazzar insulted his God, whereupon a hand appeared and wrote "Menetekel" on the wall, which the king interpreted as a warning of the imminent fall of Babylon. The king was murdered that night.

above: *Belshazzar's Feast* by Rembrandt, 17th century CE

The Tower of Babel

Nebuchadressar II's tower in Babylon, a five-tiered temple in honor of the chief god Marduk, had a square base of around 300 feet (91 m) per side and was about 295 feet (90 m) high. It was called "Etemenanki" ("House which is the foundation of heaven and earth"). The top was reached by climbing three staircases on the south side. The top levels comprised a two-story temple and were covered in blue tiles. According to Genesis 11: 1–9, it reached to heaven and was a symbol of human pride, which was punished by the Babylonian confusion of tongues.

Slaves transport a stone block, still from the film *Metropolis*, 1927

astronomy, astrology, and the mantic arts.

Militarily, Nebuchadressar II directed his activities against Egypt and then Palestine. In 597 BCE he plundered ❼ Jerusalem for the first time when it refused to make tribute payments, and in 587 he then destroyed the city. Its inhabitants were led into ❽ "Babylonian captivity" and employed as forced labor. Of the Phoenician city-states, only Tyre was able to

withstand conquest by Nebuchadressar.

His successors were weakened by family feuds, and eventually the usurper Nabonidus managed to reconsolidate the empire and repulse the invading Medes in 553 BCE. In 550 he installed his son

Belshazzar (also known as Nidintabel and Nebuchadressar III) as regent in Babylon and withdrew to the Oasis of Teima. When he returned in 539 it was already too late; the Persians under Cyrus II had annihilated the armies of Belshazzar and entered Babylon.

Reconstruction sketch of the hanging gardens of Babylon, 18th century CE

| 605–562 BCE | Nebuchadressar II | 587 BCE | Destruction of Judah | 555–539 BCE | Nabonidus | 539 BCE | Conquest of Babylon |
| 635–605 BCE | Nabupolassar I | 597 BCE | Looting of Jerusalem | 572 BCE | Conquest of Tyro | 550 BCE | Regent Belshazzar |

ANCIENT EGYPT CA. 2900–332 BCE

Ancient Egypt's civilization developed on the fertile strip of land created by the Nile in the North African desert. As a result of its relative geographical isolation, Egypt's development differed, in some respects greatly, from that of the rest of the Near East. Although Egypt was subject to outside influences as well, it appears that the principal defining characteristics of its culture remained homogeneous throughout the course of its long history. Its history is characterized by a series of ruling dynasties.

Nilometer used to measure the high-water mark of floods since 2000 BCE

The Predynastic Period

The upper and lower parts of Egypt were united as early as the predynastic period, creating a single political entity.

Egypt is located in the ❹ Nile Valley, bordered on the East and West by desert. The yearly ❶ flooding, which occurs between July and October deposits the fertile silt that is the basis of productive ❸ agriculture on the land bordering the river. The country is divided into

Upper Egypt, where the Nile flows through a narrow valley, and Lower Egypt, where the river and its tributaries form a broad delta before flowing into the Mediterranean Sea.

In the early period, ca. 2900 BCE, two warring, independent kingdoms developed in the two areas. According to tradition, it was ❷ Narmer, a Predynastic ruler of Upper Egypt, who conquered the Nile Delta and unified the two kingdoms, establishing the new capital and powerful

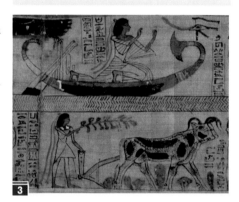

2 Votive depicting Narmer, the unifier of the Kingdoms, a prisoner, and the Horus Falcon, ca. 3000 BCE.

The Ruling Dynasties

The chronology of the Egyptian rulers before the arrival of Alexander the Great in 332 BCE is divided into 31 dynasties.

Early Dynastic Period	(1–2 Dynasty)	2900–2660
Ancient Kingdom	(3–6 Dynasty)	2660–2160
1st Intermediate Period	(7–10 Dynasty)	2160–2040
Middle Kingdom	(11–12 Dynasty)	2040–1785
2nd Intermediate Period	(13–17 Dynasty)	1785–1552
New Kingdom	(18–20 Dynasty)	1552–1070
3rd Intermediate Period	(21–24 Dynasty)	1070–712
Late Dynastic Period	(25–31 Dynasty)	712–332

"Gift of the Nile"

In the fifth century BCE the Greek historian and traveler Herodotus described Egypt as "a gift of the Nile": "It is certain, however, that now they gather in fruit from the earth with less labor than any other men, for they have no labor in breaking up furrows with a plough, nor in hoeing, nor in any other of those labors which other men have about a crop; but [they wait until] when the river has come up of itself and watered their fields and, after watering, has left."

From the History of Herodotus

above: Sailing and agriculture
left: View of the Nile showing the bordering agricultural lands

Memphis on the border of the two. Aha ruled the first dynasty, ca.2900 BCE.

The separation between Upper and Lower Egypt into autonomous regions occurred repeatedly throughout Egypt's history. Whenever central power began to decline, the individual regions would exert their independence.

The Ancient Kingdom

In the time of the Ancient Kingdom, the most famous pyramids were built. They testify to the pronounced hierarchical character of the Egyptian society.

A Nubian family with animals, ca. 1340 BCE

Pharaoh Djoser's step pyramid in Saqqara, ca. 2600 BCE

Ever since the birth of Egyptian culture, the throne was closely linked to religion. At first each pharaoh was considered to be a ❾ representative of the heavenly god Horu. From the fifth dynasty onward, however, the successive pharaohs were revered as the sons of the sun god Re.

The unification of Upper and Lower Egypt was symbolically re-enacted every time there was an accession to the throne, when the pharaoh was crowned with the double crown of both kingdoms. The ruler regularly levied taxes. These depended on the size of the fields and the ❼ amount of livestock each family owned. Furthermore,

9 Pharaoh Chephren with the Horus Falcon, ca. 2500 BCE

the population was required to absolve communal duties during the dry and flood periods. These included the digging of canals and dams as well as the construction of the royal tombs. Aside from the pharaoh, the priests, ❽ high officials, and provincial governors owned the majority of property. They were thus able to exert great political influence in the kingdom, particularly as many

8 Sitting scribe, ca. 2500 BCE

of these offices became hereditary with the passage of time.

One of the most significant pharaohs of the Old Kingdom was King Djoser of the third dynasty, who commissioned expeditions to the Sinai Peninsula where copper and turquoise were mined. He is also well known for his ❻ step pyramid at Saqqara. The architect of this structure was Imhotep, who also made a name for himself

10 The pyramids of Giza, third century BCE

as a physician, priest, and court official. He was one of history's first universal talents and was later revered as a deity.

The Old Kingdom reached its high point during the fourth dynasty. Pharaoh Snefru led raiding expeditions to ❺ Nubia (present-day Sudan) in the south and to Libya in the west, bringing back spoils such as gold, ivory, and slaves. His son Cheops left behind the ❿ Great Pyramid of Giza, the sole survivor of the Seven Wonders of the Ancient World. Cheops' successors Chephren and Mycerinus also built great burial complexes in Giza. After the reign of Pharaoh Pepy II of the sixth dynasty, who ruled for over 90 years, signs of disintegration began to appear. Power struggles, assassinations at the royal court,

and independence struggles led by regional governors led to the demise of the Old Kingdom.

7 Wood model of a livestock counting, 1990 BCE

The Pyramids

Pyramids were built from the third through the 17th dynasty, and by the Kushites. The grave mounds of the Predynastic period were the forerunners of the pyramids that developed into the right-angled tombs called mastabas (Arabic: "bench"). The step pyramids of Djoser in Saqqara were constructed by placing several mastabas on top of each other. By the fourth dynasty, pyramids with straight sides were created by filling the steps.

1785–1552 BCE | Second Intermediate Period   1070–712 BCE | Third Intermediate Period   332 BCE | Arrival of Alexander the Great

1552–1070 BCE | New Kingdom   712–332 BCE | Late Dynastic Period

View over the Sacred Lake of the Great Amun-Re Temple at Karnak, East Thebes

First and Second Intermediate Period and the Middle Kingdom 2150–1539 BCE

The Middle Kingdom era lay between two periods of weakness and division.

During the First Intermediate Period, which followed the fall of the Old Kingdom, Egypt disintegrated once again into many territories, whose rulers fought each other in a civil war. This led to a breakdown in civil administration, trade, and the economy, and the consequent neglect of irrigation and food storage systems meant the population suffered ❸ famines. The provincial governors of the eleventh dynasty of Thebes in Upper Egypt were finally able to gain supremacy in the power struggle for the reign over Egypt. They conquered Lower Egypt and founded the Middle Kingdom.

The pharaohs of the eleventh and twelfth dynasties disempowered the governors of the provinces and restored a central administration. The shift of the kingdom's capital to ❶ Thebes in Upper Egypt also affected the religious policies of Egypt. The deity Amun, who was particularly worshiped in the new capital, was combined with the sun god Re—whose main temple was in Heliopolis in Lower Egypt, near the old capital of Memphis— to become the official deity of the empire: Amun-Re. A ❷ large temple complex was erected in Thebes to honor and worship him. Thebes was on the site of the present-day villages Luxor and Karnak.

Under Pharaoh Sesostris III (1878–1843 BCE), far-reaching Egyptian influence—from Nubia across the Sinai to the rich trading cities of Lebanon—was once again restored. Sesostris' son ❹

Amenemhet III (1842–1797 BCE) diverted a tributary of the Nile to create the Fayoum Oasis. It was here that the last great pyramid was erected for the king. As Theban tradition dictated, later pharaohs were buried in underground tomb complexes in the ❻ Valley of the Kings, west of the capital.

By the dawning of the Second Intermediate Period, following the end of the twelfth dynasty, the country was divided once again into Upper and Lower Egypt. This allowed the ❺ invasion of the Hyksos (in Egyptian, Hega-khase: "rulers of foreign lands"), a group of Indo-European tribes. They entered Lower Egypt and established their capital Avaris in the Nile Delta. From here they ruled over Lower Egypt as pharaohs, while native dynasties continued to rule Upper Egypt from Thebes.

❷ A pharaoh offering a sacrifice in front of the god Amun-Re of Thebes, ca. 1440 BCE

❸ left: Emaciated man with bowl, ca. 2000 BCE
below: Invasion of Egypt by the Hyksos, woodcarving, 19th century CE

❻ Valley of the Kings, west of Thebes

❹ Amenemhet III

The New Kingdom I ca. 1539–1379 BCE

Ancient Egypt was at the pinnacle of its political power during the era of the New Kingdom. The pharaohs of the 18th dynasty turned Egypt into the dominant state of the Near East.

Thutmose III, ca. 1460 BCE

Under Ahmose I, the first pharaoh of the 18th dynasty, the rulers of Thebes were able to expel the Hyksos and extend Egyptian hegemony to the Syrian border. Ahmose's de-scendent Thutmose I (ca. 1525- ca. 1512 BCE) conquered the entirety of Nubia and integrated it into the Egyptian Empire.

Thutmose's daughter ❾ Hatshepsut (1503–1482 BCE) was married to her half-brother Thutmose II. After his death she assumed power, initially as regent for her nephew Thutmose III. She ultimately took the title of pharaoh for herself and ushered in a period of peace and prosperity in Egypt. Great trading expeditions were undertaken, for example, to the land of Punt (present-day Eritrea and Somalia). Like other pharaohs, she had a magnificent ⓫ funerary temple constructed for herself, one of the most significant structures of its kind.

After Hatshepsut's death, ❽ Thutmose III (1504-1450 BCE) eradicated all memory of his stepmother and aunt. Under him, the New King-dom was at its most extensive. It reached from the Euphrates in the north into today's Sudan in the south. To counter the growing power of the Hittites, succeeding pharaohs formed alliances with the Mitanni kingdom. This policy of alliances was reinforced through dynastic marriages; ❼ Amenhotep III (1417–1379 BCE) married not only the Egyptian Tiy but also two Mitannian princesses. The reign of Amenhotep III was noted for its ❿ construction and architecture. His long reign was also marked by the gradual decline of the 18th dynasty, which was further accelerated by the religious policies of his son Amenhotep IV (Akhenaton).

above: Giant statue of Amenhotep III and Queen Tiy, ca. 1370 BCE
below: Statues of Memnon at Thebes during the Inundation–remains of the funerary temple of Amenhotep III in West Thebes, painting, 19th c. CE

❾ Queen Hatshepsut wearing the traditional fake ceremonial beard of the pharaohs, ca. 1490 BCE

Women in Ancient Egypt

Egyptian women enjoyed rights relatively equal to men's. They could independently complete legal transactions and practice most professions. Women also had equal rights with their husbands in marriage. Polygamy was customary only in the royal houses.

Among the wives of the pharaohs, the "great royal consorts" such as Tiy and Nefertiti were able to assert enormous influence. In some cases, women themselves ruled as pharaohs. Sibling marriages were meant to ensure the purity of the divine dynasties. Usually if the pharaoh was the descendent of a concubine—which was true of most of the kings of the 18th dynasty—he would secure his rule through marriage to a half-sister from the main line. In later periods, the "godly wives of Amun" officially stood at the top of Theban theocracy in Upper Egypt.

Bust of Nefertiti, 1355 BCE

Terrace-shaped funerary temple complex of Hatshepsut at Deir el-Bahri in West Thebes, ca.1470 BCE

1503–1482 BCE | Hatshepsut

1417–1379 BCE | Amenhotep III

ca. 1525–ca. 1512 BCE | Thutmose I

1504–1450 BCE | Thutmose III

■ The New Kingdom II: The Amarna Period 1379–1320 BCE

Amenhotep IV introduced a form of monotheism and banned older cults. He thereby incurred the wrath of the priests, who feared losing their influence in Egypt.

1 Daughters of Nefertiti and Akhenaton in front of Aten's sun disk, relief, ca. 1355 BCE

Nefertiti drives through the capital, drawing, 20th century

art style became popular. In the twelfth year of his reign, however, his zeal for reform let up. **2** Nefertiti, who until then had appeared as his equal and "great royal wife," disappeared and was replaced by the Mitanni princess Kiya. A reason for this could have been the growing threat from the Hittites, which had caused Egypt and Mitanni to ally.

Soon after Akhenaton's death, the old cults were restored. Attempts were made to annihilate memory of the "Heretic King."

Both of the succeeding pharaohs married a **1** daughter of Akhenaton and Nefertiti to ensure dynastic continuity. The second of them, the young Tutankhaten, changed his name to Tutankhamun in the course of a return to orthodoxy. He was otherwise politically insignificant. The generals had steadily increased their power through continual clashes with the Hittites. Following Tutankhamun's death, military

The veneration of the sun disk, the Aten, was already common at the pharaoh's court under Amenhotep III. The new pharaoh, Amenhotep IV (1379–1362 BCE), banned all other cults. He took the name **3** Akhenaton ("He who is of service to Aten") and founded a new capital city, Akhetnaton ("Horizon of the Aten"), on the plains of Tell el-Amarna in central Egypt. In doing this, he deprived Amun-Re priesthood in Thebes of its power. Under Akhenaton, a new, more **4** naturalistic

Portrait of Akhenaton, ca. 1355 BCE

leaders usurped the throne. One of them, Ramses I, established a new dynasty about 1320 BCE.

The Curse of King Tutankhamun

The discovery of the almost undamaged tomb of Tutankhamun in 1922 was the greatest archaeological sensation of the 20th century. But soon many of those involved in the excavation died under mysterious circumstances, and the legend of the "curse of King Tutankhamun" was born. Today it is believed that the deaths were caused by rare bacteria, fungi, or viruses that were conserved in the burial chamber.

above: Sarcophagus of Tutankhamun

From Akhenaton's Longer Hymn to Aton

"Thy dawning is beautiful in the horizon of heaven,
O living Aton, Beginning of life!
When Thou risest in the eastern horizon of heaven,
Thou fillest every land with Thy beauty; . . .
For Thou art beautiful, great, glittering. . .
When Thou settest in the western horizon of heaven,
The world is in darkness like the dead. . . .
Darkness reigns,
The world is in silence.
He that made them has gone to rest in His horizon.
Bright is the earth, when Thou risest in the horizon,
When Thou shinest as Aton by day.
The darkness is banished
When Thou sendest forth Thy rays . . ."

Relief of Tutankhamun and his wife Ankhesenpaaten who ruled for eleven years, here depicted on the back of a king's throne, ca. 1340 BCE

■ The New Kingdom III: Ramessid Period 1320–1070 BCE

The pharaohs of the 19th and 20th dynasties, who almost all bore the name Ramses, were barely able to hold Egypt's great empire together.

Mummified body of Ramses II

In the confusion surrounding the throne at the end of the 18th dynasty, Ramses I was able to prevail and founded the 19th dynasty. His two-year reign was spent in heavy fighting.

While Thebes remained the religious center, the capital was moved to the Nile Delta, where the hotly contested front with the Hittites in the north was more easily accessible. The Libyan no-

The Israelites in Egypt

Among the many foreigners living in Egypt under the pharoahs were the Israelites, who were ruthlessly exploited as slave labor. At the same time, they were considered a threat:

"A new king came to power in Egypt, and he said unto his people: 'Behold, the people of the children of Israel are too many and too mighty for us . . . when there befalleth us any war, they also join themselves unto our enemies, and fight against us, and get them up out of the land. Therefore they did set over them taskmasters to afflict them with their burdens. And they built for Pharaoh store-cities, Pithom and Ramses.'"

(Exodus 1:8–11)

mads, who regularly attacked Egypt from the west, were another threat. Ramses I's son, Seti I, fought campaigns in Palestine, Syria and the Sudan, returning home to Egypt with enormous plunder. He continued to build temples, adding in particular many columns to the great edifice at Karnak.

One of the most important ❽ battles against the Hittites and their ally, the Amorite prince of

Ramses II at the Battle of Kadesh, drawing, 19th century

Kadesh in Syria, occurred in 1285 BCE. ❺ Ramses II, grandson of Ramses I, known as "the Great," a vigorous ruler but a cruel and extravagant one whose vast harem gave him 150 offspring, marched against his foes with an enormous army in order to prevent the complete loss of Syria and Palestine, but it was only by good fortune that he did not suffer a crushing defeat. The Battle of Kadesh was a draw and led to a peace treaty signed in 1259. Ramses II's foreign policy problems contrasted with his immense construction activities. The ❾ rock-

cut temple of Abu Simbel is the most famous among the many temples that he had built or restored.

Even the most significant pharaoh of the 20th dynasty, ❻ Ramses III (1198–1166 BCE), who undertook extensive social and administrative reforms, was forced to defend Egypt against fierce attacks. The sea peoples, among them the Achaians and the ❼ Philistines, allied with the Libyans and pushed forward into Egypt by land and sea. The pharaoh was unable to prevent either the Philistines from settling in Palestine or the Libyans from settling in Egypt. Trade and the tribute payments ceased. The economic problems led to social unrest, which resulted in the first documented strike in history.

Ramses III was eventually murdered, although a memorial to him remained in the form of the huge temples and palaces he had constructed. His successors lost

Ramses III and one of his sons, wall painting ca. 1370 BCE

Captured Philistines, relief on the funerary temple of Ramses III in Medinet Habu

control over the nation. The foreign peoples living in Egypt, descendants of mercenaries or slave laborers, rebelled, while the high priests of Amun in Thebes established a theocracy in Upper Egypt. With the end of the 20th dynasty, Egypt was once again divided up into parts.

Temple of Ramses II at Abu Simbel

The Third Intermediate Period and the Late Kingdom 1070–332 BCE

During the Third Intermediate Period, Egypt once again fragmented. The Late Kingdom then saw alternating periods of foreign occupation and independence.

Pharaoh Shoshenq I holds Israelite captive, hieroglyphic inscription, ca. 930 BCE

The pharaohs who followed the 20th dynasty only held sway over the lands of Upper Egypt. The leaders of the Libyan mercenary troops employed by the kings grew in power until one of them, ❶ Shoshenq I (ca. 945–924 BCE), managed to seize the throne. Through their dynastic connections, the Libyan pharaohs were initially able to exert a certain influence in Upper Egypt, but Lower Egypt eventually disintegrated into a multitude of principalities and kingdoms.

The ❷ high priests of Amun, in Thebes, had already established a form of theocracy in Upper Egypt, which they legitimized through the prophecies of the ❹ "god-wife of Amun." The functions of this high office were usually performed by the princesses of Libya, and later by princesses from the Kushite royal families.

The "god-wife of Amun" Karomama, statuette, ca. 870 BCE

The Kushites began advancing out of Nubia into Egypt in about 740 BCE. They established themselves as pharaohs, first in Thebes and then, under the ❸ 25th dynasty, in Lower Egypt as well. They succeeded in establishing a single Egyptian state in 712.

After 671 BCE, the Assyrians launched repeated invasions of Egypt. They installed Psamtik I, a Libyan prince from the Nile Delta, as governor. In 663, with the help of Greek mercenaries, he declared independence and founded the 26th dynasty. He forced the Kushite god-wife of Amun to name one of his daughters as her successor and thus brought Upper Egypt under his rule by 656. Psamtik I also brought Greek tradesmen to Egypt, who settled primarily in the Nile Delta. Over time, the relationship with the Greeks became ever closer. The pharaohs married Greek women, donated votive offerings to Delphi, and minted coins after the Greek model.

The Persians ❺ conquered Egypt in 525 BCE and incorporated it into their empire. After many uprisings, Egypt regained its independence only to fall to the Persians a second time

in 343. When Alexander the Great conquered the Persian empire in 332 BCE, Egypt also came under his rule and he founded the city of Alexandria. After his death Egypt once again rose to a position of supremacy in the Eastern Mediterranean region under the rule of the Ptolemies.

Egyptian priest reading scrolls

Taharka, from the 25th dynasty, bows before the falcon god Hemen, statue

Hieroglyphics

Egyptian hieroglyphics were a pictographic script, primarily used on monuments and for religious texts. The Egyptians continued to use simplified forms of hieroglyphics in their daily lives until the time of the early Christians, when they switched to writing the Egyptian language with the Greek alphabet. Over the centuries, the understanding of ancient hieroglyphics was lost. In 1799, a French military officer, who had come to Egypt as part of Napoleon's expedition, discovered the "Rosetta Stone." On this monument from the second century BCE he found a text chiseled in both hieroglyphics and Greek. With this new evidence, philologists finally deciphered hieroglyphics in 1822.

above: The Rosetta Stone, ca. 196 BCE

Pharaoh Psamtik III defeated and made to submit to his conqueror, Persian King Cambyses, painting, 19th century

Egyptian Religion

The Egyptian religion recognized a multitude of gods. Their relative importance was influenced by social conditions and subject to political changes.

The beginnings of the Egyptian religion can be traced to the fourth millennium BCE. At first, the gods took the form of animals, but later they also assumed human form. Often they were represented as hybrid creatures, for example the falcon-headed god Horus, or the ram-headed god ❼ Amun. Among countless deities, the gods associated with the most important religious centers and the major cities always held a special significance. They were honored across the kingdom, thus asserting a cultural and geographical hierarchy within the framework of the official cult. In the Old Kingdom the sun god Re of Heliopolis, near the capital of Memphis, stood out above all others. With the rise of Thebes during the Middle Kingdom, the city's local god Amun was elevated to the foremost rank of the deities and was then fused with Re to become Amun-Re. Pharaoh Akhenaton attempted unsuccessfully to enforce the worship of Aten, who was not represented in a humanoid form but only by the abstract symbol of a sun disk.

The Egyptians believed that the gods, too, aged and died. ❽ Osiris, represented as a mummy, symbolized death. He was killed and dismembered by his brother, the desert-god Seth, but was resurrected by his sister ❾ ❿ Isis. Osiris was thus also a symbol of ⓫ fertility and lifegiving energy. The first pharaohs were considered to be representatives of Horus, the son of Isis and Osiris. In the late Old Kingdom references first appear to a tribunal of the dead, where all the dead must account for their actions before Osiris and Re—either to continue to exist as blessed dead or to be damned, the punishment for which was severe and could mean obliteration.

Mummification, burial objects, and tombs such as the pyramids were meant to make the continuation of earthly life possible after death. ⓬ Rituals and incantations were performed for the protection of the dead. Egyptians used amulets and lucky charms such as ❻ scarabs to ward off danger or to encourage fertility.

The role played by the pharaoh, that of a link between men and gods, decreased with the fall of the New Kingdom and the disintegration of the power. Certain kinds of animals, such as cats and crocodiles, came to be venerated as spiritual mediators. Many of these animals were mummified after death and buried in graveyards or tombs. In the Late Kingdom, Greek influence led to the development of arcane cults, above all those of Isis and Osiris, that would later be popular in the Roman Empire.

Gold bracelet with scarab, ca. 890 BCE

❽ The god Osiris, Egyptian mural, ca.1306 BCE

⓫ Seed bed in the form of Osiris, second century BCE

⓬ Group of mourners, mural, ca.1370 BCE

❾ Enthroned Isis breast-feeds a young Horus, seventh C. BCE

Statue of the ram-headed god Amun, third century BCE

⓾ Isis cult, Roman mural, first century

From the Book of the Dead:

"I open the channels, in heaven as on Earth. Because I am your loving son Osiris! I have become spirit, sublimated, made holy, and with powerful chants armored...Gods of the immeasurable sky. Godly spirits! All of you, look at me! I have completed my journey and appear before you."

above: Illustration from the *Book of the Dead*, ca. twelfth century BCE

THE HITTITES CA. 1570–CA. 650 BCE

The Hittites were an Indo-European people who migrated out of the steppes north of the Black Sea and into Asia Minor during the second millennium BCE. From there they pushed into Syria and Mesopotamia, where they established an empire that competed with Egypt's New Kingdom for supremacy in the Near East. The empire came to an end under the onslaught of the sea peoples in 1200 BCE.

1 Archer and charioteer, ninth century BCE

■ The Old Kingdom ca. 1570–1343 BCE

The Hittites encountered an old, highly developed civilization in Asia Minor from which they adopted numerous cultural developments and religious concepts.

2
A Hittite couple, ca. 800 BCE

The Hittite Gods

The Hittites were called the "people of the thousand gods." Apart from their own, they took up many of the deities and religious concepts of their neighbors. A deity pair associated with the weather and the sun was always at the head of the Hittite pantheon and was worshiped in the official national cult. Above all, vegetation, mountain, and water gods also played a role in daily religious life.

Hittite gods

One of the oldest cities of the world, Çatal Hüyük, existed in Anatolia possibly as early as 7000 BCE. The city on the west coast of Asia Minor, known as ❺ Troy (Ilium) from Homer's *Iliad* and referred to as "Wilusa" by Hittite sources, also belonged to the cultural area of ancient Anatolia. The Hittites first settled, however, in central Anatolia in the land of the Hattis, from whom their name may have derived. There they lived in numerous, independently ruled communities until about 1630 BCE, when King Labarnas II established political unity and moved his capital to the ancient city of Hattusa, after which he took his name Hattusilis I.

Hattusilis expanded the borders of the Old Kingdom that he had founded through ❶ military campaigns in western Asia Minor and northern Syria. His grandson, Mursilis I, conquered the important Syrian trading center, Aleppo, and reached Babylon with his armies around 1600 BCE.

In addition to his role as commander of military forces, the Hittite king also held, together

3

with his queen, religious offices in the state cult as the ❸ weather god and sun goddess respectively. The queen participated in council meetings, had her own chancellery, and also maintained independent diplomatic relations with other princes. After the death of the king, she retained her offices and titles as his widow. In general, ❹ women, whether they were ❷ married, widowed, or divorced, were well provided for. Hittite law also appears to have been rather progressive in comparison with the other cultures of the Near

4
above: Hittite women, spinning, eighth–seventh century BCE
left: The Hittite weather god with a bundle of lightning bolts beneath the winged sun disk

East, as the death penalty was rarely imposed. The assassination of Mursilis I by his brother-in-law Hantilis around 1590 BCE led to turmoil around the throne and a revolt of the nobility. Because of the instability in the leadership, the Hittites lost control of Syria to the Hurrite Mitanni kingdom and were forced to focus on Anatolia.

5
Artist's reconstruction of ancient Troy

ca. 2000 BCE | Hittite immigration into Asia Minor   ca. 1570-1590 BCE | Old Kingdom

ca. 7000 BCE | Founding of Çatal Hüyük   ca. 1630 BCE | Political unity under Hattusilis I   ca. 1590 BCE | Assassination of Mursilis I

■ The New Kingdom ca. 1335–1200 BCE

The rise of the Hittites marked the beginning of the New Kingdom. Weakened by fierce battles with Egypt, the empire managed to settle the conflict only to ultimately be destroyed by the sea peoples.

8 Statue of a late Hittite king, ninth century BCE

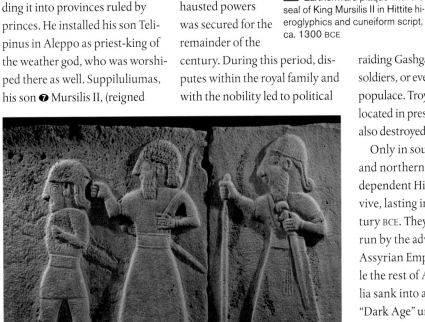

6 The Orontes River in Syria

After a transitional and chaotic phase in which the Hittites contended with enemies such as the Gashga people in their immediate vicinity, Suppiluliumas I (reigned 1380–1346 BCE), brother of Arnuwanda, established the Hittite empire by defeating the Mitannian kingdom and making vassals of the Amorite princes in Syria about 1335 BCE. He fortified his capital and organized the state, dividing it into provinces ruled by princes. He installed his son Telipinus in Aleppo as priest-king of the weather god, who was worshiped there as well. Suppiluliumas, his son **7** Mursilis II, (reigned 1345–1315 BCE), and his grandson Muwattalis (reigned 1315–1290 BCE) were all drawn into conflicts with Egypt, which had been allied with the Mitanni and also claimed hegemony over Syria. In about 1285, Muwattalis and the Egyptian pharaoh Ramses II fought at the **6** Orontes River in Syria in the **9** Battle of Kadesh. No clear victor emerged, although Muwattalis was able to maintain his hegemony over Syria. It was only after Hattusilis III signed a treaty with the Egyptians in 1259 BCE that peace between the two exhausted powers was secured for the remainder of the century. During this period, disputes within the royal family and with the nobility led to political

7 Earthenware plaque with the seal of King Mursilis II in Hittite hieroglyphics and cuneiform script, ca. 1300 BCE

disintegration. Catastrophic crop failures and famine made the import of grain from Egypt necessary and compounded the empire's difficulties. The weakened empire of the Hitttes was no longer able to withstand the onslaught of the sea peoples, particularly the Greek Achaians.

The line of **8** Hittite kings ended abruptly with Suppiluliumas II around 1200 BCE. The capital, Hattusa, was completely demolished by unknown attackers. They may have been raiding Gashga peoples, former soldiers, or even the city's own populace. Troy, a Hittite vassal state located in present-day Turkey, was also destroyed at this time.

Only in southeastern Anatolia and northern Syria did small, independent Hittite kingdoms survive, lasting into the seventh century BCE. They were finally overrun by the advance of the Neo-Assyrian Empire, while the rest of Anatolia sank into a "Dark Age" until the appearance of the Phrygians and Lydians.

The Peace Treaty between Hattusilis III and Ramses II

"Look, Reamasesa-mai-amana, the great king, the king of the country of Egypt, is at peace and fraternity with Hattusili, the great king, the king of the country of Hatti. Look, the children of Reamasesa, the great king, the king of the country of Egypt, they will be forever in a state of peace and of fraternity with the children of Hattusili, the great king, the king of the country of Hatti. They will remain in the line of our bond of fraternity and of peace; the country of Egypt and the country of Hatti will be forever in a state of peace and of fraternity as it is with us. ..."

Peace treaty in cuneiform script, 1259 BCE

9 Three marching soldiers, ninth century BCE

1335 BCE | Founding of the Hittite Empire   **1259 BCE** | Peace treaty with Egypt   **ca. 1200 BCE** | Destruction of Troy

ca. 1285 BCE | Battle of Kadesh   **ca 1200 BCE** | Last Hittite king, Suppiluliumas II

1

KINGDOMS ON THE BORDERS OF THE FERTILE CRESCENT ca. 1500–546 BCE

Besides the great empires of the Hittites, Assyrians, Babylonians, Persians, and Egyptians, there were many, often short-lived kingdoms in Asia Minor, North Syria, and Mesopotamia. They served as buffer states between the great powers and were frequently occupied by foreign soldiers. They were also sought after as partners in alliances and agreements to secure trade routes passing through their territories. During periods when their more powerful neighboring empires fell into crisis or collapsed, they sometimes won a precarious status of independence and occasionally rose to positions of considerable power and influence in the region.

Bronze helmet from Urartu, eighth century BCE

Mitanni and Urartu

In the north of the Fertile Crescent lay the Mitannian kingdom of the Indo-Iranian Hurrites. After a period of Hittite supremacy, the Kingdom of Urartu supplanted the Kingdom of Mitanni.

Around 1500 BCE, at the time of the fall of the Hittite Old Kingdom, the Hurrites founded the Kingdom of Mitanni, of which they formed only a small ruling

3

Bronze votive tablet from Urartu, showing the weather god Teisheba

elite. At its peak, between 1450 and 1350 BCE, the kingdom stretched from the Mediterranean coast through Syria to East Anatolia, Armenia, and North Mesopotamia, where Assyria was a vassal state of the Hurrites. The first written evidence, using the Akkadian alphabet, dates from the beginning of the third millenni-

um BCE, with inscriptions over the next 2000 years in Akkadian, Sumerian, Hittite, Ugaritic and Hebrew, as well as in Hurrite. At first, Egypt competed with the Hurrites for control of Syria, but then the pharaohs of the 18th dynasty formed an alliance with them against the renewed and mounting threat of the Hittites. The alliance was then sealed over many generations through marriage. Eventually, after the Middle Assyrian Kingdom had forcibly liberated itself from Mitannian dominance, the Hurrites were subdued by the Hittites under King Suppluliuna, who elevated the Hittite state to its maximum splendor, in about 1335 BCE.

In Urartu, a region on Lake Van in ❹ East Anatolia, descendents of the Hurrites established various kingdoms after the fall of the Hittite New Kingdom in 1200 BCE when it was invaded by many tribes. These merged to create a unified state around 860 BCE. The ❷ kings of Urartu expanded their kingdom into the Caucasus, East Anatolia, and northwest Iran. The

2 Inscription by Sardur III of Urartu, ca. 700 BCE

economy was based primarily on ❶, ❸ ore mining and processing, along with agriculture and trade.

Fierce disputes with the Neo-Assyrian Empire over the control of trade routes and ore deposits developed in the eighth century. The Assyrians allied themselves with the Cimmerians, an Indo-European nomadic people, and defeated Urartu in 714. The story

of Urartu comes to its ultimate end in 640 BCE with the invasion of the Scythians, who followed the Cimmerians. At the same time, Armenians entered Urartu territory from southwestern Europe. The area remained a bone of contention between the great powers, including the Roman Empire, the Parthians, and the Sassanians.

4

Landscape in East Anatolia

Phrygia and Lydia

Following the end of the Hittite empire around 1200 BCE, Anatolia experienced a cultural decline until the Phrygians in the eighth century BCE. In the seventh century the Lydians carved out an extensive area of territory in which they established powerful kingdoms.

The ❼ Phrygians emerged from the Balkans around 1100 BCE and penetrated into Asia Minor. By the eighth century, there was a thriving Phryrian kingdom in the

5
Remainder of the Temple of Artemis in the Lydian capital Sardis, steel engraving, 19th century

8
Solon before Croesus, Croesus boasts about his treasures before the Athenian lawgiver and traveler Solon, painting by Gerard van Honthorst, 1624

11
Croesus, about to be burned at the stake, is shown mercy by Cyrus, wood engraving, 19th century

center of Anatolia that maintained cultural and trade relations with the Greeks in the west and the Urartians and Assyrians in the east. The area's significant deposits of gold inspired the ❿ myth of King Midas, son of Gordius, the legendary founder of the kingdom, and the goddess Cybele. Midas committed suicide at the beginning of the seventh century when the Cimmerians, who were being driven westward by the Scythians, burned the Phrygian capital, Gordium, to the ground.

The ❺ Lydians then gained control of the western part of Asia Minor. They defeated the Cimmerians and attempted to expand their kingdom westward over the Greek colonies on the coast of Anatolia (Ionia), as well as over the entire Anatolian highlands. Their eastern border, by agreement first with the Medes and later with the Persians, was fixed at the Halys River in north-central Anatolia. The last Lydian king, ❻ Croesus—whose ❽ wealth became proverbial—conquered almost all of the Greek coastal cities. He then turned eastward after the Oracle of Delphi prophesied that a great empire would fall if he crossed the Halys. Thus feeling assured of victory, Croesus crossed the river in 546 BCE and marched against Persia but was defeated by the Persian king Cyrus II—the prophesy came true, but it was his own

great kingdom that fell. According to legend, Croesus was ⓫ pardoned shortly before he was to be burned at the stake, and he may later have become an official at the Persian court.

The Phrygians and Lydians lived on, not only in myths but also in the cultural legacy they left to the Greeks and the Romans—the cults of Dionysus and of the "Great Mother" Cybele. They also introduced the practice of ❾ minting coins to Europe.

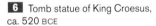

6 Tomb statue of King Croesus, ca. 520 BCE

9 Lydian gold coin from Croesus's reign, sixth century BCE

7

above: Phrygian bronze helmet, sixth century BCE
below: Midas's daughter is turned to gold by his touch, colored lithograph, 19th century

10

The Legend of Midas

The legend of Midas relates how Dionysus granted the king his wish that everything he touched would turn to gold. However, when even food and drink turned to gold, he was pushed to the verge of starvation. Then the god commanded him to bathe in the Pactolus River to be freed of his gift. It was said that this was the reason the little river in Asia Minor had such a wealth of gold. In another myth, Midas was given the ears of an ass by Apollo because he favored Apollo's rival in a contest he judged. Midas concealed his ears under a Phrygian cap. Erroneously interpreted as the cap of liberty, it later became the symbol of freedom during the French Revolution.

Statue of Paris with a Phrygian cap (fourth century BCE)

SYRIA AND PALESTINE   3000–332 BCE

❶ Syria and Palestine were of great strategic importance as military, commercial, and cultural crossroads between the early high civilizations of Egypt, Asia Minor, Mesopotamia, and the Aegean Sea. The constant wrestling for control over the area by the bordering powers prevented the formation of a unified state. Only after the upheavals caused by the sea peoples created a power vacuum was it possible for the kingdoms of David and Solomon to emerge, for a short time, as regional powers. At the same time, the Phoenicians built up a trade empire that reached from the coasts of West Anatolia to the edge of the Atlantic.

Syrian with lioness and ram, ivory statue, ninth century BCE

The Canaanites and the Amorites

The Canaanites and the Amorites developed a high civilization that fused together stylistic elements from the whole of the Ancient Orient and demonstrated the bridging role of Syria and Palestine.

The early inhabitants of Palestine are called Canaanites, those of Syria Amorites or East Canaanites. Linguistically both groups belong to the Semites. They never experienced political unity but lived in city-states ruled over by princes or priest-kings. The remains of the Canaanite city of ❷ Jericho date back to around 9000 BCE and are considered the earliest evidence of urban life. Over the centuries, the rulers of Egypt, the Hittite Empire, Assyria, and Babylon competed against each other for control of Palestine and Syria.

The trading centers situated on the Mediterranean coast held a special position among the city-states. At first, ❸ Byblos was the busiest of them. The city had enjoyed trading relations with Egypt since the third millennium BCE and was the most important port for exports of Lebanese cedar, as well as ❹ luxury goods that were

manufactured there for the Egyptian market. In the middle of the 13th century BCE, Ugarit, situated farther north, replaced Byblos as

the preeminent port city. The Mycenaean ❻ merchants had their own quarter in the city, which bears witness to trade relations with the Aegean cultures. By allying alternately with the Hittites and the Egyptians, the ❺ kings of Ugarit were able to maintain their independence until around 1200 BCE, when Ugarit was overrun by the sea peoples and completely destroyed.

Subsequent archaeological excavations of the previous site of

Foundations of a round tower in Jericho, 7000 BCE

above: Ruins of the Temple of Obelisks in Byblos
left: Example of Egyptian gold jewelry from Byblos, 19th century BCE

the city of Ugarit, present-day Ras Shamra, have uncovered a number of libraries containing ancient manuscripts written in at least four different languages.

The king of Ugarit hunting, detail on a golden plate, 14th–13th century BCE

❻ Two men agreeing on a contract, limestone relief from the city of Ugarit, 14th century BCE

Baal, bronze statue, 14th–13th BCE

Baal

Baal, or the female form Baalat, was the name of the chief deity of Canaanite and Amorite cities. They also worshiped other gods, such as the fertility goddess of war, Astarte. In Palestine, the monotheistic cult of Yahweh vied for followers with the older Baal cults and ultimately triumphed over them.

The Phoenician City-States

The Phoenicians are considered the most accomplished seafarers of antiquity. Throughout the Mediterranean and beyond they conducted trade, founded colonies, and spread their culture, which was in the tradition of the Canaanites and Amorites.

Following the devastation caused by the sea peoples, the focus of trade shifted south from Syria towards the territory of present-day Lebanon. The Greeks called this region "Phoenicia" ("purple land") after a precious dye produced there. As in Canaanite and Amorite times, Phoenicia was divided into city-states ruled by ❼ kings and great trading families. With the decline of Mycenaean and Minoan competition, the ❷ Phoenicians controlled Mediterranean trade as far as the coasts of the Iberian Peninsula and North Africa. They founded numerous ❽ colonies, including Carthage ("new city") around 814 BCE, which was later to become the most important sea power in the Western Mediterranean. The net of Phoenician ⓫ trade relations reached beyond the Mediterranean to the British Isles and the Canary Islands, and it is even possible that Phoenicians circumnavigated Africa about 600 BCE. They kept their knowledge of the ocean beyond the

"Pillars of Hercules"—the Strait of Gibraltar—absolutely secret and spread ❿ horror stories about the area to frighten off their competitors.

❾ Sidon and Tyre were the two most important Phoenician city-states, and their rulers were closely tied to the kings of Israel and Judah. In the tenth century BCE, Hiram I of Tyre supported King Solomon in the construction of a fleet for a trading expedition to the Red Sea. Tyre reached its apogee under Ittobaal I, who subjugated rival Sidon in the ninth century BCE. By this time, the Phoenicians were coming under increasing military pressure from the land powers, Assyria and Babylon, who demanded tribute from the cities. Only Tyre, situated on an impregnable island, was able to withstand the enemy forces. Phoenicia lost Sidon but remained independent despite a

13-year siege by Nebuchadressar II of Babylon that ended in 573 BCE. The Persians, on the other hand, accepted the autonomy of the Phoenicians, who made up the majority of the Persian fleet in battles against the Greeks.

It was Alexander the Great who first succeeded in conquering Tyre in 332 BCE, after a seven-month siege during which he built a causeway from the mainland to the island city. The Phoenicians were later ruled by the Diadochoi and the Romans but still managed to keep their cultural and religious identity alive.

above: Ruins of a Phoenician colony in Sa Caleta on Ibiza, founded ca. 650 BCE
left: A king with lotus stems, ivory tablet, eighth–seventh century BCE

View over Sidon with Lebanon in the distance, chalk lithograph, 19th century

The Abduction of Europa

According to Greek mythology, Zeus, the father of the gods, assumed the form of a white bull and abducted Europa, the daughter of King Agenor of Phoenicia. By him she conceived Minos, the legendary king of Crete. Much that arrived in Europe from Asia first passed through Minoan Crete, including the Phoenician alphabet.

10 Phoenician silver coin decorated with the image of a merchant ship harried by a sea monster

The Rape of Europa, painting by Rubens, 17th century

11 Phoenician merchants trade, wood engraving, 19th century

12 Phoenician merchant ship at sea, clay relief

The Israelites conquer the Canaanite city of Jericho

■ The Early Israelites and the Kingdoms of David and Solomon

The Israelites migrated into the region of Palestine in the 13th century BCE. Conflicts in the settlement areas required a military society, which extended beyond individual tribes and became the basis, around 1020 BCE, of national unity.

Many of the Canaanite city-states in Palestine were destroyed by the sea peoples around 1200 BCE, after which the ❸ Philistines settled on the coast and established a federation of individual city-states. At the same time, the Semitic Aramaeans moved in, among them the ❶ tribes of Israel. Related folk groups had previously lived in Egypt and are described in the biblical stories of Moses. These Israelite groups had in common the ❼ worship of the god Yahweh. The isolation of this god from the gods of the neighboring peoples and the maintenance of the purity of the Yahweh cult defined their society. Around the year 1020 BCE, the Israelites

David with Goliath's head, bronze statue by Verrocchio, 16th century

declared Saul their king and commander for the war against the other Aramaean tribes and the Philistines. They did not, however, grant him any internal authority, for example, to levy a general

3 A Philistine bust, relief, twelfth century BCE

tax. After ❷ Saul's death, the successful military leader ❹ David, from the tribe of Judah, was chosen as king around 1004 BCE. Unlike Saul, David relied on a private army, which he also used to seize money and estates for himself. He overrode the autonomy of the individual Israelite tribes and established a unified state, with Jerusalem as its capital and political and religious center.

David subjugated neighboring Aramaean territories until his realm eventually reached from the Euphrates River in the north to the Red Sea in the south. He was succeeded by his son ❺ Solomon, who maintained close diplomatic and trade relations with the Phoenicians, Arabs, and Egyptians. In ❽

The Philistines rob the Ark of the Covenant, the holy relic of the Israelites, painting, 19th century

Jerusalem, Solomon built a magnificent ❾ temple as the center of the Yahweh cult. There were already signs that the kingdom's power had peaked, however. Some of the Aramaean vassals regained their independence, while tax pressure, unpaid forced labor, and Solomon's tolerance of foreign cultures were stirring up discontent internally among the Israelites. Despite this, Solomon is remembered well by posterity—primarily for his proverbial ❻ wisdom.

6 Solomon settles an argument of two women claiming to be the mother of a child, book illustration, 13th c.

2 Saul commits suicide, book illustration, 15th century

The wedding of Solomon and the Egyptian pharaoh's daughter, painting, 17th century

View of the Temple Mount in Jerusalem and the so-called Dome of the Rock, built in Islamic times

David

After David killed the gigantic Philistine Goliath, Saul had him brought to his court. David was protected from the king's increasing jealousy of his popularity by his love for Saul's son Jonathan. When Jonathan fell in battle against the Philistines, Saul committed suicide and David became king. During his reign, David's own son Absalom rose up in an unsuccessful revolt against him. Later, David fell in love with Bathsheba and deployed her husband's forces in battle in such a way that he would certainly be killed. David's son by Bathsheba, Solomon, succeeded him as king.

David sees the bathing Bathsheba, book illus. ca. 1500

9 Sacrifice scene in the temple of Jerusalem

The Kingdoms of Judah and Israel

The competing claims of Solomon's successors led to a division of the kingdom. But even thereafter, the rulers of Judah and Israel were subject to strong, primarily religious opposition internally, while external pressure from the Assyrians and Babylonians increased.

After his death in 926 BCE, Solomon's kingdom collapsed. His son Rehoboam, who wanted to continue Solomon's centralist policies, was recognized as king by the tribes of Judah and Benjamin, while northern tribes instead chose **10** Jeroboam I, one of Solomon's old adversaries.

The northern kingdom, Israel, was continually shaken by dynastic change. Under King **12** Ahab and his queen Jezebel, a daughter of Ittobaal I of Tyros, social evils and the Baal cult that the queen supported provoked the resistance of the religious leader and prophet Elijah. Upon the instructions of another prophet, El-

11 King Jehu of Israel and the Assyrian king, sculpture, ninth century BCE

isha, Jehu usurped the throne about 845 BCE and killed the widowed Jezebel, her son King Joram, and many Baal adherents.

In Judah, too, where the dynasty of David had retained power, the prophets—Isaiah and Jeremiah in particular—were politically prominent. They criticized not only the religious and social conditions but also the foreign

policies of their kings. These policies were greatly influenced by the **11** Assyrian dominance of the Near East. Beginning in the ninth century BCE, the Assyrians intervened in the royal succession in Israel and then in Judah, helping enthrone their own candidates, who in return offered tribute payments.

Attempts to win independence with the aid of Egypt led to Israel's destruction in 722 BCE. The Assyrians occupied the land, ravaged Samaria, and displaced the population. After Nebuchadressar II expelled the Assyrians and Egyptians from Palestine, he installed Zedekiah as king in Judah. When Zedekiah rebelled in 587 BCE, Nebuchadressar devastated Jerusalem and annexed Judah. Most of the population was then deported into **14** "Babylonian captivity."

10 Seal of King Jeroboam I of Israel, tenth century BCE

12 Ahab and Jezebel arrange the murder of Naboth in order to steal his vineyard, book illustration, 15th century

Criticism of Rulers in the Bible

Criticism of rulers in the Near East as recorded in the Bible is unique in its sharpness. The prophet Jeremiah warned the king of Judah and predicted deportation by the Babylonians: "Say unto the king and to the queen, 'Humble yourselves, sit down: for your principalities shall come down, even the crown of your glory. . . . Judah shall be carried away captive all of it, it shall be wholly carried away.'" (Jeremiah 13:18–19)

13 Prophet Elijah kills a Baal priest, wood carving, 19th century

14 The Israelites are deported to Babylon, painting, 19th century

1

JUDAISM

Judaism is the oldest of the three great monotheistic religions and provides the historical background to Christianity and Islam. One characteristic of Judaism is an identity that involves membership in both a religion and a people. This complex dualism is embodied by the Jewish state of Israel, founded in 1948, where secularist Zionism and Orthodox Judaism coexist.

Moses sees the Promised Land

The Covenant with God

Jewish tradition teaches that God made a covenant exclusively with the people of Israel. The covenant is a central element of the Jewish religion. God, the creator of the world and of mankind, chose the people of Israel—beginning with the patriarch Abraham—as his people. Being the "chosen people" is at once equally a mark of honor

3

Moses with the Torah

and a burden. Man is directed to follow God's commandments, but, at the same time, is called upon to behave in an ethically responsible way and is accountable for his transgressions. The relationship to God is understood as a dialog between God and mankind. God often revealed himself to man through prophets who proclaimed his will. Moses stands out among them as the deliverer of the Law—the Torah—which is doctrine, law, and according to Jewish tradition, the complete revelation of God in 613 commandments and prohibitions. It was Moses who transformed the belief in the Jewish tribal god— "God, the Father"— into a belief in a universal god; "Yahweh" was at first only the mightiest among the gods, but then he became the only god.

The Promised Land and the Diaspora

❸ Moses not only brought God's law to the people of Israel but was also called to lead them out of captivity in Egypt to the ❶ "Promised Land." The concept of the Promised Land has played a significant role in Judaism. The patriarchs Abraham, Isaac, and Jacob, with whom the history of Israel begins, were nomads in the land of Canaan. Abraham received the promise that his posterity would be a great people and that God would give them the land of Canaan. The promise was fulfilled after Moses led the people of Israel out of Egypt. After a long trek through the desert, they occupied and settled in Palestine. There followed the founding of the Israelite kingdom and its capital Jerusalem, and the erection of the Jewish shrine, ❹ the Temple. To this day, Jerusalem and the Temple Mount are the most sacred sites of the Jewish faith.

Judaism was also shaped and given its decisive character by the Diaspora communities living as minorities among foreign cultures. This pattern began with the Assyrian conquest of the Kingdom of Israel, which saw the Jews dispersed around the empire. In parallel to this tradition in Palestine, another tradition, the Kingdom of Judah, developed further south in Babylon. It wavered between assimilation and segregation, and had its own liturgy and literature. By the time of Roman rule, this had become the dominant form.

4

The temple of Solomon, reconstructed model

The Torah and the Talmud: The Literature of Judaism

Judaism is the quintessential book religion, and Christianity and Islam—the other "religions of the book"—also incorporate the Torah. Christianity includes the Jewish Torah as the first five chapters of the Old Testament in its Bible, and through the founder of the religion, Jesus, it has a firm foundation in Judaism. Islam, too, recognizes many of the Jewish prophets and patriarchs. Abraham, or Ibrahim, is considered the arch-patriarch of Islam. The ❺ Torah comprises the absolute

2   The Talmud commentary by Isaac Ben Solomon, manuscript,16th c.

core of the Jewish religion. Everyday life is regulated by its laws and prohibitions. Knowledge of the Torah and Torah scholarship enjoy the greatest respect. Since the earliest times, rabbinical commentaries and interpretations have been written down in the ❷ Talmud. There are two different versions of the Talmud, the Palestinian and the Babylonian. The latter was much more influential and has been the subject of countless analyses and interpretations. In Jewish tradition, every word of the Torah has major significance.

5

Rabbi reading the Torah

19th–17th century BCE	Abraham's lifetime according to the Bible
ca. 965 BCE	King Solomon of Judea
from 9th century BCE	Scriptures of the Old Testament written
5th century BCE	Torah becomes canonical authority

Judaism under Arab and Christian Rule

In the Middle Ages, the clash with foreign cultures led to the development of various currents within Judaism. To this day, one differentiates between Oriental, Ashkenazic (Christian Europe), and Sephardic (Moorish Spain and Africa) cultures within Judaism. The influences of Islam

7 Jews depicted as profiteers, Christian book illustration, ca. 1250

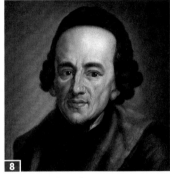

8 Moses Mendelssohn

and Christianity, as well as the circumstances in which the Jews lived in the various countries, found expression in the religious practice, theology, and self-conceptualization of the Jews.

For centuries the Jewish communities, as members of a fellow religion of the book, enjoyed tolerance under Arab rule, and this made social integration possible. Here, Jewish intellectual life experienced a golden age that radiated as far as France and Italy. The great Jewish philosopher and theologian

Maimonides wrote an important commentary to the Talmud in Moorish Cordoba, Spain. The Kabbala, a form of Jewish mysticism, emerged in northern Spain.

In contrast to this, the relationship between the Christian and Jewish communities was strained from the outset. Christianity held the Jews responsible for the death of Jesus, for which they became scapegoats. In addition, the prosperity of individual Jews aroused **7** envy and resentment, and the Church took advantage of this. In Central and Eastern Europe, the Ashkenazim were driven out of their traditional, hereditary vocations in international trade and money lending, while the skilled trades were denied to them by exclusion from the guilds. They were increasingly driven out of the cities and into the countryside. Horrifying pogroms against the Jews took place as part of the Crusades and reoccurred repeatedly into the late Middle Ages. Out of this experience with all its suffering, the renewal movement of the Chassidim developed. It lived on primarily in Eastern European Judaism. Moreover, in Poland and Russia, where the majority of the West European Jews fled, life in the *shtetl* developed.

In early modern times, the Central and Eastern European Jews continued to be subjected to in-

10 Theodor Herzl

tense repression. They were, however, allowed to return to the professions of money-lending and merchant trading. Wealthy Jews were important participants in cultural and intellectual life. In the Age of the Enlightenment, efforts toward emancipation and enlightenment, led by **8** Moses Mendelssohn, were also made in Jewish theology.

The Holocaust and Zionism

European anti-Semitism reached its horrendous climax in the 20th century. The **6** Holocaust—a product of the murderous ideology of the German Nazi regime—was the attempt to eradicate European Jewry systematically and destroy their culture.

Beginning in 1882 there were repeated waves of Jewish immigrants into Palestine, and that immigration increased dramatically with the rise of Fascism in Europe. Hopes for a Jewish state in Palestine were nurtured by the British Balfour Declaration of 1917. Zionism, a political movement seeking a Jewish homeland, was not a postwar phenomenon. Its roots date back to its 19th century founder, **10** Theodor Herzl, although the location was at that time subject to debate. Developments during and after World War II, however, accelerated the realization of the Zionist project.

6 Entrance to Birkenau, the main concentration camp at Auschwitz

In 1948 the **9** State of Israel was founded. Of the roughly 14.4 million Jews in the world today, about 4.7 million reside in Israel. A still larger community is in the United States. Religion plays a significant role in the day-to-day policies of the modern state of Israel. **11** Strict religious fractions base their nationalistic claims on their religious convictions. It has proved impossible to reconcile these claims with those of displaced Palestinian Arabs. The conflict continues to this day.

9 Foundation of the State of Israel, 1948

11 Orthodox Jews in Jerusalem, 1962

THE MEDES AND THE PERSIAN EMPIRE OF THE ACHAEMENIDS CA. 800–330 BCE

The Indo-Iranian tribes of ❶ Medes and Persians settled in the western highlands of Iran on the border of Mesopotamia beginning late in the second millennium BCE. The Persians annexed Media in 550 BCE and founded the last great empire of the Ancient Orient, which survived until it was conquered by Alexander the Great in 330 BCE. The historical assessment of the Persians' rule has often been biased and has judged them to be despotic. This is to overlook the fact that under their rule an immense integrated cultural and economic region was provided with security and stability.

Persian and Median soldiers, stone relief from Persepolis, fifth c. BCE

Clay model of two harnessed animals with a driver, art from the Persian culture, ca. 1100 BCE

Cultivated fields, landscape of the former Media, northwest Iran

Procession of archers, life-size frieze from Darius I's palace in Susa, ca. 500 BCE

■ The Medes and the Rise of the Persian Empire under Cyrus II

Building on the conquests of his Median ancestors, Cyrus II created a world empire.

The only sources of information about the early period of the Medes are Assyrian accounts of conflicts with various mountain tribes. It wasn't until the eighth century BCE that these tribes were united as a nation under a king. ❸ Media fell under Assyrian and later under Scythian domination. King Cyaxares freed himself from this rule and, together with the Babylonians, destroyed the Neo-Assyrian Empire between 614 and 612 BCE. He and his son Astyages extended their rule all the way to Asia Minor, where they agreed with the Lydians to recognize the Halys River as their common border. The ❺ Median kingdom stretched eastward to Bactria (present-day Afghanistan).

Among the vassals of the Medes were the Persians. Astyages married one of his daughters to the Persian king Cambyses I, the great-grandson of the legendary founder of the Persian ruling house, Achaemenes. Later, however, Cyrus II, the son of Cambyses I, rebelled against Astyages and by 550 had conquered the Median kingdom. From then on, the Me-

des were equals with the Persians, who adopted many elements of administration, ❼ court ceremony, and ❷ art from their former rulers.

Medians paying tribute to the Assyrians

❹ The tomb of Cyrus II, located in the royal capital city of Pasargadae

Cyrus II's conquests continued. In 546 BCE he defeated Croesus of Lydia and subjugated the Greek coastal cities of Asia Minor (Ionia). In 539 he conquered the

Neo-Babylonian Kingdom. Babylon—with the ancient Persian capitals of ❻ Susa and Pasargadae and the Median capital Ecbatana—thereafter became one of Cyrus's preferred residences. He allowed the ❽ Jews, living in Babylon since their deportation in 587 BCE, to return to their homeland. Cyrus II's last campaign took him north, where he ❹ died in 530 fighting the Massagetae.

Persian (left) and Median (right) dignitaries

Cyrus II with the Jewish prophet Daniel, painting by Rembrandt, 17th century

---

614–612 BCE | Fall of the Neo-Assyrian Empire   **550 BCE** | Achaemenids annex Media   **ca. 540 BCE** | Cyrus II rules Asia Minor

ca. 600 BCE | Foundation of the Median Kingdom   **546 BCE** | Cyrus II defeats Croesus of Lydia

The Persian Empire under Darius I

Under Darius I (the Great), perhaps the most significant ruler of the Ancient Orient, the Persian Empire of the Achaemenids experienced its golden age.

Cambyses II, the son of Cyrus II, conquered Egypt in 525 BCE. In order to foil an attempted coup, he had his younger brother Smerdis (Bardiya) secretly murdered. In the absence of the king, a Magus named Gaumâta pretended to be Smerdis and claimed the throne. Cambyses II died on the return march from Egypt in 522 BCE, but his cousin Darius stopped the crowning of the "false Smerdis" and restored the rule of the Achaemenids.

With the turmoil around the throne settled, Darius I consolidated his empire from within. He established provinces, which were required to pay taxes. Although the province governors, called satraps, had

Darius I on a throne, painted vase, late fourth century BCE

much latitude, they were controlled by a system of ❾ officials and spies. A well-developed network of roads equipped with a message and postal service and protected by patrols provided improved communications. ❿ Darius also reformed the rule of law and introduced an empire-wide coinage, the daric. In 497 BCE he completed the construction of a canal between the Nile and the Red Sea that had been begun by the pharaohs. In Persia he laid the cornerstone for the ⓭ palace city of ⓫ Persepolis, which would be developed further by his ⓬ successors. Darius I also promoted ⓮ Zoroastrianism without suppressing the other religions of his multi-national empire.

Darius I pushed the boundaries of the Persian Empire to the Indus River in the east and to the Danube in the northwest of Thrace and subjugated Macedonia in northern Greece. He was not always successful in his military undertakings, however, failing in his campaign against the Scythians in 513–512 BCE. From 500 to 494, Darius was forced to suppress the "Ionian Rebellion" of the Greek city-states in Anatolia, and a punitive expedition to Greece ended with his defeat at the Battle of Marathon in

490. Darius I died in 486 while preparing for another war against the Greeks.

9   Persian official in robes, silver statuette, fifth century BCE

11
above: The ruins of Persepolis
below: Private palace of Darius I in Persepolis

13

12

King Darius says:

"Ahura Mazda, when he saw this earth in commotion, thereafter bestowed it upon me, made me king; I am king. By the favor of Ahura Mazda I put it down in its place; what I said to them, that they did, as was my desire.

"If now you shall think that 'How many are the countries which King Darius held?' look at the sculptures [of those] who bear the throne, then shall you know, then shall it become known to you: the spear of a Persian man has gone forth; then shall it become known to you: a Persian man has delivered battle far from Persia."

Rock tombs of (from left) Artaxerxes I (or Darius II), Xerxes I (or Artaxerxes I), and Darius I at Naqsh-i-Rustam, near Persepolis

left: Darius I with crown prince Xerxes, stone relief, ca. 485 BCE
below: Darius I hunting lions, protected by the god Ahura Mazda, round seal print, ca. 500 BCE

14

■ The Persian Empire under the Later Achaemenids

Rebellion in the provinces and intrigue within the royal house weakened the power of the Persians under the successors of Darius I. Warfare against the Greeks remained inconclusive until Alexander the Great conquered the Persian Empire in 330 BCE.

At the beginning of his rule in 486 BCE, ❶ Xerxes I, the son and successor of Darius I, had to crush a rebellion in Egypt. He then attempted to carry out his father's plans for the conquest of

2

The Athenian Themistocles and Artaxerxes I, steel engraving, 1842

4

Artaxerxes III's tomb, carved into the rock face, near Persepolis

5

Alexander the Great with Darius III's body

Greece. Xerxes only succeeded in advancing as far as Athens, and ultimately his fleet was defeated at the Battle of Salamis in 480 BCE, and his army was routed at the Battle of Plataea the following year. By then, Xerxes had already returned to his ❸ capital, where he remained from then on, dedicating himself especially to building activities. He was murdered during a palace revolt in 465.

Xerxes' son Artaxerxes I ended the conflict with ❷ Greece by signing the Peace of Callias in 448 BCE. The Persians subsequently shifted their support from one belligerent to another during the Peloponnesian War and in the disputes between Athens, Sparta, and Thebes of the fourth century BCE. In return for this decisive support, the Greek powers fighting Sparta handed over the Ionian cities to the Persians in the "King's Peace" the Peace of Antalkidas.

The Persians were expelled from Egypt in 404 BCE, but ❹ Artaxerxes III recaptured it in 343 B.C. He also supported the opponents of Philip II of Macedonia, who had united the Greeks and planned to wage a war against the Persians. Artaxerxes III and his son and heir were both poisoned in palace intrigues. Whereupon Darius III, a member of a minor branch of the Achaemenids, assumed the throne in 336, becoming the last Persian king.

1

Xerxes receives a Median dignitary

In 334 BCE, Alexander the Great of Macedonia opened the campaign against the Persians planned by his father Philip II. Darius III suffered crushing defeats in 333 at ❻ Issus and in 331 at Gaugamela. Following these reverses he fled to the north of Iran, where he was betrayed and ❺ murdered in 330. By 324, Alexander had conquered the whole of the Persian Empire. The Seleucid dynasty that ruled the area after Alexander's death was succeeded by the Arsacids. They presided over a revival of Achaemenid traditions, and this continued under the Sassinian kings who overthrew them in 230 BCE.

Persia in Greek Historiography

Persian history was retold in Europe in Herodotus's Histories and in the Anabasis by Xenophon. Xenophon was one of thousands of Greek mercenaries who took part in the coup attempt by Cyrus the Younger against his brother, King Artaxerxes II, in 401 BCE. After Cyrus was defeated and killed he led the survivors back to safety.

above: Xenophon

3

The Propylaia of Xerxes I, the "gate to all countries," Persepolis, fifth c. BCE

6

Darius III at the Battle of Issus

■ Religion in the Persian Empire

Zoroastrianism flourished under the Achaemenids. The Zoroastrian concept of the afterlife had a significant influence on both Judaism and Christianity.

7 Zarathustra, mural from Syria

The ancient Iranian religion of Zoroastrianism recognized a great number of gods and was probably related to the Vedic religion of ancient India. The rituals of the Magi, a hereditary priestly cast, predominated in the cult. Their name is derived from the Magoi, a Median tribe whose members were renowned for their spiritual practices. The prophet ❼ Zarathustra (or Zoroaster in Greek) appeared around 600 BCE, probably out of the ranks of the ❽ Magi, to proclaim the teachings of the one god ❶ Ahura Mazda. Zara-

thustra criticized the Magi for, among other things, their bloody ❾ animal sacrifices and thus earned their enmity. ❿ King Darius I became a follower of Zarathustra's teachings after thwarting the coup attempt of the Magus usurper Gaumâta. Over time, the Magi adapted to Zoroastrianism and were able to defend their monopoly on religious worship.

According to Zarathustra, Ahura Mazda is the almighty creator of the cosmos and judge at the end of time. He represents the original, right, and good world order and is identified with "the Good Spirit" that opposes "the Evil Spirit." Man is free to decide between these two options but will be judged according to his deeds at the Last Judgment. Along with this dualistic value system, strict purity of ritual is particularly characteristic of Zoroastrianism. Priests were allowed to approach the ❿ eternal flame that burned in the temples in honor of the god only with their mouths covered so they wouldn't desecrate it with their breath. Fire, earth, and water were considered holy elements.

During the time of Persian dominance, the Jews came in contact with the concepts of

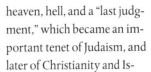

8 Praying man with goat, golden statuette, twelfth century BCE

heaven, hell, and a "last judgment," which became an important tenet of Judaism, and later of Christianity and Islam. Manichaeism was formed out of a fusion of Zoroastrianism with Christian and Buddhist teachings and was, for a time, early Christianity's strongest competitor.

Zoroastrianism once again experienced a golden period as the state religion in the Sassanid empire from the third to seventh centuries CE, only to disappear from Iran almost completely after the Arab invasions that introduced Islam. Many followers of the teachings of Zarathustra emigrated, primarily to India, where they were called "Parsis" after their land of origin, Persia. Today there are around 200,000 Parsis, about half of them in India.

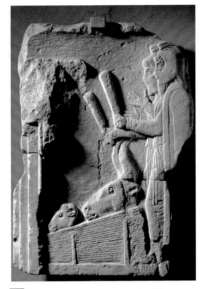

9 Ritual sacrifice of a goat, detail from stone relief, end of the fifth century BCE

10 Fire altar, Achaemenid temple, known as the Kaaba of Zarathustra, fifth c. BCE

11 Two sphinxes carry Ahura Mazda, cylindrical seal stamp, ca. 590–330 BCE

12 Lance bearers in Persian and Median dress under the winged sun of Ahura Mazda, stone relief from Persepolis, fifth century BCE

343 BCE | Artaxerxes III recaptures Egypt   **336 BCE** | Death of Philip II   **333 BCE** | Battle of Issus   **330–324 BCE** | Alexander conquers Persia

336 BCE | Darius III comes to power   **334 BCE** | Alexander the Great opens campaign against the Persians   **330 BCE** | Death of Darius III

THE NOMADS OF THE EURASIAN STEPPES

Up to the fourth century BCE, Indo-European mounted nomads ranged the wide steppes of the Ukraine, southern Russia, and Kazakhstan until the advancing Huns triggered the "Great Migration of Peoples." But even before this, individual tribes left the region and moved into the Mediterranean area, the highlands of Iran, or India. Some, such as the Hittites, Medes, Persians, or the later Parthians, settled down and established kingdoms. Others stayed on the move and were, like the Cimmerians, eventually annihilated by enemies or withdrew back to their original territory of settlement, as the Scythians did.

■ The Scythians, Sakians, and Sarmatians

Outsiders have frequently sought to divide nomads of the Eurasian steppes into various peoples and tribes. Greek and Roman authors, in particular, attempted to transcribe the flexible organization of these peoples into categories familiar to them.

3 Sarmatian cavalrymen on armored horses, detail from Trajan's Pillar, Rome, 113 CE

2 Fight between a tiger and wolf, Scythian gold plate, sixth c. BCE

The homeland of the ❶ Scythians is thought to have been in the area of present-day Kazakhstan. Some began to move westward in the first millennium BCE while the rest—the Sakians—remained. The Scythians drove the Cimmerians, another nomadic people, out of their homeland north of the Black Sea. They ❸ crossed the Caucasus and pushed down into Mesopotamia and Asia Minor.

The Persian kings were constantly at war with the various nomadic peoples on the northern borders of their kingdom. In 530 BCE, Cyrus II fell in battle against Tomyris, the Queen of the Massagetae, part of the Sarmatian tribe related to the Scythians and Sakians. Darius I's attempt to subjugate the Scythians in 513–512 BCE also failed. The Persians and other Near East rulers recruited

nomads as mercenaries for their armies or made alliances with them. Even in Athens, Scythians were used as police. These peoples and tribes never formed fixed units for a long period of time, but rather joined into confederations under a common figure when an outside threat made it necessary. The Scythian high king Atheas, who died in battle in 339 against Philip II of Macedonia, was one such leader.

Starting in the third century BCE, the Scythians were slowly absorbed by the Sarmatians, and

by the first century BCE only a small group in ❹ Crimea remained. During the "Great Migration of Peoples," most of the Sarmatians merged with the Goths and the Huns. The Sakians arrived in India around 100 BCE, where they established kingdoms that survived for centuries.

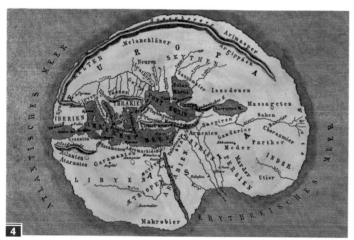

4 The Earth according to Herodotus, showing the Scythians and the Massagetae in the far northeast, wood carving, 19th century

5 Scythians offer milk to the Roman poet Ovid living in exile on the Crimean Peninsula, painting by Delacroix, 19th century

530 BCE Death of Cyrus II		**ca. 450 BCE** Herodotus writes about the Scythians	
from ca. 1000 BCE Scythians immigrate into Asia Minor	**513–512 BCE** Persia attacks the Scythians	**ca. 350 BCE** The Scythians and Sarmatians settle	

The Scythian Culture and Society

The Scythians left no written records of their own. Greek and Roman sources, along with archaeological finds, provide the only information about their lives.

6
Beard comb with a carved handle showing Scythian soldiers in combat, ca. 500 BCE

The leaders of the Scythians were princes and were buried in elaborate burial mounds called kurgans. The dead were often embalmed and interred in a central burial chamber. Many times, the horses of the deceased were bu-

ried with them in adjoining chambers, highlighting the importance of these animals to the Scythians. Weapons and finely worked ❺, ❻ gold objects were common burial gifts; other items included drinking ❽ vessels, jewelry, and armor, and pictures of hunting, battles, or banquet scenes. Domesticated animals seem to have frequently accompanied the dead to their tombs. ❾ Women were also buried with weapons of war, which seems to suggest that not only queens like Tomyris but also common Scythian women may have fought in conflicts. Some historians have cited this as

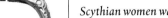

7 Gold armband, sixth–fifth century BCE

8
The Battle of the Amazons, painting by Rubens, ca. 1600

a possible historical basis for the Greek myth of the Asiatic women warriors, the ❼ Amazons.

One of the main facts known about the Scythians was their custom of "blood brotherhood," which was widespread among warriors and formed the basis for lifelong fighting bands. The ❷ mounted warriors were lightly armed and wore coats of chain mail for protection. In the hands of skilled archers, poisoned arrows could do great damage from a distance. For close combat, the short sword, battle-axe, and spiked mace were the preferred weapons. Their battle technique—a short, fast attack followed by immediate retreat—was widely feared and gave them the advantage over unwieldy armies of infantry. The Scythians also practiced trade, agriculture, and herding. Scythian grain, furs, live-stock, and slaves were exported through the Greek colonies on the Crimean Peninsula.

The "Wild" Scythians

Come, friends! let's not shout and scream /
like Scythian drunks
but let us study our wine, friends/
and accompany its drinking
with beautiful songs.

(Anacreon, Greek lyric poet, sixth century BCE)

9 **above:** Scythian warriors, gold vessel, fourth century BCE

10
Women riding on horses in a procession, stone relief, fifth century BCE

Amazons

Scythian women warriors, who even led armies, perhaps served as a model for the Amazons of Greek mythology. Like the Scythians, the Amazons were supposed to have lived on the shores of the Black Sea. They only temporarily lived together with men. Of their children, they only raised the girls. The girls' left breasts were burned off so that later they would not hinder them shooting the bow and arrow—thus, perhaps, the origin of the name Amazon, from amazós (Greek for "without breast"). Herodotus in the fifth century BCE, however, wrote about a matriarchal society in Asia Minor that also could have served as a model for the Amazons.

THE RELIGIONS OF INDIA, CHINA, AND JAPAN

All present-day world religions originated in Asia. The three major monotheistic religions Judaism, Christianity, and Islam originated in the Near East, and Hinduism and Buddhism, both polytheistic religions, find their roots in India. While ❶ Buddhism has also become popular in the Western world today, religions such as Hinduism in India, Confucianism in China, and Shinto in Japan are closely tied to, and have also significantly influenced, the cultures and social structures of their respective countries and regions.

Shakyamuni Buddha with Confucius and Lao-Tzu, the three teachers

Hinduism

Hinduism is a religion of India that has diversified into many forms. It resulted from the merging of the Vedic religion, which was introduced by the Aryans, and the religion of the native peoples, but had no known founder. It is difficult to comprehend for members of other religions as it has neither a standardized canon of scripture nor a fixed pantheon of gods, nor an organizational structure that can be compared to that of a church, for instance. Hinduism has no uniform philosophy, and the forms of belief and cult are extremely multifarious. The polytheistic belief in gods such as ❸ Vishnu, Shiva, and Shakti is only one of its manifestations. Coexistent with these are, for example, monotheistic tendencies alongside philosophical speculations that completely reject a personified cosmic guiding force. The one conviction common to all variations is the belief in an all-encompassing world order (dharma) that structures human life and its environment, which Buddhism also adopted. Another characteristic is the belief in the eternal cycle of birth, death, and reincarnation, based on the assumption that the conduct and deeds in each life influence the form of existence in the next. Hinduism developed complicated sacrificial rituals, and the

Shiva, Brahma, Vishnu, and another deity with the goddess Devi

priest caste of Brahmans' exact knowledge thereof ensured their considerable influence in Indian society.

The caste system is one of the pillars of ❹ Hindu society. It possibly originated from the partition of immigrants from the indigenous population. The individual castes differentiate themselves through specific customs and responsibilities in society. Although social differences between the castes were officially abolished with India's independence in 1947, in effect they continue to exist. Today, Hinduism once again plays a significant role in the national identity of India.

Buddhism

In the sixth century BCE, the "reformer" Siddhartha Gautama (Buddha) rejected the caste system associated with Hinduism and propagated universal compassion and nonviolence toward all living things. He did not see himself as the founder of a religion but rather as an advocate of a self-redeeming doctrine that had strong ethical traits. The underlying belief of Buddha's philosophy was that human existence, fundamentally, meant suffering. His goal was to overcome suffering, which he believed was caused by worldly desires and passions. This goal could be achieved, he believed, by immersion in the true nature of things and the rejection of self and would culminate in nirvana. Nirvana, directly translated as "nothing," is the cessation of the reincarnation cycle and

❷ Shakyamuni Buddha, Tibetan statue, eleventh century

the liberation from suffering as a result of this release from existence on Earth.

As Buddhism spread through Asia, and the monks and laity built their own organizational structures, it absorbed elements of folk religions. The development of the compassionate redemption figure (bodhisattva) was one result. Gradually Buddhism

Sacrificial ceremony with Buddhist priests and monks in the temple area of Swayambunath in Kathmandu, Nepal

❹ Hindus doing their ritual washings in the Ganges River in Benares (Varanasi), India

evolved into a religion with its own temples and cults.

The early rulers of India, from the sixth century BCE on, installed Buddhism as a form of state religion, so that Hinduism was, at times, completely suppressed on the subcontinent. Buddhism split into several differing schools: Hinayana ("lesser vehicle") Buddhism, with its ❺ austere monks, and the more diverse and liberal Mahayana ("greater vehicle") Buddhism are two of the most significant schools. Contemporary ❷ Tibetan Buddhism headed by the Dalai Lama represents a form of Vajrayana Buddhism.

The Religions of China

The folk religion of China, in which ancestor worship and belief in spirits and nature deities played a large role, is strongly represented to this day. Other important religious currents in China, which have mixed with the folk religion, include Taoism, the teachings of Confucius, and Buddhism.

One characteristic of Chinese thought is the belief in the designed and universal harmony of heaven, Earth, and man. The cosmos is considered a well-ordered organism that is governed by a "Supreme Master," who is not always conceived as a personified unity. People were thought to be linked to and able to communicate with the supernatural world at first through shamans or priests, and

6 Lao-Tzu on his way to the mountains, from a Chinese bronze group

later through the emperor. He was the recipient of the "Mandate of Heaven" and was political and religious guarantor for cosmic order on Earth.

Taoism developed in the sixth century BCE and is attributed to ❻ Lao-Tzu. In his book *Tao Te Ching* ("The Book of the Way and Its Power"), written in the third or fourth century BCE, he described the Tao, or "the Way," as the original source of all existence and power possessed by living things. The T'ai Ch'ai, originally presented as a unity, was split into the opposite forces of ❽ *yin* and *yang*, through whose interplay creative forces resulted. Taoism propagated a withdrawal from the world of human reality and an immersion in nature. It very soon merged with the idea of the deities in the folk religion, stressed magic elements such as the search for the "elixir of life," and developed its own temples.

8 Plate with yin and yang, symbol of the principle of Tao

9 Heaven's king standing on a demon, Tang dynasty

Confucianism

The teachings of China's most successful political philosophy opposed Taoism's retreat from society. The philosophers ❼ Confucius and Mencius (Meng-tzu) developed a doctrine of lifelong learning and personal modesty without withdrawal from the world. The ideal human, according to the philosophy, was the aristocratic "noble" who lived a "humanitarian" life. He would be educated and active as councilor and servant of the state, which needed his service. Confucianism stressed the ritual of ancestor worship and a deep sense of hierarchical family unity. As a result, it quickly became the leading state doctrine of China after 200 BCE. Soon the Confucian attitude and training was compulsory for all civil servants.

The doctrine eventually stagnated within a hierarchy, and the state-celebrated Confucius worship took on religious traits, despite Confucius's assertion that he knew nothing of the gods. He did, however, consider religious rites to be of importance, as they strengthened order.

7 Picture of the Chinese philosopher Confucius, ca. 551–479 BCE, stone engraving in Ch'ue-fou

Shinto

The ❿ Shinto religion was tied to the national identity and monarchy of Japan. The story of Japan's origin and the ❾ descent of the emperor Jimmu Tenno from the sun goddess Amaterasu plays a determining role in the religion. Ancestor worship, along with the worship of innumerable deities (kami)—primarily clan divinities and spirits of nature—is the most important element of Shinto. The values and behavioral forms transmitted by the Shinto belief system characterize many of the traditions of Japanese society. When Buddhism reached Japan, the two belief systems became closely intertwined, and both continue to coexist to this day.

10 Gate leading to Shimogamo Shinto temple in Kyoto, Japan

INDIA FROM THE BEGINNINGS TO THE INVASION OF ALEXANDER THE GREAT

From very early times, the culture of the Indian subcontinent was marked by the great number of ethnic and linguistic groups living in the region. This diversity was the result of the many waves of migration that settled the subcontinent. Aryan immigrants put their stamp on the first civilization by introducing into it their gods, caste system, and political order. More complex state structures gradually developed out of the original tribal societies.

Citadel of Mohenjo-Daro, Sind Province, Pakistan—after Harappa, the most important excavated city of the Indus culture

India's Early Period and the Indus Culture

A great variety of cultural forms took shape early in the history of the subcontinent. The first major culture to assert itself was the Harappa, which arose in the area of present-day Pakistan.

Evidence shows that humans settled India between 40,000 and 30,000 BCE at the latest. These first inhabitants probably migrated out of Africa by way of the Arabian Peninsula. Several waves of migration followed, resulting in numerous, diverse ethnic

Bronze figurine, Harappa culture, ca. 2500 BCE

Indra, Nepalese sculpture, 15th century

groups settling in India. Among the inhabitants, five great language groups developed. The Indo-Aryan (predominantly Hindi) or Indic language, which became the language of religious texts, emerged in northern Sri Lanka and the Maldives. Dravidian, the language of archaic literature, appeared in the south of India and (as Tamil) in parts of Sri Lanka. The other, less widespread language groups

were the Austro-Asiatic languages, composed of the Munda tongues; the Sino-Tibetan languages in Kashmir, Nepal, and Bhutan; and the autochthonous remnant languages.

The first inhabitants of the subcontinent were hunter-gatherers, who were superseded by farmers and herdsmen from 7000 BCE By 6000 BCE the emergence of a discernible proto-culture began. From this, the ❶, ❽ Indus or ❷, ❸ Harappa culture, which flourished between 2600 and 1900 BCE, evolved on the plains of the river Indus. It is named after the city of Harappa, which was discovered in 1921 CE in northeastern Pakistan. The civilization was characterized by advanced agriculture, as evidenced by a highly developed irrigation system and large granaries.

The society's administrators used standardized weights, measurements, and ❺, ❼ seals. The Harappa script, which is etched

into about 5000 surviving seals and tablets, was in use around 3300 BCE and has not yet been deciphered. There were large settlements with planned streets, public buildings, and fortified citadels. Archaeological finds indicate sophisticated commercial structures.

In around 1900 BCE, the settlement suddenly fell after being struck by floods and attacked by outsiders. The southern Indus plains were completely given up as a result, but Indus culture lived on in the animal and sacrificial cults of later groups. An example of this is the cult surrounding the ❾ sacred cow.

2 Harappa royal priest, limestone carving, ca. 2500 BCE

5 Official seal with animal heads, Indus culture

6 Chariot, bronze model, Harappa culture

The Arrival of the Indo-Aryans

The invading Indo-Aryan peoples were organized into tribal monarchies. When they arrived, they dominated the culture of India. Nevertheless, there was ultimately an intermixing with the native population.

7 Seal decorated with unicorn, Harappa culture

Among the Indo-Aryans moving into India in the second half of the second millennium BCE was the Sintasha culture from the eastern Ural mountains. Like the Hurrites of the Mitanni kingdom in northern Iraq and northern Syria, their military superiority was based on their early use of the ❻ chariot. As they pushed into northern India, they introduced the early Aryan gods (Mithra, Varuna, ❹ Indra) to the cultures they encountered.

How the Aryan invasion actually took place is disputed among experts. It was most likely a case of migration rather than conquest. The resettlement probably took place in several waves, coming from the West through Iran.

Along the way, the Indo-Aryans picked up elements of the Oxus culture, which had flourished in southern Tajikistan from around 2400 to 1600 BCE. The greater part of our knowledge about the arrival of the Aryans, and the oldest literary work written in an Indo-European language, comes from the Rig-Veda. Vedism was the earliest Aryan religion of India. In its verses we learn, for example, that the Aryans were cattle breeders. The Aryans did not see themselves as a race—in contrast to later Aryan ideologies of the 19th and 20th centuries—but as members of a particular cultural group who spoke the Vedic (Sanskrit) language. They were soon the dominant class in North India and spoke of other peoples as "enemies" or "slaves." Only after a long period of time did an accommodation with the native population occur.

The Vedas are considered religious texts of purely Aryan origin, although India's early ❿ religions probably arose through a process of fusion of Aryan and native elements. The Rig-Veda refers to the native people as "idol" and "phallus" worshippers and the veneration of the stone Phalli (*lingam*) as fertility symbols can be traced to them. The Rig-Veda also describes the early organization of the Aryans into tribal monarchies, and mentions the Bharata people in Punjab. The Bharata king Sudas is said to have defeated his enemies in the Battle of the Ten Kings by bursting the dams (Rig-Veda 7, 18). Poets played a major role in the Aryan culture as chroniclers of the lives and deeds of the kings.

The Four Vedas

The Vedas ("knowledge") constitute India's oldest literature, a collection of religious hymns and verses. They contain the religious, philosophical, and ritual knowledge used by the priests and poets of the Vedic period (between 1500 and 500 BCE). The canon of the Vedas was compiled around 1000 BCE. The oldest Veda is the Rig-Veda. The Sama Veda, which follows, is made up of melodies and texts to accompany sacrificial rituals. The Yajur Veda contains verses and dietary requirements to go with the sacrifice. The Atharva Veda is primarily composed of magic formulas and poetical-philosophical speculation.

above: Boy receives lessons in the holy Vedas in a Brahman school in Trichur

8 Brick-lined well that supplied the Mohenjo-Daro Citadel, in today's Sind Province, in the southeast of Pakistan

9 Holy zebu bull in India, decorated with richly embroidered cloths

10 Religious scene depicting Indra appealing to the goddess, Indian miniature

◼ The Nations of the Middle Vedic Period

In the Kuru period, India's caste system and complex religious rituals developed. The hierarchical society spread throughout the entire subcontinent.

Around 1000 BCE India entered the Middle Vedic period. This began in northwest India with the unification of 30 Aryan tribes from the Rig-Veda era to form a great tribal entity: the Kuru-Pancala. The leading tribe, from

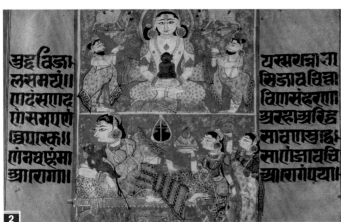

2 The birth of Mahavira, Indian miniature, ca. 1400

which the kings were drawn, was the Bharata. Their capital was situated in Hastinapura, present-day Delhi.

During this period, the transition to iron working began and the distinctive "Painted Gray Ware" pottery became prevalent. The Vedic Indians retained a seminomadic lifestyle; even the kings did not lead fully sedentary lives. Lower down the social structure, rice farmers were forced off their

land to make way for grazing and had their provisions stolen.

An important aspect of the Kuru period was the development of the caste system. There were originally four castes. Two upper classes, the ❺ priests and the nobility, ruled over the two lower castes, which were made up of the farmers, craftsmen, and laborers, and the outcasts (Pariah, or "untouchables").

In religious practice the sacrificial rites, considered to be exchanges of food between the gods and men, became progressively more complex. This practice was thought to preserve the cosmic order. A Brah-

man was required for the interpretation of the holy texts.

This social system spread to north and east India, including Kashmir and Nepal. Brahman texts speak of a "ritual taking-possession" of the country and the "civilizing" of barbaric tribes by the Brahmans around the year 800 BCE. The tribes of the east were "adopted" into the caste society. The major kingdoms of the northeast, the Kosala and Videha, produced "Black and Red Ware" pottery. The kingdom of Videha, under King Janaka, soon became a model nation of the Vedic order.

1 Buddha with disciples

3 Buddha, relief from the Jaulian monastery, ca. third–fifth century

4 Buddha in contemplation

5 *The Priest and the Believer*, Indian miniature, 18th century

■ The Later Vedic Period and the Eastern Nations

In the sixth century BCE, Buddhism and Jainism emerged as religious reform movements. The rise of Buddhism began as the cultural center of gravity shifted toward the eastern Indian states.

6 The gods Brahma and Krishna, scene from the *Ramayana*

In the Later Vedic period, around 600 BCE, the cultural and political focus of India shifted to the northeast. Concurrently, new groups began moving into the eastern states from Iran and Afghanistan. The kings of Videha and Kosala sent for Brahmans from western India to instruct them in the Vedic laws. Around this time, two

reform movements emerged in the east. Both were critical of the caste system and the bloody animal sacrifices that it demanded. The reform movements were the Buddhism of Prince ❶, ❸, ❹ Siddhartha Gautama (Buddha) and the Jainism of ❷ Mahavira.

The Later Vedic period came to an end somewhere around 450 BCE, at least partly due to the Persians' invasion of the Gandhara and Sindh regions of present-day Pakistan in 530 and 519 BCE. New cities and centers of commerce developed. An ambitious class of dealers and merchants prospered, as the luxurious vessels of the "Black Polished Ware" testify. The culture opened itself to the world and flourished. In Gandhara, the alphabet borrowed

7 The monkey kingdom, scene from the *Ramayana*

from further west was modified into a new script: the ❾ Brahmi alphabet from which all present-day Indian alphabets derive. The grand Indian national epic ❻, ❼, ❽, ❿ *Ramayana* was written between 400 and 300 BCE by the legendary poet Valmiki.

While western India had been under Persian influence since the end of the sixth century, the east developed its own structures. In 500 BCE the kingdom of Maghada, under King Bimbisara, was in a position of dominance. Bimbisara had professed his faith in Buddhism around 525 and sought to promote it, while pursuing a strategy of conquest and marriage. His son Ajatashatru extended the empire to include the tribal federation of the north, and his successor continued this effective strategy. In 364 the usurper, Mahapadma Nanda, toppled them and expanded the empire into central India and Orissa. He and his successors, the Nanda kings, reigned almost up until the invasion of Alexander the Great between 327 and 325 BCE.

The True Brahman

"The Brahman, truly, was this world in the beginning, the One, the Unending: Unending to the East, unending to the South, unending above and below, unending on all sides. For him there is no ... location of heaven, not across, nor below, nor above."
From the Upanishads following the Vedas.

9 Characters of the Brahmi alphabet, second millennium BCE

8 The testing of Sita in the fire, illustration of a scene from the *Ramayana*

10 Rama and Krishna, illustration of a scene from the *Ramayana*

4th–3rd century BCE	*Ramayana* compiled		364–321 BCE	Period of the Nanda kings
ca. 500 BCE	Rise of Maghadas	ca. 450 BCE	End of the Later Vedic Period	327–325 BCE	Alexander the Great invades India

EARLY CHINA UP TO THE PERIOD OF THE "WARRING STATES" 5000–221 BCE

Although China was one of the first places of human habitation, its civilization is relatively young compared with other ancient high cultures. In the third millennium BCE, the first communities with a sophisticated civilization began to emerge. From around the 18th century BCE, the ruling Shang and Zhou dynasties centralized power and presided over a period of considerable technical innovation. The empire perceptibly decayed from the eighth century BCE on and finally ended in a war between its constituent parts.

Bronze vessel decorated with human masks and used for ritual meals during the Shang dynasty era, ca. 1766–1100 BCE

China's Early Period and the Shang Dynasty

Even the earliest cultures in China produced great technical achievements. These early people and their rulers would later be much celebrated and attain a mythical status in Chinese history.

The ❷ "Peking Man" is among the oldest hominid finds made in China. His remains were found in a cave near Beijing (Peking) and are between 300,000 and 400,000 years old. Subsequently, remains of a 700,000-year-old hominid were discovered near Lantian. Cattle breeders and farmers are known to have settled in villages along the larger rivers in China as early as the Neolithic period. One

Skull of the "Peking Man" (*Homo erectus pekinensis*), discovered in the 1920s

of the cultures of this period was the Yang-shao culture (ca. 5000 BCE) in northern China, which produced significant pottery. Around 3000 BCE the group was supplanted by the Lung-shan culture, which was characterized by permanent settlements and technical refinements for predominantly domestic purposes.

In Chinese tradition, the first state was formed at the end of the third millennium BCE. According to mythology, it was ruled by the sage-kings Yao, Shun, and Yu. They are said to mark the arrival of civilization, particularly through innovations in agriculture and management of water resources, in the region.

Yu is credited with founding the Xia dynasty, which gave way to the ❶, ❺, ❻ Shang dynasty at the start of the Chinese bronze age around 1800 BCE. During the

period of the Shang dynasty (ca. 1766–1100 BCE), the emperor became the political and cultural leader. He was considered the "representative of heaven" and surrounded himself with a great caste of priests. Permanent walled cities were built, some of them at amazing expense, with palaces and temples. The emperor often shifted his ❸, ❹ richly appointed residences. The houses of tempered clay had subterranean

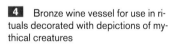
Bronze vessel used for ritual use with the inscription "Father Chi"

storage rooms for food supplies. Among the many technical advances developed in this period were polished ceramics, the farming of silkworms, spoke-wheeled wagons and the plow. The Shang script, pictographic with more than 3000 characters, is a direct predecessor of the modern Chinese writing system.

4 Bronze wine vessel for use in rituals decorated with depictions of mythical creatures

Bronze wine vessel in the shape of a pair of owls, Shang dynasty

Bronze knife and dagger, Shang dynasty

The Zhou Dynasty and the "Warring States"

The victory of the Zhou dynasty over the Shang ushered in important changes in China's social structure. The feudal system that developed precipitated a decline in central political authority as regional states asserted their autonomy.

Bronze vessel, Western Zhou dynasty, ca. 1050–771 BCE

Richly decorated dagger handle, made of plaited gold and turquoises, Eastern Zhou dynasty, 771–ca. 256 BCE

The Zhou, who ruled a small kingdom in the west of China during the Shang dynasty, defeated the Shang around 1050 BCE and assumed power. They ruled their vast lands through vassals, awarding land to loyal clan chiefs and above all to their family members. Thus historians have traditionally ascribed the emergence of China's characteristic feudal system to the Zhou period. The decentralization of power inherent in this system paved the way for the later formation of more than 1000 "small nations" under the autonomous rule of the local elite. The period also saw traditional social divisions solidify into feudal ones, between the nobility, the military caste and the administrators on the one hand and the serf farmers and craftsmen (the overwhelming majority) on the other. The Zhou are also credited with introducing the concept of a "mandate of heaven," whereby emperors ruled by divine right. The political fortunes of the Zhou dynasty can be divided into two phases. During the first, known as the ❼, Western Zhou period (ca. 1050–771 BCE), a strong central government ruled. During the second, known as the ❽, ❿ Eastern Zhou period (771–ca. 256 BCE), only a puppet ruler, or symbolic figure, remained. He had no real power and was manipulated by rival regional lords. Some sources divide the Zhou dynasty into three phases: the "Early" period (771–722 BCE); the "Spring and Autumn" period (722–481 BCE), in which a few larger, autonomous vassal states developed; and the period of the "Warring States" (481–221 BCE), which takes its name from the *Book of the Warring States* written

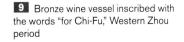

Bronze wine vessel inscribed with the words "for Chi-Fu," Western Zhou period

during the later Han dynasty. A period of forced consolidation left seven large states to fight for dominance over China's vast territories. Although marked by violence and war, the period was also notable for its intellectual and technological advances. Perhaps most significant was the transition to a more intensive use of agricultural land, including the introduction of new varieties of crop, in particular rice and wheat.

Irrigation techniques and road construction methods were substantially improved, and knowledge of ironworking spread. The period of the "Warring States" was also the golden age of classic Chinese philosophy. It ended with the establishment of the Qin military state.

War drum decorated with dragon handle, from the Eastern Zhou dynasty

---

The Time of 100 Schools of Thought

In the shadow of the rival lords' conflicts during the period of the Warring States, a number of philosophical schools developed. Almost all of these schools took a position on political questions and endeavored to gain the favor of the rulers. Nine of these schools eventually came to dominate. Among them were the School of Literati (Confucianism); the Taoists; the Mohists, whose moral code shows many parallels with utilitarianist thought; and the Legalists, who advocated strong leadership with strict legal controls. Legalist teachings became state dogma under the Qin dynasty while Mohism died out.

The Ancient World

ca. 2500 BCE–900 CE

In ancient Greece and the Roman Empire, the epics of the Greek poet Homer, the wars of Caesar, and temples and palaces characterize the image of classic antiquity and culture. They are the sources from which the Western world draws the foundations of its philosophy, literature, and, not least of all, its state organization. The Greek city-states, above all Athens, were the birthplace of democracy. The regions surrounding the Mediterranean Sea and great parts of Northwest Europe were forged together into the Roman Empire, which survived until the time of the Great Migration of Peoples. Mighty empires also existed beyond the ancient Mediterranean world, however, such as those of the Mauryas in India and the Han in China.

In the famous Battle of Issus in 333 BCE, Alexander the Great defeats the Persians under Darius III, detail from a Roman mosaic crafted during the period of the Dominate, found in Pompeii.

1 Greek theater in Syracuse

2 Forum Romanum

3 The Roman theater of Leptis Magna, Libya

THE CULTURE OF THE GREEKS AND ROMANS

The ❶ Greek and ❷ , ❸Roman civilizations of antiquity are regarded today as the origins of Western civilization. The Greek thirst for knowledge and structure and the Roman achievements in political organization have shaped European culture to the present day, and their influence has radiated out to other parts of the world as well.

Greek Literature and Philosophy

There are vastly differing opinions concerning the essential nature of ancient Greek culture. The Greeks are regarded as the true inventors of political and historical thought, but also as the proponents of rationalism and science. Their complex system of myths and gods continues to fascinate, and their sense of art and aesthetics is admired.

In addition to their contribution to political evolution, the Greeks influenced Western attitudes and literature with their early epics, particularly ❹ Homer's *Iliad* and *Odyssey* (ninth century BCE). While ❺ Hesiod, in his *Theogony*, wrote about the fates of the gods, Homer made the human and social aspects of individually fashioned figures the focus of his epic tales. For this reason, the Greeks are considered to be the forerunners of later Western Individualism.

The Greek culture, with its thirst for knowledge, was the first to make the conceptual transition from myths to Logos. The Greeks no longer believed in a world ordained solely by the gods, but sought to understand the world around them by inquiring into the origin of things and the ordering structure of the cosmos.

5 *Pandora in front of Prometheus and Epimetheus, from Hesiod's Theogony*

7 Anaximander, natural philosopher from Milet, with sundial, ca. 610–546 BCE

From the ❼ Ionian natural philosophers of the seventh and sixth centuries BCE, the search for the primary building blocks of life and for the governing principles that guide nature dominated Greek thought through the appearance of Socrates, Plato, and ❻ Aristotle. These three great philosophers replaced the capricious gods with natural laws and so stimulated the development of sciences, including mathematics, physics, and engineering.

4 Homer, Roman marble bust

As a result of intensive observation of nature, biology developed, along with a self-awareness of humans as observers and manipulators of nature. This self-awareness found expression in a desire for political freedom and independence, which for a long time hindered the creation of a united Greek state. It took the wars against Persia and pressure from Macedonia under Philip II and Alexander the Great to bring about a cosmopolitan Hellenism that culturally overarched and politically united the city-states. It was the formation of the Diadoch empires of Alexander and the Diadochi that first made possible the link between Eastern and Western cultural influences that went on to characterize the Mediterranean area.

6 *The school of Aristotle*, fresco by G. A. Spangenberg, 1883–88

The Achievements of Roman Civilization

Roman culture appears more "practical" than that of ancient Greece. Its outstanding contributions to intellectual-historical development lie more in state administration and law—areas in which they shaped subsequent history—than in philosophy. Collections of laws were written

| ca. 2500 BCE | Minoan culture | ca. 470 BCE | Roman Republic founded | 336–323 BCE | Alexander the Great's reign |
| 800 BCE | Homer's *Iliad* and *Odyssey* | ca. 387 BCE | Plato's Academy founded | 335–334 BCE | Aristotle's school in Athens founded |

8 Villa Hadriana in Tivoli, built under Emperor Hadrian

9 The Roman aqueduct Pont du Gard, first c. CE

10 Arch of Titus, part of the Forum Romanum, 81 CE

and then continually supplemented—from the biblical Ten Commandments to the comprehensive Justinian Codes. Even the ethical philosophy of **12** Cicero or Seneca was written in the service of the Roman Empire and Rome's claim to political and cultural world dominance.

In its early period, **4** Rome was a small, free republic with an almost puritanical code of laws. In the course of its ambitious expansion, Rome gradually overwrote its own laws in favor of foreign, particularly Hellenistic, ideas of governance, which it then integrated into its concept of empire; this was particularly the case under the rule of Julius Caesar. The adoption and integration of foreign cults and ideas eventually allowed for the ascendancy of Christianity, a sect of Judaic origin, until it was established as the religion of all territories of the empire. Within its vast realm, Rome projected the image of a disciplined and militarily invincible organizing power.

11 Gladiators, relief, ca. 50 CE

Proof of the Roman Empire's impressive engineering capabilities can be seen not only in the many **10** temples and magnificent buildings in Rome and other important centers but also in the garrisons and settlements constructed throughout the empire, the well-developed road networks, the **9** aqueducts, the luxurious thermal baths and **8** villas, and even the capital's ingeniously devised **13** sewage system.

Roman culture demonstrated the intense interaction of the empire's center and its provinces. Rome exported its state and administrative structures and imported finished products, luxury articles, and art—along with ideas and religions. The innumerable military triumphs of the consuls and emperors were celebrated with imposing state celebrations. Under the motto of "bread and circuses," the emperors

13 "Cloaca Maxima" in Rome, sewage pipe leading to the Tiber River

of Rome, and later also of the Byzantine Empire, entertained the masses with chariot races and bloodthirsty **11** gladiatorial combat in great arenas such as the "Circus Maximus" or Colosseum.

The long existence of the Roman Empire is impressive considering the many upheavals, political reorientations, and the constant social unrest that shaped its history. It developed from a republic founded in the sixth century BCE to a sprawling world empire by the beginning of the Christian era and survived even the fall of the city of Rome itself in 476 CE. The Roman legacy was carried on not only by the Byzantine Empire, lasting until 1453, but also by Charlemagne at his coronation in 800 as emperor of the Frankish-German Holy Roman Empire. Charlemagne combined the Roman idea of a universal emperor and belief system of Christianity, with its supranational and intercultural ideals, and thereby ushered in the first renaissance of classical thought in the transition from Roman antiquity to the European Middle Ages.

12 Marcus Tullius Cicero, Roman orator, politician, and writer

14 The center of ancient Rome during Emperor Septimus Severus's reign, artist's reconstruction

CRETE AND MYCENAE – THE BEGINNINGS OF GREEK CULTURE 2500–750 BCE

Greece was the earliest influential culture of the West. The Minoan and Mycenaean cultures were its first manifestations. The Minoan culture on Crete was characterized by palace cities, extensive trade networks, and sophisticated artwork, while the mainland culture of Mycenae was warlike and its architecture dominated by castles and defensive structures. The myth of the Trojan War, set in the Mycenaean era, clearly illustrates ancient Greece's self-image as a fiercely protective defender of its honor and freedom. The Trojan episode facilitated Greece's assertion of its cultural independence.

1 The Phaistos Disc, burnt clay impressed with Minoan hieroglyphics, 1700–1600 BCE

Minoan Crete

The **1** Minoan culture is the oldest precursor of Greek culture. Minoan Crete maintained intensive trade contacts throughout the Mediterranean area. The characteristic cult symbols of the Minoans were the double axe (the sacred labrys) and the bull.

3
Sculpture of a goddess, 17th century BCE

2 Clay vessel, example of Kamares ware, ca. 1800 BCE

4
Minoan vessel, decorated with the double axe motif

Between 2500 and 1300 BCE, Minoan culture developed on the island of Crete on the southern edge of the Aegean Sea. The oldest high civilization of the area, it has been named after Minos, a mythical ruler of Crete in the city of Knossos. The settlements of the first Minoans—farmers who probably emigrated from Asia Minor—were situated in the east of the island. From here, the Minoans spread throughout Crete.

Crete's favorable geographical position encouraged a flourishing trade with Phoenicia and the states of the ancient Near East. Cultural influences and important raw materials reached Crete from Egypt and Mesopotamia. On Crete, there is evidence of metalworking and the production of faience such as **2** Kamares ware, which was exported throughout the Mediterranean. The Minoans had a developed commercial and urban life, while they cultivated vines and olive orchards to produce wine and olive oil.

The head of the Minoan pantheon was a great **3** goddess, so it is often assumed that the original culture was a matriarchy. The Minoan religion, in which the king acted as high priest, had its shrines on mountains or in caves, and practiced human sacrifice to pacify the gods. Nevertheless, there were no monumental statues of deities. The symbols of the great goddess were the **4** double axe (labrys), the **5** bull, and stylized **7** bull's horns (bucrania). The bull had great significance as a sacrificial animal. The **6** wall paintings from this period often depict humans leaping over the backs of charging bulls. Indications of a warlike tradition that was characteristic of the later Greeks are less apparent on Crete.

5
Late Minoan vessel for donatives, shaped like a bull's head

6
Acrobats leap over the back of a charging bull, Minoan fresco, 16th century BCE

7
Set of bull's horns decorate the entrance to the palace of Knossos

| 2500–1300 BCE | Formation of the Minoan high culture | ca. 2000–1550 BCE | First unfortified palaces on Crete |
| from 2000 BCE | Evidence of Minoan arts, crafts, and trade | ca. 1750 BCE | Earthquake destroys the first palace at Knossos |

The Palace Cities of Crete

The Minoan palace cities on Crete were political, economic, and cultural centers and were laid out according to a uniform pattern. The most significant of these was the capital palace city of Knossos.

9
Minoan prince carrying lilies and wearing a feather crown, Minoan relief, 16th century BCE

11
Frescoes in the throne room, Knossos

12
Ceiling frescoes depicting dolphins in queen's Throne Room in the palace of Knossos

The Minoan social order, which centered on the ruler, was reflected in the layout of their cities. The king's palace was always at the center. It served as a political, economic, and cultural focal point. The king probably exercised religious functions, but neither the names nor representations of the rulers have survived. The palaces had a uniform layout. The palace wings contained a great number of rooms in a labyrinth arrangement and were grouped around a rectangular interior courtyard, complete with a modern drainage system providing flushing latrines. Notable colorful ⓫ fresco wall paintings dating back to 2000 BCE display a wide range of subjects. Art had a primarily decorative function in the early periods, but naturalistic representations of plants, ❾ people, and animals, for example ⓬ dolphins, later came to predominate.

The most important palace on Crete was that of ❽, ❿ Knossos with its two- to four-story palace wings. It was first discovered by archaeologists in 1834 and is situated around four miles (6.4 km) from Candia. It was excavated in 1900 by British archaeologist Arthur Evans. Villas and houses were arranged around the palace, while the burial sites were located outside the city. At its height, 80,000 people probably lived in Knossos. There may have been as many as a thousand rooms, all skillfully lit by natural light. An earthquake destroyed the early palace at Knossos about 1750 BCE. It was rebuilt and encompassed more than 200,000 square feet, which suggests that the ruler of Knossos had a position of supremacy on Crete. Subsequent earthquakes on Crete also leveled a portion of these buildings.

Besides Knossos, palace cities existed in Mallia in the north, Zakros to the east, and Phaistos farther south. This last was built on terraces at different levels. There was also the "summer residence" of Hagia Triada. Minoan settlements were found outside Crete on Santorini (Thera), but the island was destroyed by a volcanic eruption around 1628 BCE. About 1450 BCE Crete, including Knossos, was overrun by the Mycenaeans. The assault of the Dorians around 1230 BCE led to the destruction of the Mycenaean culture, including the high civilization on Crete. By 1100 BCE, Crete had become part of mainland Greek culture.

8
"Hall of the Double Axes" in the palace of Knossos

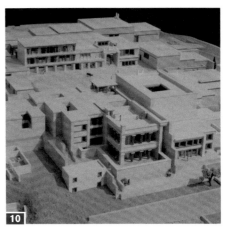

10
Palace of Knossos ca. 1520 BCE, model

Minos and the Minotaur

According to legend, King Minos of Crete was the son of Zeus and Europa. He failed to sacrifice a white bull sent from the sea by Poseidon, and for this the sea god took revenge. He made Minos's wife Pasiphae fall in love with the bull, and she bore a half-man, half-bull monster, the Minotaur. The king confined the Minotaur in the Labyrinth constructed by Daedalus. Seven youths and seven maidens were sacrificed to him annually until Theseus finally defeated and killed him. Minos died in Sicily and became a judge of the underworld.

above: Theseus slays the Minotaur, detailed miniature painting on the inside surface of a clay bowl

---

ca. 1628 BCE | Volcanic eruption destroys Santorini   **ca. 1230 BCE** | Dorian occupation of Mycene

ca. 1450 BCE | Mycenaean occupation of Crete   **from 1100 BCE** | Crete becomes a part of mainland Greek culture

The Mycenaean Culture and Troy

The Mycenaean civilization was characterized by its warrior aristocracy and its fortified cities. The saga of Troy plays an essential part in illustrating the character of these warrior kingdoms.

Around 1600–1200 BCE, the Achaians migrated from the north into Greece, where they established city-states in the Aegean islands, in Attica, and on the Peloponne-

Decorated dagger made of bronze, gold, silver, and niello, 16th century BCE

sus. Homer uses the term Achaians to refer to all the Greeks. They maintained a ❷ martial social structure, which was mirrored in the arrangement of their palaces, castles, and cities. Most of the castles in which the warrior ari-

stocracy resided were fortified and the cities enclosed by walls. For a long period of time, the most important city was ❹,❻ Mycenae, after which the whole Aegean culture of this period is named.

Little is known of the social organization of the Mycenaean city-state. It was probably a centrally administered palace bureaucracy with close ties between the religious cult and its rulers such as Atreus and his son ❺ Agamemnon. The economy was based primarily on agriculture and ❶ metal-working. There were military conflicts among the various Aegean seats of power, as well as with Minoan Crete and the states of Asia Minor, such as Troy. There is still no clear consensus about the causes behind the fall of the Mycenaean culture. Natural catastrophes or internal social upheaval may have led to the demise of this civilization some-

time between 1200 and 1000 BCE.

The destruction of Troy by the Greeks, as immortalized by Homer's *Iliad*, is undoubtedly connected with the migratory movements of aggressive sea peoples such as the Philistines, who drove whole populations from their territories. Nevertheless, the sagas of heroism in the battle for Troy became a model for the whole culture of classical Greece.

German archaeologist Heinrich Schliemann began the ❼ excavation of Troy in 1870 in the mound of ruins at Hissarlik, in modern

Mycenaean warriors mount wooden chariots and prepare for battle

Turkey. He believed the account in the *Iliad* to be historical reality and therefore dated his finds—treasures of gold and silver from the second stratum of his excavation, which he reached in 1873, including what he believed to be the ❸ "Mask of Agamemnon"— to the time of the Trojan War. However, his oldest finds were distinctly older (ca.2500–2200 BCE) than this chronology suggests. In 1874, Schliemann also started excavations of Mycenae, where he found relics of a civilization which linked Greece and Cyprus.

The Lion Gate at Mycenae

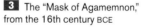
❸ The "Mask of Agamemnon," from the 16th century BCE

❺ The "treasury of Atreus" or the "tomb of Agamemnon," tomb, 14th c. BCE

❻ Fortified castle in the area of Mycenae, second century BCE

ca. 1400 BCE | Enlargement of castle of Mycenae

7

Excavation works in Troy, led by Heinrich Schliemann, 1870–1882

From Homer's *Iliad*

"And then, last, Achilles drew his father's spear / from its socket-stand –weighted, heavy, tough. / No other Achaean fighter could heft that shaft, / only Achilles had the skill to wield it well: / Pelian ash it was, a gift to his father Peleus / presented by Chiron once, hewn on Pelion's crest / to be the death of heroes."

The Trojan War

According to Homer's Iliad, the Trojan War began with the abduction of Helena—the wife of Menelaus of Sparta—by Paris, the son of King Priam of Troy. Under the leadership of Agamemnon, king of Mycenae and brother of Menelaus, the Greeks began a ten-year siege of Troy. The climactic episode in Homer's account is the victory of the Greek hero Achilles over the Trojan hero Hector. A ruse by Odysseus (Ulysses in Latin)—the "Trojan horse"—decided the war in favor of the Greeks. The partisanship of the gods and the moral ambiguity of the conflict characterize Homer's work.

Achilles kills Hector outside the walls of Troy

above: *The Rape of Helena,* oil painting by Guido Reni, 1631
below: The Trojan Horse stands amid the ruins of the fallen city

The Dorian Migrations

The migration of the Indo-European Dorians into Greece led to the gradual settlement of the whole region. Individual clans and communities developed, and these eventually merged together into cities.

The immigration into Greece of Indo-European Dorian tribes out of the Balkan region followed in the wake of the sea peoples around 1000 BCE. In a series of waves, the Dorian Greeks settled first in central Greece and then, about 1150 BCE, also in the Peloponnesus. Dorian tribes settled in the Cyclades, on Crete, and on the coast of Asia Minor as well. They vied with with the Phoenicians for maritime supremacy.

The tribes soon divided into separate subgroups: the Spartans, the Messenians, the Argives, and the Northwestern Greeks, among others. With the development of individual clans and distinct communities came the beginnings of the later city-states and their struggles for independence.

The day-to-day lives of these early Greeks were described by Homer: The house (*oikos*) was the family's living space, and the lot (*kleros*), a clan's or family's portion of land, was the nucleus of its private property. Family members were subordinate to the head of the family. This world was confined within strict boundaries; warfare and cults led to personal ties to aristocracy or warlords. However, with a modicum of politics and administration, several families or communities could ultimately unite and form a city (*polis*), usually located on a fortified elevation.

CLASSICAL GREECE FROM THE CULTURE OF THE POLIS TO THE END OF INDEPENDENCE 8TH–3RD CENTURY BCE

In the wake of the Dorian invasions, city-states with a high degree of political organization developed in the Greek territories. These city-states proliferated around much of the Mediterranean and the Greeks combined their resources in the defense of their territories against the Persians. However, tensions soon developed between the major powers of Athens and Sparta, culminating in the Peloponnesian Wars. The war left Sparta with hegemony over Greece, but eventually its strength also collapsed, sapped by numerous minor wars against other states. After a short period of rule by Thebes, the system of city-states disintegrated as the Greek peninsula was caught up in Macedonian plans for a great empire.

Greek warrior, statuette, mid-seventh century BCE

top right: Greek youth playing with hoop

■ The Organization of the Polis

The polis (city-state), where public life was governed and precisely regulated by laws, was based on the political participation of its citizens. The conception of freedom associated with the city-state was central to Greek identity.

The early Greek cities were settlements of between 500 and 1500 ❶ men fit for military service, who lived in the surrounding area. Most of the city-states had a central acropolis ("upper city"). In

The Temple of Apollo at Delphi

the eighth century BCE, religious and communal sites and festivals linked the cities. The oracle of ❹, ❺ Apollo at Delphi and the Olympic games of ❸, ❻ Olympia are examples of this tendency.

Relations between citizens, who were the minority of a city's population, were regulated by es-

tablished laws. The proportion of the population that qualified as citizens, and thus participated actively in public life, varied between city-states. Polis was a legal term that described the city and its surrounding area. A council of elders and officials was elected for a fixed period of time by a public assembly of citizens to which they were accountable. The cities demonstrated a large degree of internal cohesion in defending their ideal of self-sufficiency (autarky) against foreign domination. The Greeks considered themselves "politically free"—superior to the "bound barbarians" of the Eastern monarchies.

Greek ❷ society was nonetheless divided into the aristocracy and the non-aristocracy. The aristocracy was distinguished by high levels of property ownership and

proficiency in warfare. The non-aristocracy was made up of the rest: free peasants, tradesmen, the landless, and slaves. Slaves became an integral part of Greek society's economic structure at an early stage. They tended to be either former inhabitants of colonized lands, prisoners of war, or indentured servants. Most performed manual labor, but an educated minority held

Extract from Aristotle's *Politics*

"He who has the power to take part in the deliberative or judicial administration of any state is said by us to be a citizen of that state; and, generally speaking, a state is a body of citizens sufficing for the purposes of life."

above left: The Column of Zeus in the Temple at Olympia, one of the Seven Wonders of the Ancient World
left: The Temple of Apollo, Delphi

positions as private tutors or secretaries in their master's household. Greek society was patriarchal, though the private ideal was that of a harmonious family life.

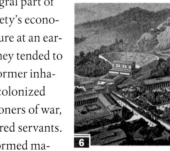

Olympia, from left: gymnasium, theater, old wall, Heraion, Kronos Hill, Zeus temple, treasure house, stadium, ceremonial gate

ca. 776 BCE | First Olympic games   ca. 800 BCE | Homer writes epics *The Iliad* and *The Odyssey*   ca. 735 BCE | Foundation of Naxos

8th century BCE | Building of first centers of worship   750 BCE–500 BCE | Wave of Greek settlement in the Mediterranean area   ca. 735 BCE | Foundation of Syracuse

The Colonization of the Mediterranean Region

An agrarian crisis in Greece led to mass emigration and the colonization of most of the Mediterranean area. Some colonies, particularly those in Sicily, became leading cultural centers.

Greek theater in Syracuse, originally constructed in the time of Hieron I, ca. 470 BCE, partially rebuilt in 238 BCE

The Greeks had long demonstrated an interest in surrounding lands, but it was not until the agrarian crisis of the eighth century BCE that large-scale colonization began. Increasing indebtedness and servitude among the farmers led to uprisings in many regions and ultimately to migratory pressures.

Between 750 and 500 BCE, a wave of sea-borne migration began, from Greece to islands and coastal areas throughout the Mediterranean. In about 735 BCE, colonists founded Naxos at the foot of Mount Etna in Sicily, followed by Syracuse. From 650 BCE, Greeks settled the coasts of Thrace, the Sea of Marmara, and the Black Sea, as well as Asia Minor. Between about 550 and 500 BCE, Ionians occupied Sardinia and Corsica, while Athenians moved into the Tyrrhenian Sea and reached as far as present-day Nice and Barcelona. With a growing population and booming Mediterranean trade, the colonies flourished.

Most colonies continued to consider themselves part of the Greek cultural world and maintained contact with their parent cities. In the fourth and third centuries BCE, favored by wars on the Greek mainland, ❼, ⓫ Syracuse and Agrigento on Sicily became the leading ❽ cultural centers of the "West Greeks." At the same time they were forced to defend themselves against the growing threat posed by the ❾ Carthaginians and Etruscans.

The presence of numerous profiteers and exiles contributed to political conditions in the colonies that were frequently unsettled. Military and political leaders often seized power and were known as "tyrants." The tyrants of Sicilian Syracuse— such as Dionysius the Elder, who extended his power into Sicily and southern Italy, or Agathocles, who is remembered for his struggle against the Carthaginians—are a well known group.

Battle of Himera against the Carthaginians, Sicily, 480 BCE

The Charioteer of Delphi, votive tribute from Polyzalos of Sicily

Dionysius the Elder of Syracuse

Dionysius (ca. 430–367 BCE) took the rich of Syracuse to court on behalf of the populace, who elected him to a generalship in 405 BCE. He seized power as tyrant the same year, strengthening the army and fortifying Syracuse against the Carthaginians. Dionysius succeeded in conquering Sicily and concluding peace with powerful Carthage in 392. He invited philosophers, including Plato, and poets to his court and became well known as a writer of tragedies.

above: Plato at the court of the tyrant Dionysius in Syracuse

The *ekklesiasterion*, where citizens' assemblies (*ekklesia*) took place, built in the sixth century BCE in Agrigento

Temple of Apollo and Artemis in Syracuse

after 550 BCE | Athenian colonies stretch from Tyrrhenian Sea to Barcelona   **405–ca. 367 BCE** | Reign of Dionysius the Elder of Syracuse

after 650 BCE | Colonization of the Black Sea coast, Thrace, and West Asia Minor   **ca. 500 BCE** | Ionian occupation of Sardinia and Corsica

■ The Omnipresence of War

Due to the regional organization of the city-states, war and conflict increasingly defined the lives of the Greeks. As a result, methods of warfare evolved rapidly.

1 Hoplite with shield, helmet, and spear, Greek vase painting

The self-contained organization of the polis, and the struggle of each for autarky or hegemony, created shifting alliances and led, as is vividly illustrated in Homer's epics, to constant wars, which came to overshadow the lives of the Greeks. There was an underlying sense of Greek cultural homo geneity and unity, but this was not reflected by their political alliances. Thus, the strength of the tightly-bound communities also proved a weakness for the Helle-

2 Iron weapons, ca. 820 BCE

nic world. Greek city-states fought among themselves over land, influence, and privileges. Local conflicts often spread rapidly when neighboring cities intervened. Undeclared minor wars consisting of raids and the theft of goods were commonplace.

With the increasing size and importance of the cities, warfare with rivals—both on land and at sea—became the main focus of the politicians. Men capable of military service, who usually joined the battles for a couple of months each year, began to enter the service of the warring states as mercenaries, even joining the army of the Persian king.

By the seventh century BCE, individual combat as described by Homer had disappeared in favor of battles between armies. The Greeks adopted the chariot from the East and attacked with ❷ heavily armed and well-armored warriors called ❶, ❹, ❺ "hoplites." They advanced in groups of hundreds—units known as "phalanxes." The art of war increasingly became a profession, with professional strategists and tacticians taking the place of military leaders who had traditionally

3 Rowers on an Athenian trireme

led the charge. From the sixth century on, the narrow and maneuverable ❸, ❻ trireme ("three-oared") vessel—with 170 oarsmen on three decks and a pointed bow—redefined marine warfare. The ship itself had become a weapon that could ram into other vessels and cause huge damage. Shipbuilding experienced an enormous upswing and brought great prosperity to those cities with shipyards. The procurement of wood, however, cost vast sums of money.

4 Hoplite with shield and spear, marble relief, ca. 500–490 BCE

5 Hoplites putting on armor, Greek vase painting

6 Greek triremes carry out maneuvers in the fifth century BCE

525 BCE Cambyses II of Persia subjugates Egypt	**490 BCE** Destruction of Eretria	**483–82 BCE** Fleet construction launched by Themistocles
539 BCE Cyrus II of Persia conquers Babylon	**500–494 BCE** Ionians revolt against the Persians	**490 BCE** Battle of Marathon

The Persian Wars

The threat of Persian expansion led to the first military alliance among the Greek city-states. This Greek alliance succeeded in preventing the Persians from entering Europe.

The political changes that took place throughout the Middle East after 550 BCE finally forced the Greeks to abandon their inward-looking policies. After the Persian kings Croesus and Cambyses II had brought the Middle East—including Egypt and Asia Minor—under their control, Darius I (the Great) sought to ex-tend his realm into Europe. Many of the smaller Greek cities had already sought protection under his rule, and the Greek exiles also counted on him to subjugate the city-states. The Greeks regarded the Persians with a mixture of admiration and contempt; admiration for their ❽ fighting strength and

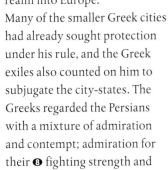

8 Persian archer

cultural wealth, but contempt for their despotic political system.

In 500 BCE, Greek cities in Anatolia, under the leadership of Histiaeus, ruler of Miletus, attempted to revolt against Persian rule. The rebellion failed in 494, but it provided Darius with a reason to move his armies west. In 491, Persian messengers demanded the submission of all Greek cities. When these demands were rejected, the Persian army and fleet were dispatched across the Aegean Sea in 490 to punish Eretria and Athens. The Persians subjugated the Cyclades, destroyed Eretria, and then advanced into the Bay of Marathon. In the face of this threat, Athens and Sparta buried their rivalry and fought together. Under the leadership of the Athenian general Miltiades they defeated the Persians at ❼, ❾ Marathon. A messenger is supposed to have run all the way to Athens with news of the victory, collapsing dead after

delivering the message; he was the first ❿ "Marathon runner."

⓫ Xerxes I, whom the Greeks particularly despised, continued the work of his father, Darius, and marched his troops across the Hellespont into Greece in 481 BCE. Responding to the renewed threat, the Athenian statesman Themistocles oversaw the construction of a new war fleet, and once again a Greek alliance was formed, this time led by Sparta. The large Persian army advanced along the Greek coast accompanied by a large fleet. After a dramatic land-battle in the narrow pass of Thermopylae, the Greeks were forced to retreat. The Persians then captured and burned Athens in 480 BCE, marking a low point in the fortunes of the Greeks. Later in the year a Greek victory in a pitched sea battle at ⓬, ⓭ Salamis changed the course of the war. The Greeks chased the demoralized

7 Battle of Marathon, October 9, 490 BCE

9 Burial-mound of the Athenians who died in the Battle of Marathon in 490 BCE

10 Messenger brings news of the Greek victory from Marathon to Athens, painting, 1869

Persian army to Plataea, in Boeotia, where they won a crushing victory in 479 BCE. The Persian threat was thus averted and the episode entered Greek folklore as a glorious triumph.

From Aeschylus's
The Persians

"Advance, ye sons of Greece, from thraldom / Save your country, save your wives, your children, / The temples of your gods, the sacred tomb / Where rest your honour'd ancestors."

11 Xerxes at the Hellespont

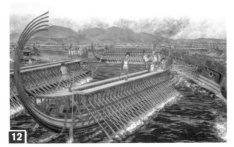

12 Ships engage in the Battle of Salamis, September, 480 BCE

13 Main forces in the Battle of Salamis, the Greek fleet shown in green, the Persian fleet shown in red

481 BCE | Xerxes I of Persia marches into Greece   late 480 BCE | Greek naval victory at Salamis

481 BCE | Formation of the Greek alliance under Spartan leadership   480 BCE | Persians burn Athens   479 BCE | Greeks rout Persian army

The Rise of Athens

From the beginning Athenian political life was shaped by the legal system. The famous lawmaker Solon was the architect of numerous reforms. After a period under the rule of the tyrants, Cleisthenes broadened citizen participation in government to weaken the aristocracy.

Athens, the city under the protection of the goddess ❷ Athena, whose symbol was the ❸ owl, always held a special position in Greece. It was considered the "cradle of democracy." The highest organ of Athenian government was the *Areopagus* (council). Its members were initially confined to the aristocracy, but later *archons* (rulers)—magistrates who were elected annually for six centuries, came to predominate between 683 and 84 BCE. In 630 BCE growing social unrest and an attempt to dislodge the council prompted the lawmaker Draco to draw up a harsh code of laws (from which the word "Draconian" derives).

The Athenian lawmaker, Solon

In 594, the Athenians elected ❶, ❹ Solon as archon. He championed the notion of the "rule of law" on all levels and introduced wide-ranging legal reforms. In the sixth century, Athens was suffering from a social crisis brought on by spiralling debt among the poorer classes. Solon sought to remedy this with reforms, establishing legal protection against the arbitrary use of power and abolishing the enslavement of the indebted.

Although Solon worked for the balance of the interests of all groups, Peisistratus seized power in Athens as tyrant in 556 BCE. Peisistratus

❸ Owl of Athena and olive branch on an Athenian coin

extended Athens's influence beyond the Aegean, laid the foundation for the city's economic rise, further reformed the legal code, and erected grand public structures such as the Temple of Zeus in Athens. His sons Hipparchus (assassinated in 514) and Hippias succeeded him, but when he was deposed and driven out in 510 the old system was restored.

In 508–507 BCE the new archon, Cleisthenes, brought about a complete change in the political structure. He divided Attica into ten geographical sections, called "phyles," which elected their own administrators and provided their own hoplite regiments. Each of

From
Solon's *Fragment*

"My heart commands me to instruct the Athenians thus: Where no law is given, much evil will befall the state. Where there is law, the whole is united in beautiful order. Those who do wrong, shackle it by doing so."

(3, 30)

❷ The Goddess Athena, bronze statue, ca. 375–340 BCE

these phyles sent 50 representatives to the newly created "Council of the Five Hundred," the highest political assembly, which convened on the Athenian ❺ Agora. In this way Cleisthenes created a system of local administration and severed the ties between the citizens and the aristocracy. Cleisthenes is also credited with instituting ❻ "ostracism," by which supporters of tyranny could be temporarily exiled from the city.

Solon defends his laws against criticism from Athenian citizens, painting by Noël Coypel, 1699

above: Shards of pottery inscribed with the name of Themistocles, an Athenian who was exiled under the ostracism law in 470 BCE
left: Stele, found on the Agora, celebrating the anti-tyrant law of Eucrates, 337–336 BCE

7
Pericles

Themistocles

An Athenian army commander, statesman, and archon, Themistocles designed the Piraeus naval harbor in 493–492 BCE. He was never popular with his fellow citizens, despite playing a crucial role in Athens's rise to power, most notably as a commander during the the Battle of Salamis. His enemies and critics managed to have Themistocles ostracized in ca. 470 BCE, and this was followed by the pronouncement of a death sentence. He died or committed suicide abroad sometime after 460 BCE as a vassal of the Persians.

above: Themistocles

Athens as a Great Power

Athens came to dominate Greece through the Delian League, originally established to fight the Persians. This hegemony inevitably provoked resistance from other city-states, most notably Sparta. Domestically Athenian democracy reached its high point under Pericles.

Athens emerged from the Persian Wars in a position of considerable strength. Under archon ❾ Themistocles, Athens exercised a growing dominance over the Delian League, which had been founded in 477 against the Persians.

9
Themistocles flees to Artaxerxes

By extorting financial contributions from the league's members, Athens extended its hegemony over most of Greece. Conflict with the stronger members, above all Sparta, became inevitable. Athens used force to crush revolts in league member cities. Meanwhile, the smoldering war with the Persian Empire finally ended with the Peace of Callias in 448, under which Athens abandoned the attempt to drive the Persians out of the Mediterranean and the Persians agreed to respect the independence of all the Greek cities in Anatolia.

While Athens was pursuing aggressive policies against neighboring states, internally it continued to move towards democracy. Under the leadership of Ephialtes, the Athenians stripped the judicial power from the *Areopagus* in 462–461 BCE and gave it to the jury courts, thus placing judicial power in the hands of the citizens. Six thousand lay judges were drawn by lots. This was implemented by Ephialtes' protégé, ❼ Pericles, who, beginning in 443, was re-elected each year as the strategist who guided Athens's destiny. He established equality before the law and made the city assembly a democratic council before which every citizen had the right to petition. Officials were appointed by drawing lots. The impressive ⓫, ⓬ public buildings and ❽, ❿ theater plays ensured that Pericles' period in office would be considered Athens's golden age.

8
The Dionysios Theater in Athens

10
The Dionysios Theater in Athens today

11
View of the Acropolis in the fifth century BCE, artist's reconstruction

12
The Parthenon or Temple of Athena the Virgin, on the Acropolis, Athens

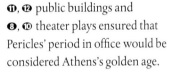

The Military State of Sparta

Sparta, the most powerful state on the Peloponnesus, was significantly more traditional than other city-states. Its public life was characterized by austerity and martial order, and the state boasted a formidable military force.

The landscape of ancient Sparta

The Agora of Sparta, artist's reconstruction

Spartan communal meal

Alongside Athens, ❶, ❷ Sparta played a dominant role among the city-states of Greece. Due to the conflict between the two powers, which emerged in the fifth century BCE, comparisons of their political structures and lifestyles have often been drawn that do not do justice to their dissimilar development and background. Sparta's expansion in order to solve its demographic problems began around 720 BCE when the Spartans occupied Laconia and invaded Messenia. The Messenians rebelled between 660 and 640, which led to the city's subjugation, giving Sparta control over the whole of the Peloponnesus. The conquered peoples became helots, or serfs. Individual tribes of helots were able to gain their freedom through bravery in war, however, and later even acquired the right to Spartan citizenship.

Sparta's social order rested on the upholding of traditional tribal customs such as the petitioning of the gods, communal meals, and the raising of boys from the age of seven by the state rather than the family. The Spartans were famed for their discipline, the austerity of their lives and their obedience to authority. The consequences, however, were that Sparta remained socially and economically backward, for example, not even minting a coinage. By the sixth century BCE the rule of the aristocracy had been abolished and replaced by a society of equals (Homoioi) composed of all able men. They ate their ❸ meals—for example, the notorious Spartan "black soup"—communally. Fifteen men comprised an eating community and undertook the training of their adolescents (ephebi). Until the age of 30, the men lived with their military unit and underwent continuous training. This led to the sidelining of marriage and family life and encouraged homosexual relationships. As the men were frequently absent due to war or military training, the women of Sparta led a more liberated life than women in other cities. Aristotle even spoke of an "unbridled regiment of women" in Sparta.

Sparta's political goal was military effectiveness and readiness for battle against outside enemies as well as against possible revolts of the helots. Through physical and weapons ❹, ❻ training, young Spartans were disciplined to fight, kill, and die for the good of Sparta. This archetypal character—readiness for battle and fearlessness in the face of death—is history's image of Sparta.

Gymnastic exercises of Spartan youths

Youths wrestling, marble relief, ca. 500 BCE

❺ Ephebe with pole and sling

Translated from Herodotus' History:

Inscription on graves of Spartans killed defending the Pass of Thermopylae

"Go, stranger, and tell the Spartans that we lie here in obedience to their laws."

ca. 720 BCE | Conquest of Laconia and Messenia   660–640 BCE | 2nd Messenian War   521–490 BCE | King Cleomenes I

ca. 900 BCE | Foundation of Sparta in the Eurotas Valley   ca. 700 BCE | Lycurgus's constitution   550 BCE | Foundation of the Peloponnesian alliance

The Political Organization of Sparta

Sparta was ruled by two royal dynasties, though the ephorate occasionally seized the reins of power. The original harmonious relationship with Athens turned into rivalry and confrontation after the Persian Wars.

Sparta's form of government was a monarchy with two lines of kings, the Agiads and the Eurypontids, sharing power between them. The Spartan aristocracy dedicated itself to **7**, **8**, **11** warfare and was supported by the taxes of the helot peoples. In the first half of the seventh century BCE, the lawmaker **10** Lycurgus instituted a political code called the Great

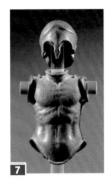

7 Greek helmet and armor

Rhetra ("agreement" or "law"), which listed Spartan customs and traditions. A council of 28 aristocrats, elected for life, governed with the kings. Beside the council was an assembly (*apella*) of male citizens that approved or vetoed council proposals.

A new institution called the *ephorate* ("overseers") emerged in the fifth century BCE: this group of five men was at first elected annually by the apella, but soon usurped the leadership of both the council and the apella and eventually displaced the kings

8 Duel or ritualized combat between hoplites armed with spears and shields, painting on a Greek vase, ca. 560–550 BCE

from power. It wasn't until 226 BCE that King Cleomenes III was able to break the power of the ephorate.

Sparta established its domination over the whole of the Peloponnesus, and only few dared to rebel against the powerful state. In contrast to Athens, Sparta was wise enough to demand only men and weapons from other city-states and not to interfere otherwise in their internal affairs.

Sparta's relations with Athens were good at first; the Spartans, under Cleomenes I, helped the Athenians dispose of the tyrant Hippias in 510 BCE. Furthermore, given the Spartans' military capabilities, they carried the burden of the heaviest fighting during the Persian Wars. This is illustrated by the Spartan king **12** Leonidas, who in 480 BCE blocked the advance of the vast Persian army

9 Leonidas and his companions before the Battle of Thermopylae, 480 BCE

with a tiny force of warriors at the Pass of **9**, **13** Thermopylae, buying time for the other Greeks to arm themselves for the Battle of Salamis. The Spartans fought and died to the last man. Afterwards, harmony between the two city-states was replaced by rivalry as Athens sought to expand. The resultant tensions eventually led to the Peloponnesian War.

10 *Lycurgus Demonstrates the Meaning of Education*, painting by Caesar van Everdingen, 1660–61

Cleomenes I of Sparta

Cleomenes I of the Agiad family was king in Sparta from ca. 521 to 490 BCE. He played an important role in deposing the tyrants in Athens. Later, however, he came into conflict with the Athenians. In 494, he dealt Argos, Sparta's traditional enemy, a crushing defeat at Sepeia, and he intervened in several other conflicts. As he wanted to restore a strong monarchy, the ephorates used his absence in war to depose him in 491 and he committed suicide a year later.

11 Spartan hoplite wearing a Corinthian helmet and greaves

12 Leonidas, King of Sparta

13 *Leonidas at Thermopylae*, painting by Jacques-Louis David, 1814

5th century BCE | Creation of the *ephorate*   **480 BCE** | Battle at the Thermopylae Pass

494 BCE | Spartan victory over Argos   **480 BCE** | Alliance made against the Persians   **226 BCE** | Reforms of Cleomenes III

The Peloponnesian War

Athens's abandonment of its previous alliance system led to conflict with Sparta. Its ruthless expansionism led to the Peloponnesian War on the periphery of the Greek world.

Greek warrior wearing light armor, greaves and helmet with a shield and javelin

In 464 BCE, Sparta suffered a severe earthquake followed shortly afterwards by a helot revolt. An appeal to Athens for help was answered in 462 by Athens's leading statesman and military leader, Cimon, who dispatched ❶ hoplite troops to the aid of Sparta. The democratic forces in Athens used Cimon's absence, and the crushing defeat of his troops suffered at the hands of the helots, to implement a radical change in policy. ❸ Cimon was banished by ostracism, and Athens left the anti-Persian alliance with Sparta in 461. The Delian League was then created, and other states were forced to join and support Athenian expansionist designs. The first inconclusive military conflict with Sparta was settled by a peace treaty in 446–445 BCE, in which both powers agreed not to extend their influence and to allow the neutral Greek states to remain aloof. In the years that followed, however, Athens continued to extend its influence while Sparta sought to maintain the status quo. Thus, the peace became increasingly unviable, and the move to armed conflict was swift.

The devastating ❷ Peloponnesian War between the two most powerful city-states began with a flare-up on the fringes of the Greek peninsula between minor powers. However the two giants, Athens and Sparta, were quickly drawn in by their conflicting alliances. ❺ Corinth and Corcyra were quarreling over the possession of their common colony Epidamnos (modern Durrës) on the Adriatic Sea. Corcyra, a neutral power, then sought an alliance with Athens, and Athens—wanting to extend its sphere of influence to include the Adriatic

❸ Clay shard inscribed with the name of Cimon, who was banished under the ostracism law

❷

Two hoplites greet each other before entering battle, Peloponnesian War, marble relief, ca. 420 BCE

coast—agreed. In 433 BCE the first clashes occurred at sea, between Athenian and Corinthian ships. In 432, Athens imposed a blockade on Corinth's ally Megara and its Pontian colonies, whereupon Corinth and Megara, both allies of Sparta, pressed for support. After some hesitation, Sparta declared war on Athens in the summer of 432, citing the breach of earlier peace treaties.

❹
Athenians and Corinthians in battle near Potidaea, 431 BCE

❺
Corinthian helmet

462 BCE | Cimon sends troops to aid Sparta   446–445 BCE | Peace treaty between Athens and Sparta   431–421 BCE | First phase of the war

464 BCE | Earthquake disaster in Sparta   461 BCE | Athens cancels alliance with Sparta   432 BCE | Sparta declares war on Athens

The Course of the War

The first phase of the Peloponnesian War was confused, with neither side gaining a decisive advantage. However, once Sparta concluded an alliance with the Persians, Athens was caught on the defensive and ultimately had to capitulate.

The Peloponnesian War (431–404 BCE) drew most of the surrounding states into one camp or the other. In the first phase (431–421 BCE), Athens, under Pericles, with its powerful navy, fought defensively on land and

Foundation of the Heraion of Argos

Alcibiades, marble bust

offensively at sea. Sparta, under Archidamus II, with its formidable warriors, concentrated on the land war in 431–427 and ravaged Attica in 425. Ultimately the two powers' differing strengths brought the first phase of the war to a stalemate. Pericles' successor, Cleon, continued Athens' imperialistic policies. After gaining an impressive naval victory over Sparta near the island of Sphacteria in 424, he gambled away the chances for a peace agreement by

making excessive demands. Negotiations only became possible once Cleon fell in battle at Amphipolis in 422.

The peace faction in Athens came to power under Nicias and managed to conclude the Peace of Nicias with Sparta in 421 BCE. This restored the territorial boundaries to their prewar locations. Nonetheless, the main powers' allies continued the conflict. In 420 the prowar faction, led by ❼ Alcibiades, regained power in Athe-

ns and formed an alliance with Sparta's archenemy, the city ❹, ❻ Argos. This did not prevent the latter's defeat by Sparta in 418.

In 415 BCE a new phase of the war began, as the theater of conflict shifted to ❾ Sicily. However, in 413 the war once again returned to Attica. Athens's situation seemed perilous when Sparta allied itself with the Persians, who supplied large amounts of gold to finance the construction of a Spartan fleet. ❿ Alcibiades was able to defeat the Spartans and the Persians in 411 at Abydus and in 410 at Cyzicus. However, the Athenian naval defeat at Notium in 407 made it evident that the powerful city-state was militarily and financially exhausted.

The destruction of the mighty Athenian fleet by the Spartans at Aegospotami in 405 BCE proved decisive. The Spartan admiral ❽ Lysander was able to blockade Athens and force the city to capitulate. Athens's dominions were reduced to Attica and Salamis,

Lysander orders the walls of Athens to be torn down

and it was forced to dismantle its fortifications and relinquish its fleet to the Spartans. The balance of power had shifted; Sparta was now supreme in Greece.

The Greek Historian Thucydides

Thucydides, the Athenian historian and onetime general, is the main source of information for scholars about the various phases of the war between Sparta and Athens. Between 431 and 411 BCE, he wrote The History of the Peloponnesian War in eight books, a meticulous account of events. This strategist of Athens was defeated by the Spartans near Amphipolis in 424 and was forced into exile for 20 years. The historian Xenophon took up where Thucydides left off and provided us with the final phase of the war (411–404 BCE) in his Hellenica.

above: Thucydides, sculpture

The Battle of Syracuse, Sicily, 413 BCE

Alcibiades' victory over the Spartans

Intellectual Innovations in the Fifth and Fourth Centuries BCE

In the two centuries after 500 BCE, significant intellectual developments took place in Greece. This was initiated by the great tragedians and early historians and by the Sophists, whose philosophy was answered by that of Socrates, Plato, and Aristotle.

 **1** Sophocles
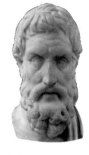 **2** Euripides
 **3** Aristophanes
 **4** Plato
 **5** Aristotle

From Herodotus' *History*, **Book 1:**

"I shall go forward with my history, describing equally the greater and the lesser cities. For the cities which were formerly great have most of them become insignificant; and such as are at present powerful, were weak... I shall therefore discourse equally on both, convinced that human happiness never continues long in one stay."

The fifth and fourth centuries BCE were a time of **⓾** intellectual regeneration in many fields. In the fifth century, the three most important tragedians of antiquity—**❾**Aeschylus, **❶** Sophocles, and **❷** Euripides—were all working in Athens. They used myths and historical tales to illustrate subjects such as man's inconstant fate, guilt, and atonement. In the fourth century, similar subjects—but with an emphasis on human weaknesses—were dealt with in comedies, most notably by **❸** Aristophanes.

In parallel to this creative effervescence, the first philosophy of history, or historiography, emerged with Herodotus in the middle of the fifth century. He was followed by Thucydides a few decades later. Herodotus is credited as the

6 Logic and Dialectic, typified by Aristotle and Plato, relief by Luca della Robbia, 1437

"father of history" for his original use of universal historical contexts in writing on the Greco-Persian wars. History was no longer seen as merely "a game of the gods" but rather became a combination of forces and people actors; causes and motives were examined and suggested.

In philosophy, the Sophists ("teachers of wisdom") renounced the natural philosophy of the sixth century and set out in a new direction, which led to the end of the old order. As provocative philosophers of enlightenment, they saw thought, critical reasoning,

and rhetoric as the basis of all knowledge, behavior, and customs. Man became "the measure of all things." Complementing this, the three great Greek philosophers began the development of ethical thought. **❼** Socrates, who was preoccupied with the moral responsibility of the individual, was put on trial in 399 BCE and sentenced to drink a cup of poisonous hemlock for "corrupting the youth of Athens." His student **❹**, **❻**, **⓫** Plato was inspired by the unjust death of his teacher, and took Socrates' teachings, notably his dialogues, as a principle from which he designed

an ethics-based, hierarchically structured order of all that exists. In his Politeia ("Republic"), Plato contemplated the nature of the ideal state and developed the idea of philosopher-kings. Around 385 BCE he founded **❽** an academy of philosophy in Athens, where he taught for many years.

Later **❺**Aristotle, whom Plato "converted," took as his starting point individual things and created an all-encompassing system of the sciences. He introduced the thought processes of natural science and the observation of nature into the history of ideas.

7 Socrates

8 *The School of Athens*, fresco by Raffael, 1508–11

ca. 445 BCE | Herodotus' History   **ca. 412 BCE** | Euripides' *Iphigeneia in Tauris*   **410 BCE** | Sophocles' *Oedipus the King*

458 BCE | Aeschylus's *The Oresteia* first performed   **423 BCE** | Aristophanes' *The Clouds*   **ca. 411 BCE** | Thucydides' *History of the Peloponnesian War*

Performance of Aeschylus' Agamemnon in Athens; the play recounts the return of the King of Argus from the Trojan War, colored wood engraving, ca. 1865

Significant artists, poets, and philosophers of the Age of Pericles, print with color added later, ca.1852

Plato and his scholars in the academy of philosophy that he established in Athens, steel engraving, ca. 1850

The Political Environment

After the Peloponnesian War, Sparta was forced to defend its supremacy in Greece against the struggle for autonomy by the city-states. It was eventually defeated by Thebes.

The Peloponnesian War altered the balance of power. Athens had failed in its imperialist ambitions and was forced to relinquish hegemony to Sparta. However, a

Naval engagement during the second Battle of Coroneia in 394 BCE

general peace on the Greek peninsula proved elusive. The war had left deep scars on almost all of the cities allied with the two main combatants. In virtually every polity, citizens were divided into pro-Athenian advocates of democracy or pro-Spartan advocates of the old oligarchic order. There was social unrest—for example, in Corcyra—and small civil wars.

Following Athens's capitulation in 404 BCE, Sparta's allies—above all Corinth and Thebes—demanded the destruction of the city to break Athenian power once and for all. Sparta, which

had already achieved its objectives, opposed this. Meanwhile, the cities formerly under Athenian rule demanded the autonomy that Sparta had promised them during the war—and showed little inclination to exchange Athenian domination for Spartan. However, Sparta removed the democratic governments in these cities and reinstated the old oligarchic parties.

Fresh unrest also broke out on the Peloponnesus. Around 400 BCE, the Persians again occupied the Greek cities in Anatolia. Sparta attempted to force the Persians out with military action in 400–394, but with money and promises of liberation, the Persians persuaded Thebes, Argos, Corinth, Athens, and the central Greek states to side with them against Sparta. Although Sparta had some success against the individual city-states, as in the **12**,**13** second battle of Coroneia (394 BCE), the alliance backed by Persian gold was too large to overcome. In the ensuing King's Peace of 387–386, Sparta was forced to recognize Persian supremacy in Asia Minor and the autonomy of

the other Greek cities. Sparta was visibly weakened—a signal for its former allies to shake off Spartan control once and for all. Thebes took the initiative. Under the command of General **4** Epaminondas, who developed a new military strategy

Victory of the Spartans at the second Battle of Coroneia, 394 BCE

with an attack from the left flank, the Theban army defeated the Spartans at Leuctra in Boeotia in 371. Sparta was broken, and within a few decades, Thebes became

the leading state in Greece. This lasted until a new power—Macedonia under Philip II—challenged the order.

The Death of Epaminondas after the battle against the Spartans led by Mantineia in 362 BCE., painting by Louis Gallait

THE RISE AND FALL OF A WORLD POWER: FROM MACEDONIA TO THE DIADOCHOI 7TH–1ST CENTURY BCE

Initially, the Greeks hardly took note of the Macedonians and regarded them as useful "semi-barbarians" who shielded their civilization from invasions from the north. In the fifth century BCE, however, the Macedonians began to unify as a cohesive nation under a strong monarch and eventually, under Philip II, became the leading power in Greece. From Macedonia, Philip's son ❶ Alexander the Great conquered the known world, although his empire did not survive his death. His successors, the Diadochoi, carried the Hellenistic culture throughout the empire and into the Near and Middle East.

1 Alexander the Great of Macedonia during the Battle of Issus against the Persians in 333 BCE

The Rise of Macedonia

Starting in the fifth century BCE, Macedonian rulers were able to develop a relatively cohesive state structure. Macedonia was thus able gradually to build up its influence and become a great power.

In its early period, Macedonia, in the north of Greece, did not play a strong role in shaping Greek culture. Its populace, predominantly peasants, spoke a distinct dialect and did not regard itself as Greek. Macedonia's early history was characterized by conflicts with the Illyrians and Thracians, its neighbors to the north and south, respectively. By the seventh century BCE, the Argead dynasty ruled in

2 Philip II of Macedonia, coin

Macedonia. The king was commander of the army, supreme judge, and ritualistic religious leader in one, with his power held in check by an assembly of the army and the warrior aristocracy.

By the fifth century BCE, Macedonia had become a cohesive state. ❹ King Alexander I (the Philhellene) supported the Greeks in the Persian Wars and had, by 480 BCE, extended his kingdom to Mo-

unt Olympus and the Pangaion region. He gave his kingdom a more stable structure through military, administrative, and coinage reforms. His successor, Perdiccas II, used clever tactics between the sides of the Peloponnesian War. The rise of Macedonia as a military power began under Archelaus, who made Pella his capital, occupied parts of Thessaly around 400 BCE, and invited famous Greek artists, Euripides foremost

3 Young Macedonian warrior, relief

among them, to his court.

Macedonia faced catastrophe in 359 BCE when its king was killed: Perdiccas III, who had won a victory over the Athenians in 360, fell in battle against the Illyrians along with 4,000 of his ❸ warriors. His son and heir Amyntas IV, was still a child, and the Illyrians and Paionians took advantage of this to enter Macedonia. In desperation, the fallen king's younger brother and the child's regent, ❷ Philip II, was raised to the throne and the situation immediately changed.

4 Alexander I of Macedonia has Persians killed by youths disguised as girls, during a feast organized by his father, Philip II

5 Method of attack used by basic unit of the Macedonian phalanx as it was organized under both Alexander the Great and his father Philip II

ca. 5th century BCE	Macedonia becomes a unified state
from 7th century BCE	Rule of the Argead dynasty
413–399 BCE	King Archelaus

359–336 BCE	Philip II reigns
348–342 BCE	Occupation of Thessaly, Chalcidice, and Thrace

Macedonia as a Great Power under Philip II

Within a few years, Philip II turned Macedonia into the leading military and political power in Greece. He sought a political and cultural union between the Greeks and the Macedonians under his own leadership.

6 The Greek orator Demosthenes rails against Philip of Macedonia

8 Macedonian phalanx

10 The Philippeion, commissioned by Philip II after his victory at Chaeronea in 338 BCE in honor of his family

11 Mercenaries fighting for Philip II, wood engraving, 1867

❼ Philip II (359–336 BCE) was an outstanding statesman and also a brilliant ❾ military commander. After the death of his brother he governed the country as guardian of his young nephew. Once on the throne, he resolved to capture the various Greek cities. First, he drove the Illyrians and the Paionians out of the country and in the following years conquered a large part of Thrace and the Pangaion. Beginning in 354 BCE he pushed ever farther into Greece and in 351 conquered the Bosporus. Between 348 and 342 he occupied Thessaly, the Chalcidice, and the entirety of Thrace and incorporated them into his kingdom. Philip built up the Macedonian fleet and reorganized his army. He backed ⓫ mercenaries and professional officers, chose capable generals, and made use of his own military engineers to construct siege devices such as battering rams and catapults. However, the primary reasons for Philip's successes were the weakness and internal strife of the Greek states that had resulted from the Peloponnesian War. The Athenians were particularly anxious about the liberty of the Greek cities. The orator ⓬ Demosthenes warned the Greeks of the "Macedonian barbarian," in his four ❻ Philippics ("speeches against Philip"). Philip's advances led to open war in 340 BCE, during which the Athenians

initially gained an upper hand due to their superiority at sea. In the ❿ Battle of Chaeronea in August 338, however, the ❺, ❽ Macedonian phalanx under Philip and his son Alexander won a crushing victory over the "Hellenic League" of Greek cities led

9 Reconstruction of armor from the grave of Philip II in Vergina

by Athens and Thebes. Philip, who called himself the "unifier of Greece," dictated moderate peace terms that allowed the illusion of autonomy, and Athens, Thebes, and most of the other cities joi-

7 Gold medal with a portrait of Philip II, 336 BCE

ned the Corinthian League and a "Common Peace." Philip then became the undisputed sovereign of the first truly united Greece.

In 337 BCE Philip called for a war against the Persians to extend his power eastward. In the spring of 336, a great army of Greeks and Macedonians crossed the Hellespont into Anatolia. However, Philip was assassinated in the middle of preparations for war during the wedding feast for his daughter's marriage.

12 Demosthenes

The Panhellenic Movement

The term "Hellenes" was taken from Hellen, a mythical patriarch. His sons gave their names to the Aeoleans, Dorians, and Ionians. At first it referred to a tribe in Thessaly, but was later extended to include all Greeks. "Zeus Panhellenios" was declared the universal godhead of all Greeks and was honored in rites on the island of Aegina. Philip II and Alexander used Panhellenism as a political integration strategy and intervened as arbitrators in internal Greek conflicts in its name.

347 BCE | Demosthenes' Philippics   **338 BCE** | Macedonian victory in the Battle of Chaeronea   **336 BCE** | Murder of Philip II

346 BCE | Peace of Philocrates between Athens and Macedonia   **337 BCE** | Corinthian League

Alexander the Great and His Campaigns

Alexander rapidly conquered the Near East and Asia as far as India. He was prevented from marching farther by a mutiny of his troops.

❸ Alexander III, son of Philip II, is one of the outstanding personalities of world history. His youthful élan and tactical genius were admired by his contemporaries; his personality and aims continue to present riddles to this day. With his campaigns and his plans for a world empire, he altered Greek identity and Europe's world view, yet ultimately failed as a result of his excesses. Alexander, who was educated by the philosopher ❶ Aristotle, was entrusted by his father with important duties as early as 340 BCE, at age 16, but felt slighted when Philip remarried in 337. Possibly Alexander and his mother Olympias were involved in Philip's murder.

As the new king, Alexander suppressed rebellion in various Greek cities and demonstrated his strength by destroying the city of Thebes in 335 BCE, then took up

Aristotle and his student Alexander

the aggressive ❺ war against the Persians planned by his father. He crossed over to Asia Minor and defeated the Persian army under Darius III at ❹ Issus in 333, then occupied Syria and Phoenicia in 332. He entered Egypt peacefully in 332–331, had himself crowned ❷ pharaoh, and founded Alexandria. In 331 Alexander crossed the Euphrates and Tigris Rivers into

❸ Alexander the Great

Persia, defeated the Persians once more, and proclaimed himself "king of Asia." The subjugations of Babylon, the imperial capital Susa, and Persepolis were symbolic acts that strengthened his claim as ruler of Persia.

In 327 BCE Alexander pushed further east, into India, occupying the areas through which he proceeded. He defeated the Indian king ❻ Porus at the Hydaspes River in 326, but as he was preparing to press on to the Ganges, a mutiny of his soldiers forced him to turn back. The army marched along the Indus to the delta, where it split up in 325. Alexander continued back to Iran through the desert of Gedrosia with the major part of his army, while the

Alexander the Great depicted as a pharaoh greeting the god Amun

fleet was sent to explore the sea passage through the Persian Gulf. Alexander's plan to integrate the cultures in his vast empire by making Macedonians and Persians equal in the army and government met with an army mutiny and resistance in Macedonia and the Greek city-states.

The Gordian Knot

After Alexander the Great had subjugated Phrygia, he found, in Gordium on the Persian "Royal Road," in the Temple of Jupiter in Gordium, the royal chariot of King Gordius, the yoke of which was knotted up with a rope. According to the oracle, whosoever loosened the knot would rule over Asia. Alexander shouted, "What does it matter how I loose it?" and cut through the legendary Gordian Knot with his sword.

above: Alexander cuts through the Gordian Knot with his sword

Battle of Issus between the Macedonians under Alexander and the Persians, stone relief, 333 BCE

The aftermath of the conquest of the Persian Empire by Alexander the Great, 334–331 BCE

Alexander and Porus, painting by Charles Le Brun, 1673, showing Alexander the Great and the captured Indian king

335 BCE | Destruction of Thebes   332 BCE | Occupation of Syria and Phoenicia

336–323 BCE | Alexander III (the Great) rule   333 BCE | Battle at Issus   332–331 BCE | Occupation of Egypt and founding of Alexandria

Alexander's Goals and Failure

Alexander alienated himself from his troops by demanding he be revered as a deity. His ambitious goal was the cultural unification of East and West in his world empire. Alexander's plans became increasingly unrealistic and his grip on power loosened.

7 Alexander depicted as Amun, coin

Like his father, Alexander went to great lengths to achieve his ambitious goals. He presented himself as liberator of the peoples he conquered and observed their traditions. Along the way, he became increasingly fascinated with

8 Marriage of Alexander the Great to Roxana, Roman mural

Oriental cultures. When he began demanding the Oriental custom of prostration before the king (*proskynesis*) from his subjects, he alienated himself from his old Greek and Macedonian comrades-in-arms, who resisted this "custom of slaves." After the death of his friend Hephaestion in 324 BCE, the king became increasingly isolated and indulged in heavy bouts of drinking. In that same year he declared himself the **7** son of the Egyptian national deity Amun and forced the Greeks and Macedonians to worship him as a god.

Alexander's plans for a cultural fusing of East and West were far reaching. He himself married the Bactrian princess **8** Roxana in 327 BCE, and he then arranged the **9** mass marriage of 80 of his close associates and military leaders with Persian noble-women in 324. These marriages were part of a long-term plan to provide a future elite for his empire that would be personally bound to him and carry the legacy of both cultural areas. Exactly how far his plans extended for a world empire—which also included the founding of a large number of cities—is disputed.

Ultimately, Alexander had to give in to reality and the demands of his army. The situation in Europe and, above all, in Macedonia eventually slipped out of his control. Antipater, Alexander's governor in Europe, was strong enough to resist his command that the Greek cities readmit all their exiles who had served in his army. The last months of his life were overshadowed by megalomaniacal plans, feverish delirium, and contradictory political goals—such as an expedition for the conquest of Arabia. On his deathbed, Alexander took leave of his army

Quintus Curtius Rufus, *The History of Alexander*

"To be sure, it is obvious to anyone who makes a fair assessment of the king that his strengths were attributable to his nature and his weaknesses to fortune or his youth."

and passed his signet ring to Perdiccas, one of his generals, yet he failed to designate a successor to rule Macedonia or any other part of his empire. In June of 323 BCE, Alexander **10** died in Babylon at the age of 33 from a fever or (as many historians suspect) as a result of being gradually poisoned by one of his many enemies.

9 From the throne, Alexander watches the mass wedding at Susa with Stateira, the daughter of Darius, at his side

10 A gravely ill and feverish Alexander takes leave of loyal members of his army from his deathbed

331 BCE | Alexander proclaimed "king of Asia" after his victory at Gaugamela   **326 BCE** | Victory at the Hydaspes River

327–325 BCE | March into India   **324 BCE** | Mass wedding in Susa

The Kingdoms of the Diadochoi

After his death, Alexander's generals divided his empire among themselves. Only those who limited themselves to a distinct territory were able to assert themselves as founders of a dynasty.

1 Roxana, the widow of Alexander the Great, with her son Alexander IV Aigos are received by the Macedonian commander Eumenes

2 Tetradrachmon commissioned by a Macedonian or Seleucid dynasty, ca. 311–280 BCE

As Alexander had designated no successor, a power struggle erupted immediately after his death in 323 BCE at the early age of 33. He had succeeded in making the concept of monarchy, which had been peripheral to the Greek world, a model for the succeeding Hellenistic kings. The diadem became the symbol of monarchy.

Each of his generals wanted a share of his crumbling empire. Among these *Diadochoi* (successors) there were plenty of strong leaders—in fact, there were simply too many competing against each other. At first, Perdiccas of Orestis, a general who had distinguished himself in the Indian campaign, attempted to use the signet ring he had received from Alexan-der to legitimize a role as "regent of the empire" until Alexander's young ❶ son, Alexander IV Aigos, came of age. However, those Diadochoi who sought to uphold Alexander's plans for a world empire were defeated, and Perdiccas was murdered in 321 BCE. Only tho-se who chose a specific country in which to build up their power base succeeded. The Diadochoi also carried the cosmopolitan Hellenistic culture, which in many areas fused Greek-Macedonian and Oriental elements, into the empire. Thus Greek culture and philosophy influenced societies in countries far from Greece. The Diadochoi states were strongly aligned with the personalities of the rulers. Each king legitimized himself as a conqueror and military leader who was able to hold and manage his territory. His power was not limited by a constitution. The successful Diadochoi established ❷ dynasties. These, however, were often characterized by family feuds among the descendants, the *Epigones*.

Many of Alexander's officers established small kingdoms, primarily in Asia Minor. One of these was the Macedonian Philetaerus who, in 283 BCE, founded the kingdom of the Attalids of Pergamon, which has become particularly well known due to its impressive buildings such as the ❹, ❺ "Pergamon altar." ❸ Pergamon became a leading power in Asia Minor, made an alliance with Rome to help bring peace to the region, and brought forth significant cultural achievements. Its library was founded by Attalus I (241-197 BCE), Philetaerus's grandson. Pergamine parchment was pioneered when supplies of Egyptian papyrus for manuscripts were cut off. In 133 BCE when Attalus III died, Pergamon fell to the Romans.

3 Statue of a dying warrior, found in Pergamon ca. 210 BCE

4 Pergamon altar, the lower section of which is a frieze depicting mythological scenes of gods fighting animals and giants, reconstruction of the western section

5 Eastern frieze of the Pergamon altar, showing a battle of gods and Titans

The Seleucids and the Ptolemies

The two most important and longest lasting of the Diadochoi kingdoms were those of the Seleucids in Syria and the Ptolemies in Egypt. These kingdoms were ended by Roman conquest.

8 Sphinx on the Serapeion in Alexandria

6 Seleucus I Nicator

7 Ptolemy I Soter

❻ Seleucus I Nicator, founder of the Seleucid dynasty, received the province of Babylonia after Alexander's death. Starting in 312 BCE, he extended his rule through Syria and Mesopotamia and eastward into India. In 305 Seleucus took the title of king and solidified his domain through numerous alliances and military expeditions. He brought Greek and Macedonian settlers into his realm and founded many cities. His son Antigonus I Soter (king from 280 BCE) introduced the Seleucid ruler cult, settled Celts in Galatia, and founded Antioch. The most prominent of his descendents was ❾ Antiochus III the Great (king from 223 BCE), who subjugated the Armenian, Bactrian, and Parthian kingdoms and, between 202 and 194, occupied Phoenicia, the western and southern coasts of Anatolia, and Thrace. War with Rome in 192–189 resulted when he crossed over to Europe and forced the Greek cities of Asia Minor under his rule. In 189–188 BCE Antiochus had to withdraw from Asia Minor down to Taurus.

His successors dissipated their powers in fratricidal wars until the Roman general Pompey dethroned the last Seleucid ruler in 64 BCE and made a Roman province of what was left of the empire.

As a friend of Alexander, ❼ Ptolemy I Soter, founder of the Ptolemaic dynasty, wrote Alexander's biography and started the state cult around him. He won Egypt in 323 BCE and took the title of king in 305. In alliance with Seleucus I, he attacked Macedonia several times. Ptolemy solidified his rule in Egypt, generally adopting Egyptian religious concepts and the image of sovereign. He founded the Mouseion, the ❽ Serapeion, and the great ❿ library of Alexandria. His son Ptolemy II installed the Egyptian national cult around his own dynasty and constructed the ❿ Pharos lighthouse of Alexandria, one of the Seven Wonders of the Ancient World. ⓫ Ptolemy III Euergetes (king from 246 BCE) advanced to the Euphrates and Asia Minor and defended the empire against the expansionist ambitions of the Seleucids. After him, insignificant and often short-lived kings reigned until Ptolemy XII Neos Dionysos (king 80–51 BCE), who completely relied on the power of Rome. The story of his daughter Cleopatra VII, the last of the Ptolemaic dynasty, belongs to the Roman era under Julius Caesar.

Ptolemy II Philadelphus

Ptolemy II (308–246 BCE, king from 285 BCE) married his sister Arsinoe II (ca. 316–271 BCE) according to old Egyptian custom. He extended the kingdom from Egypt into Nubia and the Arabian Peninsula and gained maritime strength in the Mediterranean. The couple, deified as the "Theoi Adelphoi," were generous patrons of the arts and sciences and made Alexandria a cultural center of the world.

above: Ptolemy II Philadelphus and his wife Arsinoe II

9 Antiochus III the Great

10 The Pharos lighthouse in Alexandria, one of the Seven Wonders of antiquity

11 Ptolemy III Euergetes

12 The destruction of the Royal Library of Alexandria by a fire in 47 BCE

Macedonia after Alexander's Death

The struggle of the Diadochoi for Macedonia and Greece was played out through family intrigues. Alexander's dynasty fell, and almost all of the Diadochoi joined in the scramble for power in Europe.

1 Olympias, wife of Philip II and mother of Alexander the Great

2 Dying Alexander, marble sculpture, second century BCE

❶ Olympias, Alexander the Great's mother, tried to secure influence as head of the dynasty.

Antipater decided on the loyal general Polyperchon as his successor, but his own son Cassander wanted control and allied himself with Antigonus I, who had established an empire in Asia. Cassander and Antigonus unseated Polyperchon and allied themselves with King Philip III and his wife Eurydice. Polyperchon in turn allied himself with Olympias, and together they had the royal couple killed and from 317 ruled as regents in the name of the child Alexander IV. Thereupon, Cassander started a campaign of revenge against the royal house. He marched out of Athens with the army at his side in 316, had Olympias executed, and drove out Polyperchon. He took the young Alexander IV and his mother Roxana as prisoners and put them to death in 310. With this, Cassander had annihilated Alexander's dynasty. Through shifting alliances with other Diadochoi rulers (Lysimachus, Ptolemy I, and Seleucus I), he was able to gain recognition from all as "viceroy of Europe" by 311 BCE After engaging in serious clashes with Antigonus beginning in 307, Cassander's position finally became untenable around 300 BCE.

❺ Thessalonica, Cassander's wife, who had tried to decide his succession, was murdered by her son Antipater. In 294 Antipater was finally deposed by Demetrios I Poliorcetes, who gave way to the rule of the Antagonids over Macedonia and Greece. The peace between the successors of Alexander recognized the effective division between Antigonus, who was supreme in Asia; Cassander, who dominated Greece and Macedon; Lysimachus, who ruled Thrace; Ptolemy, who governed Egypt; and Seleucus, who ruled the eastern satrapies. Soon after his death in 297, his dynasty came to an end.

Upon Alexander's death in 323 BCE, his strongest generals proceeded to divide power. They controlled the richest satrapies, leading the strongest and largest armies, and fought for control of the empire. **❹** Antipater, whom Alexander had appointed viceroy, ruled **❸** Macedonia until his death in 319 B.C. The Macedonians in Alexander's army wanted to hold on to the Argead dynasty and chose Alexander's half-brother Philip III Arrhidaeus as king in 323 BCE. Alexander IV, who was born after the **❷** death of his father, also had dynastic claims. Antipater became regent of the empire in 321, while at the same time

3 Map of ancient Greece showing Macedonia in the north in red, Thracia in yellow, Epirus in green, copper engraving, 18th century

4 King Antipater in battle, copper engraving, 17th century

5 King Antipater I kills his mother Thessalonica

316 BCE | Murder of Olympias by Cassander during the war of succession   **310 BCE** | Murder of Roxana and Alexander IV

323 BCE | Election of Philip III to the throne   **315–01 BCE** | Diadochoi war   **301 BCE** | Battle of Ipsus

Macedonia under the Antigonids

The descendents of Antigonus I finally succeeded in gaining power in Macedonia and thus over Greece. Their successors waged war against the growing power of Rome.

6 King Philip V forces Theoxena and her husband Poris to commit suicide for fleeing Macedonia

7 King Perseus of Macedonia in profile, contemporary cameo

Antigonus I Monophthalmus ("the One-eyed," ca. 382–301 BCE) and his son Demetrius I Poliorcetes—"the Besieger"—were the last of the Diadochoi to hold on to Alexander's plans for a world empire. From their power base in Asia, they invaded Greece and took Athens claiming to be "liberators." After the expulsion of Cassander, Antigonus assumed the title of king in 306 BCE and revived the Corinthian League for the liberation of all of Greece. In 301 Antigonus fell at Ipsus against Lysimachus and Seleucus I. Demetrius was able to bring a large part of Greece, Macedonia, and Asia Minor under his control but was captured by Seleucus I in 285 BCE.

His son Antigonus II Gonatas (king 283–239 BCE), however, was able to maintain Antigonid control of Macedonia and most of the Greek cities through alliances until the country was invaded and conquered by the Romans in 168 BCE.

By about 250 BCE the situation was generally settled, and Macedonia was again the undisputed master of Greece. Demetrius II (king 239–229 BCE) son of Antigonus I, secured victories over the Celts and the Dardanians and dominated the Aegean Sea, defeating the battle fleets of the Egyptian Ptolemies at Cos in 258 BCE and at Andros in 245 BCE. Antigonus III Doson (regent, then king 229–221 BCE) brought Sparta under their sovereignty, and Antigonus united almost all of the Greek peninsula in the "Hellenic League" in 224.

However, conflict began to develop with the rising power of Rome, which sought to hinder Macedonia's consolidation of its strength in Europe. **6** Philip V of Macedonia (king from 221 BCE) allied himself with the Carthaginian general Hannibal in 215 BCE to expand westward against Rome. During the First Macedonian War (215–205 BCE) Philip was relatively successful, gaining access to the Adriatic Sea, but when a few Greek cities pulled out of the **8** Second Macedonian War (200–197 BCE), he was defeated by the Romans. In the following years he became entangled by internal Greek unrest. Philip's son **7**, **9** Perseus was the last king of Macedonia. After suffering several **10** defeats by Rome, Perseus was captured in 168 and paraded through the streets of Rome in a victory procession in 167. Macedonia was then divided into four republics and finally made part of the Roman Empire as a new province.

The Athenian Philosophy

During the period of Antigonid rule over Greece, Athens remained a center of culture and philosophy. In 306 BCE, Epicurus founded his school, whose followers strove for individual happiness and peace. The Stoics, named after their meeting place in the columned hall on the Agora of Athens, first met around 300 BCE and with their austere rationalism stood in opposition to the hedonism of the Epicureans.

left: The Stoa Poikile ("painted colonnade"), at the Agora in Athens, where philosophy was taught and after which the Stoics were named
above right: The philosopher Epicurus, ca. 270 BCE

8 The Greeks are set free at the Isthmic Games, 196 BCE, after the Second Macedonian War

9 Perseus marches through the Thessalian canyons to Illyria during the Third Macedonian War

10 Roman legionnaires break the Macedonian phalanx in the Battle of Pydna, 168 BCE

JUDEA AND ARABIA BEFORE THE ROMANS

CA. 1100 BCE–136 CE

As the Babylonian exile ended in 539 BCE, the returning Jews installed a priestly principality in Palestine, later taken over by the Maccabees. Herod the Great first established a secular kingdom. The ancient Arabian kingdoms benefited from the ❷ Incense Road trade route connecting India and the Persian Gulf with the Mediterranean. These states, and the Nabataea of ❶ Petra, acquired great wealth and made significant cultural developments. While Petra fell to Rome, southern Arabia was occupied by the Sassanids.

The "Shelter of the Pharaoh" of Petra, capital of the Nabataea

■ Palestine from the Persians to the Maccabees

After their return from Babylon, the Jews were able to maintain their cultural and religious autonomy under changing regimes. The Maccabees finally established the first king/high priest monarchy.

High priest and minor priest

When the Persian king Cyrus II conquered Babylon in 539 BCE, he ended the "Babylonian captivity" of Jews captured by Nebuchadressar II in 588 BCE. Most of the Jews returned to the vicinity of Jerusalem, where they erected a shrine to Yahweh. They came into conflict with the Samarians and the Ancient Judeans who had settled there in the meantime. It wasn't until 520–515 BCE that the Jews were able to reestablish a central Yahweh cult in Jerusalem under a ❸ high priest, who was simultaneously political leader of the Jews.

Palestine remained a province of the Persian Empire until 332 BCE, when Alexander the Great incorporated it into his growing empire. After Alexander's death, it ultimately came under the rule of the Egyptian Ptolemies in 301, who allowed the Jews complete religious freedom. Around 200 BCE a strong Hellenization of the Jewish culture began. In 198, Palestine and Phoenicia came under the domination of the Seleucid Antiochus III of Syria, who confirmed their religious freedom and constitution. His son ❹ Antiochus IV Epiphanes, however, deviated from this policy when he inter-

4 Antiochus IV Epiphanes' portrait on a coin

2 Perfume flacon from Jerusalem, first century CE

Judaized the regions of Samaria, Idumaea, and Galilee.

Power struggles in the first century BCE allowed the Romans to intervene in Judea, installing Hyrcanus II (76–40 BCE) but granting him only limited powers. When the Maccabean king ❻ Antigonus Mattathias allied with the Parthians, he was captured and executed in 37 BCE.

vened in the conflicts between Jewish priestly families, attempted to introduce the Seleucid cult, and plundered the temple in 168 BCE. A Jewish revolt in Jerusalem was crushed and an altar to Zeus was installed in the temple. The Maccabee family overthrew the high priests in charge and led an uprising of the people. ❺ Judas Maccabee ("the Hammer") drove the Seleucids from Jerusalem and restored the Yahweh cult in 164. His successors extended their rule over Judea, made the high priest office hereditary, and

5 Judas Maccabee defeats the enemies and purges the temple

Antigonus Mattathias calls the Jews to arms

Herod the Great and His Successors

Herod the Great conclusively did away with the rule of the Maccabees and allied himself with Rome. Following rebellions by the Jews, Judea was completely integrated into the Roman Empire.

❼ Herod the Great was from a family that was loyal to the Romans; his father Antipater had been appointed procurator over Judea by Julius Caesar. Herod

8 The ruins of Masada, in the background the Dead Sea

10 Believers during Passover in front of the temple of Jerusalem

eliminated the last of the Maccabees and assumed the throne in 37 BCE. Although he married the Maccabean princess Mariamne, his rule was secularly oriented, following the Roman model.

Herod suppressed the religious agitators in the land, as well as intrigues in his palace, and was thus able to maintain peace. Under him Judea's economy blossomed, as evidenced not least by his monumental construction projects. He had the ❿ temple erected anew, yet his attempts to culturally unify the Jews ultimately failed. The birth of Jesus Christ falls within his reign, but the ⓫ murder of innocent children of which he was accused is probably a Christian myth.

Upon his death in 4 BCE, Herod's kingdom was divided among his three sons, the Tetrarchs. One of them, Herod Antipas (ruled 4 BCE–39 CE), who received Galilee and Peraea, is known to this day for his marriage to his niece and sister-in-law Herodias and the dance of his stepdaughter, ❾ Salome, performed for the head of John the Baptist. His nephew, Herod Agrippa I, ruled once more over the reunited realm of Herod the Great with great support of Judaism and as a friend of the Romans from 41 to 44.

In 66 CE, Jewish religious zealots initiated a revolt against Roman rule. The king, Agrippa II, who while of Jewish faith had been raised in Rome, sided with the Romans against the zealots. The revolt led the Roman emperor Titus to seize control of Jerusalem and to order the ⓬ destruction of the temple in 70 CE. The last stronghold of the Jewish zealots, ❽ Masada, fell in 73 CE after the suicide of all the defenders. Judea was made a Roman province with limited autonomy. But even that was permanently lost after the revolt of Bar Kokhba in 132–135, led by the Jewish military commander Simon Bar Kokhba, establishing the independent state of Israel. The Jewish people were then driven out of Judea by the Romans three years later into the Diaspora.

7 Herod the Great conquers Jerusalem in 37 BCE with the help of the Romans

9 Salome dancing in front of king Herod Antipas

The Rebellion of Bar Kokhba

Simon Bar Kokhba ("the Son of the Star") led the last revolt of the Jews against the Romans in 132 CE. The catalyst was the ban on circumcision and the Roman attempt to construct a temple to Jupiter in Jerusalem. Bar Kokhba captured Jerusalem and ruled as "prince of Judea," with messianic traits as defined by ancient Jewish laws. In 135 CE he was vanquished by superior Roman strength at Bethar. Thereafter the Jews were forbidden to enter Jerusalem.

above: Silver coins (tetra drachmas), distributed by Bar Kokhba

11 The Bethlehem infanticide, painting by Alessandro Turchi, 1640

12 Destruction of the temple of Jerusalem by the Romans under Titus, 70 CE

164 BCE | Reintroduction of Yahweh cult and reconstruction of the temple   **70 CE** | Conquest of Jerusalem and destruction of the temple by Titus

167 BCE | Maccabee Revolt   **37 BCE** | Herod named king of the Jews   **132–135 CE** | Revolt of Bar Kokhba

The Kingdoms of South Arabia

Kingdoms in South Arabia grew rich from the ❶ caravan trade of the Incense Road. In the first century CE, the Himyars of Saba (Sheba) were able to bring the whole region under their control.

The Arabian Peninsula, inhabited since the Paleolithic age, has been home to Semitic tribes since the third millennium BCE. These peoples have generally been referred to as "Arab" and are mentioned in Assyrian sources as early as the ninth century BCE. While the inhospitable central desert was largely crossed only by nomads, a number of city kingdoms devel-

2 Dam of Marib, in present-day Yemen, an irrigation plant, which leads the water out of the wadi to the fields

oped in the more favorable climes of the south (present-day Yemen and Oman along the coast). Very early on, they built irrigation systems like the ❷ dam of ❸ Marib and profited from the incense trade. They connected the Persian Gulf with India and even China by caravan and shipping trade routes. Incense, myrrh, and spices reached the Mediterranean by way of the militarily guarded caravan

5 Depiction of a goddess carrying an ear sheaf, found in Qataban first century BCE

4 Figure with sword and dagger, found in Qataban, first c. CE

stations and cities built on rocky hilltops.

The South Arabian empire of Saba, or Sheba, initially ruled by priest-princes and then from the fifth century BCE by kings, developed in the tenth century. Its capital was Marib. The visit of the ❼ queen of Sheba to King Solomon, as reported in the Old Testament, reflects Israel's trade relations with the southern Arabian area. Another state that is mentioned in inscriptions dating back to the tenth and ninth centuries BCE is ❹, ❺ Qataban, with its capital Timna. This kingdom reached its height in the second century BCE but was conquered by the ❻ Hadhramauts about 20 CE. The kingdom of the Hadhramauts, whose capital was Shibam, began its ascendancy at the beginning of the first century CE, and by 50 CE was sovereign over all of southeastern Arabia.

At this time, the kingdom of Saba, under the tribe of Himyars, was regaining importance. The Himyars made the rocky fortress Zafar their new capital and conquered the Hadhramauts, bringing all of South Arabia under their rule by around 300 CE. Following the destruction of Jerusalem in 70 CE, the Himyarite kingdom

1 Caravan on its way to the Red Sea, painting by Alberto Pasini, 1864

3 Terracotta statuettes from Marib in Yemen

experienced a strong influx of Jewish communities and, from the fourth century on, of Christian communities. Originally the Himyarite kingdom had good relations with Christian Abyssinia, but the persecution of Christians by the last Himyarite rulers, who were religiously inclined toward Judaism, resulted in an attack by the Abyssinians in 525. The kingdom was subsequently conquered by the Persian Sassanids in 575.

7 The queen of Sheba at Solomon, painting by Veronese, 16th century

6 The village Kawkaban in western Hadhramaut

The Nabataea of Petra

The kingdom of the Nabataea also became wealthy through its position on the Incense Road. It had become a leading power in the region by the second century BCE, but ultimately succumbed to the power of Rome.

Ed-Deir ("the Convent") of Petra

Three containers for incense from the Ancient East, tenth–sixth century BCE

The Nabataea migrated out of the Arabian Peninsula and into the territory of present-day Jordan in the fourth century BCE. They

The gorge Siq is the main entrance to Petra

founded ❽, ❾ Petra (today Wadi Musa) in a rocky basin of soft red sandstone that was accessible only through a narrow ❸ gorge. Up until the second century BCE they remained without political ambitions and lived in their secluded valley as herdsmen, caravan guides, and traders, maintaining good relations with Egypt, Persia, and Greece. The Nabataea controlled an important section of the incense route and built warehouses for goods and foodstuffs in the rock faces. Some of these became multistoried dwellings, burial complexes, and shrines in which, at first, ❶ stone idols and later deified rulers were worshiped. The Nabataea produced finely decorated ❿ pottery, which became a sought-after article in the Orient.

Nabataean politics changed in the second century BCE and the kingdom began to expand. The kings proceeded cautiously in the power struggles between the Seleucids and the Ptolemies, aiding the Jews in their revolt against the Seleucids in 164 BCE.

New times came with Aretas III, who

11 Anthropomorphic idol with a Nabataean inscription

conquered half of Palestine and a large part of Syria from the Seleucids in 84 BCE. The inhabitants of Damascus chose him as king. He went on to besiege Jerusalem in 65 BCE but was forced to withdraw when threatened with war by the Romans. Still, Aretas III had extended his kingdom from Damascus in the north to Egypt in the west.

Aretas IV (9 BCE–49 CE) conducted a victorious campaign in Ju-

Petra Rediscovered

Petra became the capital of the Roman province Palaestina Tertia in 106 and was still the seat of a Christian bishopric into the fourth century. After being overrun by the Arabs in the seventh century, the city decayed and lay completely forgotten in its inaccessible rocky valley until it was identified in 1812 by the Swiss Orientalist Johann Ludwig Burckhardt, following up on reports of indigenous nomads.

9 View of Petra, colored chalk lithograph, 1839

12 The amphitheater in Petra, built in the first century BCE and extended by the Romans

dea against Herod Antipas, who had divorced his wife, Aretas's daughter, to marry his niece Herodias. Aretas ruled in harmony with the Romans and, with the construction of an aqueduct and the ❷ amphitheater in Petra, achieved a cultural merging of Nabataean, Hellenistic, and Roman building styles, which is characteristic of the surviving structures that were cut from the living rock. The death of the Nabataean king Rabel II (70–105) provided Rome with the excuse to occupy the kingdom in 105, resulting in Petra's destruction. Emperor Trajan turned it into a Roman province.

CARTHAGE: WORLD POWER AND RIVAL OF ROME 814–44 BCE

The Phoenician colony of Carthage, traditionally founded in 814 BCE, rose, through trade and shipping, to become the leading power of the Western Mediterranean. Facing conflicts with the Greek colonies on Sicily and later with Rome, Carthage also armed itself militarily. The struggle between Rome and Carthage under ❶ Hannibal was a battle for survival. It culminated in the defeat and destruction of Carthage.

Hannibal crossing the Rhone in 218 BCE

2 Pendants in the form of bearded heads, ca. fourth/third century BCE, found in Carthage

The Rise of Carthage to Military and Economic Power

After Carthage's ascendancy as a trading power, it also became an important military power as a result of its clashes with the West Greeks and Romans in Sicily.

Dido

According to the myth, it was the Phoenician princess Dido who founded Carthage. The Roman poet Virgil tells of her love for the Trojan hero Aeneas. When Aeneas only stops briefly in Carthage on his way from the defeated Troy and then leaves the queen in order to fulfill his destiny and found Rome, she immolates herself on a burning pyre. The story has been a very popular subject among writers, composers, and poets since.

Originally settled by Phoenicians from Tyre, ❹ Carthage was initially very much under Phoenician cultural and religious influence. Its highest god was ❸ Baal

Hammon, joined in the fifth century BCE by the goddess Tanit. The cult was practiced in cavelike ❻ shrines (*tophets*), but whether child sacrifices were made—as was reported—is disputed. Grotesque ❷ clay masks that have been found in the area possibly belonged to a cult of the dead.

In the sixth century BCE, the politically independent Carthage began setting up trading colonies in North Africa and on the Mediterranean coasts. Carthage became a great city with, at its zenith, 400,000–700,000 people living in buildings up to six stories tall. The heart of

3 Statue of Baal Hammon

the city was the double harbor (Cothon)—a circular inner ❺ military harbor enclosed by an outer harbor for trading vessels—and a city wall 20 miles (32 km) long was constructed. Carthage was ruled by elected shophets (chief magistrates)— who were both head of state and military leaders— and a senate composed of members of the nobility.

The conflicts with the West Greeks, primarily with the tyrants of Syracuse, began in the fifth century BCE, over bases and trading settlements in Sicily and Sardinia. After several wars and sieges, the Halycus River was set as the boundary line in Sicily in 374 BCE. From the sixth to the third centuries, the Carthaginians maintained trade relations with the Etruscans and the Romans, to whom they were tied by alliance treaties. When the

Romans took control of Messina in northeast Sicily in 264 BCE, a conflict ensued. In the First Punic War (264–241 BCE), the Romans drove the Carthaginians out of Sicily, although a Roman landing in Africa in 256–255 was repelled. In 241, Rome destroyed the Carthaginian fleet. Forced to sue for peace, Carthage withdrew from Sicily and Sardinia in 237.

4 Ruins of Punic Carthage

6 Shrine (*tophet*) of Carthage

5 Punic defensive military harbor with docks that cannot be observed from the sea, artist's reconstruction

| 264–241 BCE | First Punic War | 218–201 BCE | Second Punic War | 216 BCE | Victory at Cannae |
| 814 BCE | Carthage founded | 41 BCE | Destruction of Carthaginian fleet | 218 BCE | Hannibal crosses the Alps | 215 BCE | Alliance with Macedonia |

Hannibal and the End of Carthage

In the Second Punic War, Hannibal was able to win several victories against Rome but was then forced onto the defensive. Carthage was totally destroyed in the Third Punic War.

7 Obliteration of Carthage in 146 BCE in the Third Punic War

Hannibal's suicide in Libyssa in Bithynia in 183 BCE

In 237–236 BCE the Carthaginian general Hamilcar Barca occupied the south and west of Spain as a power base against Rome. His son-in-law Hasdrubal advanced up to the middle of Spain but concluded a moratorium with Rome in 226. With Hasdrubal's murder in 221, command fell to ❾ Hannibal, the son of Hamilcar

10 Mosaic with scenes of country life on a Roman estate near Carthage

Barca, who had ⓬ sworn deadly enmity against Rome as a boy. Hannibal had enormous talent for military and tactical thinking, and he immediately began with the conquest of the area north of the Ebro River in Spain, provoking the Second Punic War (218–201 BCE). Hannibal famously crossed the Alps with his army and the legendary elephants in 218 and defeated the Romans under Publius Cornelius Scipio, later known as Scipio Africanus, on the Trebia River in 218 and again on Lake Trasimene in 217. By encircling the Romans, he won a major victory at the ⓫ Battle of Cannae in 216. He then tried to force the northern Italian peoples such as the Celts to join him against the Romans, but was only partially successful. However, in 215 he was able to form an alliance with Philip V of Macedonia, another enemy of Rome.

Under the Roman consul and dictator Quintus Fabius, known as "*Cunctator*" ("the delayer"), the Romans consistently avoided direct battle with the Carthaginians and limited themselves to guerrilla attacks. Conse-

9 Portrait bust of Hannibal

quently, Hannibal moved toward Rome in 211 BCE but was stopped and soon forced out of most of Italy and Spain in 206. In 204, P. Cornelius Scipio landed in North Africa with his Roman legions. Hannibal returned to defend Carthage but was defeated in battle at ⓭ Zama by Scipio in 202. Hunted by the Romans, Hannibal fled through Syria to Bithynia. Threatened with extradition to Rome, he ❽ ended his own life in 183.

Total submission to the power of Rome saved Carthage at first. But the fear of the once powerful city-state, stirred up primarily by Cato the Elder, led to the Third Punic War (149–146 BCE). Carthage was taken and ❼ obliterated in 146 BCE—the

Cato's closing words

Cato the Elder's closing words of every one of his speeches before the Roman Senate: "Ceterum censeo, Carthaginem esse delendam."

("I declare that Carthage must be destroyed").

above: Cato the Elder

11 Battle of Cannae, 216 BCE

ground of the city strewn with salt to render it infertile. Resettled under Julius Caesar, in 29 BCE ⓾ Colonia Julia Carthago became the capital of the African province.

12 Hamilcar Barka lets his nine-year-old son swear enmity to the Romans, painting by Johann Heinrich Schönfeld, ca.1662

13 Scipio conquers Hannibal in the Battle of Zama, 202 BCE, painting 1521

206 BCE | Loss of Spain   **202 BCE** | Carthage's catastrophe at Zama   **146 BCE** | Destruction of Carthage
204 BCE | Scipio invades North Africa   **183 BCE** | Suicide of Hannibal   **29 BCE** | Colonia Julia Concordia Carthago

THE ETRUSCANS: THE LEAGUE TO THE ROMAN EMPIRE 7TH CENTURY BCE–1ST CENTURY BCE

Between the seventh and first centuries BCE, the ❶ Etruscans thrived as an independent culture in central Italy. Whether they were indigenous to Italy was unclear even in antiquity, as the Etruscans had assimilated the Roman myth about Aeneas and the founding of Rome. The Etruscans believed in predestination and that life was totally controlled by the gods, which is why sacrificial cults and cults of the dead played a special role in their culture. From the fifth century on, their history was closely tied to that of Rome.

Terra-cotta model of an Etruscan temple, first half of first century BCE

The Culture of the League of Twelve Cities

A confederation of twelve Etruscan cities controlled Mediterranean trade at first but were forced onto the defensive by the West Greeks of Sicily.

The Etruscan necropolis at Cerveteri

The Etruscans in Italy can be traced back to the seventh century BCE. Today they are no longer regarded as immigrants from the East, although there was a close cultural proximity to the early Greek world as seen in their ❹ script and ❸ vase painting. Evidence of their culture is found primarily in house-like tombs and in the form of ❺ burial objects found in chamber tombs, which were decorated with ❻ frescoes. They built necropolises, for example, at Orvieto and ❷ Cerveteri, with their own road networks. The Etruscans worshiped a number of gods, which were later mixed with the Roman gods. The highest god was Varro, the god of war and vegetation. The prophecies of the ❼ haruspex, who read omens in sacrificial livers and interpreted lightning and bird flights, played a large role in the cult.

The Etruscans were politically organized as a league of twelve city-states, which were ruled by priest-kings. This league was primarily a community based around the shrine to the god Voltumna at Volsinii, but it also pursued common political goals. In the seventh and sixth centuries BCE, the Etruscans pushed out of their core territory, pres-

3 Etruscan vase painting, ca. 500 BCE

ent-day Tuscany, into southern Italy and over the Apennines to the north, and they founded the city of Rome about 650 BCE by combining existing settlements.

Because of Etruria's wealth of ore, it had many trade contacts, including trade agreements with the Phoenicians, Carthaginians, and Greeks—particularly Sicily, beginning in the fifth century. Over time, the Etruscans increasingly intervened in Sicilian political affairs and came into conflict with the tyrants of Syracuse when the Sicilians extended their sphere of power to the Italian mainland. The destruction of the Etruscan fleet at Cumae in 474 BCE broke Etruscan political power and made Rome's subsequent rise possible.

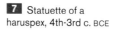

4 Sheet of bronze with Etruscan script, end of the third century BCE

5 Etruscan animal figures, found in the Tomba Bernadini in Palestrina, ca. 640–620 BCE

A Life of Luxury
The flourishing trade in mineral resources and other raw materials provided the Etruscan upper class with great prosperity and wealth, as testified to by the luxury articles they left with their dead for the next life. However, the Etruscans also knew how to enjoy this life. Sumptuous celebratory feasts with music and sporting competitions were held. Greek and Roman writers took exception to the loose morals of their neighbors but at the same time admired their cultural achievements.

Etruscan mural in the Tomba dei Leopardi in Tarquinia depicting servants and musicians, first half of the fifth century BCE

7 Statuette of a haruspex, 4th-3rd c. BCE

The Etruscans under Roman Rule

As Rome gained power, the Etruscan cities increasingly lost their independence, and the Etruscans became allies—Roman citizens, but without the right to vote. They were later completely integrated into the world empire.

Initially, Rome was part of the Etruscan world and was ruled over by the Etruscan Tarquin dynasty. When they were driven out by the Romans in 510 BCE, the king of the Etruscans, **⑩** Porsenna of Camars (modern-day Chiusi)—who is frequently mentioned in ancient literature—is said to have besieged and taken the city. But his efforts proved in vain. Rome became a republic, and when the people rebelled against the powerful patrician families around 500 BCE, the monarchic form also came to an end in other Etruscan cities.

During the fifth century, the Etruscan cities came under attack by both the **⑪** Celts and an expanding Rome. The clashes between Rome and Tarquinia, the leader of the League of Twelve Cities, spread in 353 BCE to all the cities of Etruria. The Etruscan city-state of Caere was quickly captured and assimilated by the Romans. Its inhabitants became "allies," Roman citizens with all privileges except the vote. This was the model by which succeeding Etruscan and Italian cities were taken into the Roman Empire; the Etruscan cities of Veii (396), Nepete (386), and Sutrium (383), which had already been conquered, received the same status. Between 310 and 283 the last **⑧**, **⑨**, **⑫** Etr-

8 Statuette of an Etruscan warrior, fourth century BCE

Etruscan chariot from Castro

uscan coalition army suffered crushing defeats against the Romans at the Vadimonian Lake. This sealed their fate as an independent polity.

Economic and cultural decline followed the political fall when the Etruscan cities, now under Roman rule, experienced destruction by attacking Gauls in 225 BCE and the advance of the Carthaginians under Hannibal in 218–207. The areas around the cities became extensively depopulated as a result of the pillaging and brutal conquest by the invaders, and many Etruscan peasants were forced by poverty into lifelong servitude. The social misery of the Etruscan territories provided a mass base for Roman social reformers like the Gracchi in the second century BCE and Marius, who built up a voluntary army of poverty-stricken Etruscans, in 87 BCE. The revenge of its enemy Sulla thus hit the region of Etruria particularly hard. Under Emperor Augustus, Etruria was fully incorporated into the Roman Empire and was granted the status of Regio VII, making it a Roman voting district.

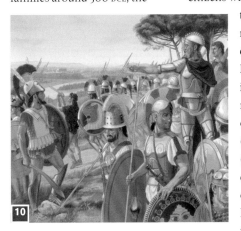

10

11

Battle between the Etruscans and the Celts, urn, second century BCE

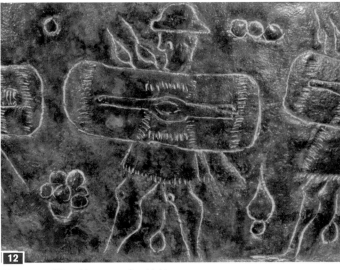

12

Etruscan soldier with rectangular shield

from 353 BCE | Battles between Rome and Etruscan cities **225–207 BCE** | Destruction by the Gauls and Hannibal's advance

474 BCE | Etruscan defeat at sea at Cumae / Rise of Rome **310–283 BCE** | Etruscans defeated by the Romans at Vadimonian Lake

ROME: FROM THE BEGINNINGS TO THE END OF THE REPUBLIC 753–82 BCE

Aeneas pays tribute to the Penates, who accompanied him from Troy to Rome

Rome's early self-conception was derived primarily from the republican myth of its ❶ founding. Its rise followed the political fall of the Etruscans and their incorporation into the new Republic. Rome first gained control of all of Italy, then spread its hegemony throughout the Mediterranean area and into the Near East. The two pillars of Roman rule were, internally, its republican constitution, and, externally, its expansion. The first crumbled through social unrest, making possible the emergence of military dictators from Marius to Julius Caesar, but the second continued unabated as Rome continued to expand its sphere of influence.

■ Myth, Founding, and Early Period

The myth of its founding shaped Rome's self-image and its identity as a state. Out of the battle for military power came the disparity in status between the upper (patrician) and the lower (plebeian) classes.

Romulus and Remus decide where to build the city of Rome by reading the flight of birds

Reconstruction of the antique Forum Romanum as it looked after its completion, wood engraving, ca. 1880

Reconstruction of the Capitol with the temple of Jupiter and Forum Romanum, end of second c. BCE

In no other world empire did the myth of its creation play such a pivotal role in the state as in Rome. The Romans traced their ancestry back to the Trojan hero Aeneas, who—according to Virgil's *Aeneid*—landed in Italy and founded Alba Longa, the mother

The rape of Lucretia by Tarquinius Superbus's son, *Tarquin and Lucretia*, painting by Tintoretto, 1559

city of Rome. ❸ Romulus, however, is regarded as the founder—on the traditional date of April 21, 753 BCE— and first king of Rome.

Altogether, seven kings ruled over Rome, the last of which, Tarquinius Superbus, was toppled in 510 BCE. The cause was, among other things, his son's ❺ rape of Lucretia, the wife of the nobleman Collatinus. It was his nephew, ❻ Junius Brutus, who was said to have initiated the reforms instrumental to the creation of the consulate.

In reality, ❷, ❹, ❼ Rome was founded as an Etruscan colony

Bust of Junius Brutus

around 650 BCE, perhaps even as late as 575 BCE. At first it was ruled by Etruscan kings from the Tarquin royal family, but after the defeat of the Etruscans at Cumae in 474 BCE, Rome disposed of their rule. Even during the time of the monarchy, Rome was characterized by the division of its citizens into "horsemen" (knights), from whom the later patrician families descended, and the masses (plebs) who made up the lower military ranks. The supreme commander of the army (*praetor maximus*) made the decisions concerning military leadership posts, all of which were soon filled by patricians. With the adoption of the Greek phalanx form of warfare, the lower ranks became increasingly important; competition for military leadership positions thereafter evolved into a struggle between patricians and plebeians over access to political offices in general and came to characterize

Roman history. Early Rome, like the Greek cities, experienced severe social conflicts when, through agrarian crises and overpopulation, farmers and peasants became increasingly impoverished and were forced into bonded servitude.

Romulus and Remus

Romulus and Remus were the twin sons of Rhea Silvia and Mars. They were abandoned at the Tiber River and suckled by a she-wolf—which became the symbol of Rome. Romulus later struck his brother dead for jumping over the foundation walls of Rome, as no one was ever supposed to "vault" the impregnable city walls of Rome.

above: *The Capitolian She-Wolf,* Etruscan sculpture, 500 BCE

The Struggle over the Constitution of the Republic

The early laws of Rome and political leadership by two consuls worked towards the realization of the balance between the patrician and the plebeian classes, which was always threatening to tip.

7
Forum Romanum: View of the temple of Saturn, built 498 BCE

10 Roman soldier, colored litho-graph, ca. 1860

The first Roman law code, the Twelve Tables, was drawn up around 450 BCE under pressure from the plebeians. It remained the basis of Roman law up until the early emperors. It guaranteed, among other things, wide-ranging legal equality of ⓫ patricians and plebeians. The class struggle did not come to an end until 300 BCE, however, when the plebeians were granted access to the higher state offices (magistrate) and positions in the priesthood.

The political system of the new republic was geared toward creating a political balance between the patricians and the plebeians. The ❽ Senate, the supreme advisory body to the magistrate, was forced to accept plebeians. However, as the Senate remained dominated by patricians, the plebeians were granted the influential office of "tribune of the people," which publicly represented the rights of the people and allowed them their own assembly. Rome now had a mixed constitution with monarchic (magistrate),

aristocratic (Senate) and democratic (people's assembly) elements.

The seminal event in the struggle for equal rights was the consulship constitution of 367 BCE. It allowed for the ❾ election of two consuls—ideally one patrician and one plebeian—for a one-year term. These two principal magistrates were joined by a *praetor* ("he

9 Dinar depicting a voter submitting his vote for an election

who goes ahead") as the highest civil court officer and "arbitrator." The two counsuls were each elected for one year during the time of the Roman Republic. They were, in case of war, also joint supreme commanders of the armed forces, as long as no dictator was elected. The two-counsul system remained in force as well during the Roman Empire.

When internal stability had been reestablished after the ⓬ Gauls sacked the city in 387 BCE, Rome began building up its world empire in the third and second centuries. By subjugating the Etruscans, and with the victory over the central Italian Samnites, Rome gained control over all of Italy and was also able to assert itself in the Mediterranean against the sea powers of Sicily

8
Senators with the son of a senator or philosopher, fragment of a sarcophagus

and Carthage. In numerous wars, Rome was able to extend its power from western Europe into Greece and the Near East. The last deadly threat to Rome was the unsuccessful Carthaginian expedition led by Hannibal against Rome between 218–201 BCE.

With its well-equipped and disciplined ❿ army, its system of Roman colonies, and its practice of conferring Roman citizenship or perpetual alliances on defeated and subjugated foes, Rome could concentrate, as Athens had done before it in the fifth and fourth centuries BCE, on the development of internal republican freedom and external expansion.

12
Conquest and plundering of Rome by the Gauls under Brennus, 387 BCE, wood engraving, 19th century

11
Romulus divides the population into patricians and plebeians

367 BCE | Constitution creates the consulship   **from 3rd century BCE** | Roman expansion in the Mediterranean region

387 BCE | Looting by the Celtic Gauls   **300 BCE** | Plebeians gain access to priesthood and high offices   **218–201 BCE** | Hannibal's campaign against Rome

The Crisis in the Republic

The rapid expansion of state power exacerbated the social disparities in Rome. The Senate's brutal suppression of the Gracchi land reform further aggravated the general crisis and led to social unrest that threatened to overwhelm the political structures of the Republic.

The death of Tiberius Gracchus, 132 BCE, steel engraving, 19th century

By the second century BCE, Rome had built a world empire, but culturally it leaned on the traditions of other peoples. In the early period, ❹ Greek cultural influence was significant, while later the Hellenistic culture with its Oriental aspects was more important. Leading patrician families, such as the Fabians, the Julio-Claudians, and the Scipiones, who provided consuls and generals in every generation, enjoyed high esteem and ❺ wealth as a result of military fame and the spoils of war. They ruled the city with their network of clients.

The tributes of subjugated peoples and allies brought enormous amounts of money and precious metals to the city of Rome. Corruption scandals, primarily in the provincial administration, shook the republic. The inequality between the large landowners and the destitute city plebeians threatened to shatter the internal peace of Rome yet again.

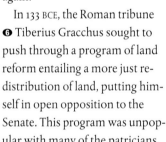

❸ Coin portrait of Jugurtha, king of Numidia

In 133 BCE, the Roman tribune ❻ Tiberius Gracchus sought to push through a program of land reform entailing a more just redistribution of land, putting himself in open opposition to the Senate. This program was unpopular with many of the patricians, and Tiberius was ❷ killed in 132, along with a majority of his sup- porters, in the civil war–like battles between the plebeians and Senate troops. His younger brother Gaius Gracchus then took over his reform proposals and planned a plebeian colony in the provinces. He provoked a national crisis when he promised full citizenship for Roman allies. Renewed attempts to revolt were crushed by the Senate and patricians, who forced Gaius to commit suicide.

Ultimately, the Senate and the consuls came out of the conflict weakened, as they had made themselves the advocates of patrician interests against the plebeians.

In this situation, external threats, especially the Jugurthine War (111–105 BCE) against King ❸ Jugurtha of Numidia and the attacks of the Germanic ❶ Cimbri and Teutoni in northern Italy (113–101 BCE), highlighted an unexpected explosive force with the state of Rome.

Battle between the Cimbri and the Romans under Marius in northern Italy, near Vercelli 101 BCE

P. Cornelius Scipio Africanus the Elder

Publius Cornelius Scipio Africanus the Elder (ca. 235–183 BCE), the most significant Roman general before Julius Caesar, participated in the battles against Hannibal. Entrusted with the command of the Roman troops in Spain as proconsul in 210 BCE, he drove the Carthaginians out by 206 and landed in North Africa in 204, where he defeated Hannibal at Zama in 202. Afterward, he fought in Rome's wars against Antiochus III of Syria.

The Hercules temple on Forum Boarium in Rome, built in the second century BCE

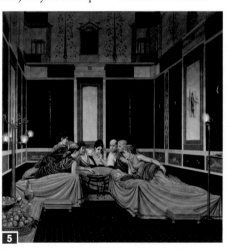

Roman banquet feast in the house of a wealthy citizen of Pompeii

Gracchus, tribune of the people, wood engraving from 1873, from a play by Adolf von Wilbrandt

133 BCE | Land reform proposals by Tiberius Gracchus   111–105 BCE | Jugurthine War   107 BCE | Marius appointed consul

from 133 BCE | increased patrician–plebeian tensions   132 BCE | Death of Tiberius   113–101 BCE | Battle against the Cimbri and Teutons

The Civil War

The political clashes of the generals Gaius Marius and Lucius Cornelius Sulla resulted in the Roman Civil War that divided the state. After the rule of Marius and Cinna, Sulla established a dictatorship that led to the fall of the republic.

In 107 BCE, the Senate appointed the ambitious general ❾ Gaius Marius to lead Rome in the struggle against external enemies. He completely destroyed and defeated King Jugurtha and the Germanic tribes who threatened Rome from the North. At the same time, he strove for political office, supported by the military power of his troops. He occupied the office of consul several times. Marius took up the cause of the plebeians, formed a volunteer army of semiprofessionals—with a single ensign, the Roman eagle— and opened its ranks to the innumerable destitute plebeians. After military service, these volunteers were given their own land, creating plebeian and soldier colonies in the provinces.

The Senate was split over the issue of land reform when the Italian allies revolted against Rome in 91–89 BCE and were pacified only when granted full Roman citizenship. During these battles ❽ Lucius Cornelius Sulla particularly distinguished himself as a commander of the troops and the name "Felix"—the fortunate— was added to his name in reference to his luck in war. Sulla was

8 Lucius Cornelius Sulla, marble bust, ca. 50–40 BCE

elected consul in 88 BCE, but the Senate relieved him of supreme command in the war against Mithradates VI of Pontus in favor of Marius. Sulla then marched to Rome at the head of his troops, expelled ❼ Marius to Africa, and restored his command. For the first time, a military leader had dared to force his will upon the Senate through military means. The civil war had begun.

❿ Sulla had hardly marched off again to resume the war against Mithradates, when ⓫ Lucius Cornelius Cinna (consul 87–84 BCE), an ally of Marius's, led his own army against Rome in a bid for power. Cinna occupied the city in 86 and ruled alone as dictator until he was murdered in an uprising of his troops in 84. Sulla returned to Italy the next year, and

a majority of the patricians and Senate defected to his side.

In 82 BCE Sulla entered Rome as dictator and "restorer of the state and the Senate's power." In the following years he ushered in an era of brutal persecution of his opponents. He had the followers of Marius and Cinna hunted down and killed, which led to the bloody extermination of whole families (the "proscriptions"). In

9 General Gaius Marius, marble bust, ca. 90 BCE

81–80 Sulla rewrote the constitution, strengthening the Senate and limiting the tribunate. Individual state offices and courts were allotted far-reaching new authority and jurisdiction. At the same time he settled 120,000 army veterans in Italy. In 79 BCE, Sulla voluntarily resigned his offices and retired to the country. He died shortly thereafter. Sulla's restoration of the old Roman constitution did not long outlive him—but the example set by him and by General Marius set a precedent for later dictatorships.

7 Marius after his exile by Sulla to Carthage in 87 BCE

Description of the
Proscriptions:

"Sulla now busied himself with slaughter, and murders without number or limit filled the city. Many, too, were killed to gratify private hatreds, although they had no relations with Sulla, but he gave his consent in order to gratify his adherents."

From Plutarch's Parallel Lives

10 Sulla triumphs over Mithradates VI's army in 86 BCE

11 Cinna, depiction from Pierre Corneilles's drama, 1640

88 BCE | Civil war between Sulla and Marius   **82 BCE** | Sulla claims dictatorship   **79 BCE** | Resignation of Sulla

89 BCE | Voting rights granted to Italian allies   **86–84 BCE** | Dictatorship of Cornelius Cinna   **81–80 BCE** | Realignment of constitution

1

Gaius Julius Caesar

THE RULE OF THE GENERALS AND IMPERIAL ROME 74 BCE–192 CE

The civil war destroyed the structure of the Roman republic. The seizure of power by the generals Pompey, ❶ Caesar, and Antonius prepared the way for the transition to autocratic imperial rule finally accomplished by Augustus. The era of imperial Rome had begun. After the dynasty of Augustus, other dynasties ruled including that of Julius Caesar and Octavian, with the emperors increasingly coming from the provinces of the empire rather than from the city of Rome itself. Diocletian's tetrarchy restored a strong system of government to the late Roman Empire.

Pompey, Caesar, and Crassus

The alliance of the generals Pompey and Caesar with Crassus, the richest man in Rome, ended the Republic. In the ensuing power struggle between Caesar and Pompey, it was Caesar who ultimately triumphed.

3 Gnaeus Pompeius Magnus

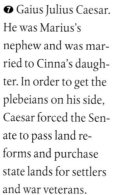

2

Armor and weapons of Caesar's army in the Gallic War, 58–51 BCE

4

Murder of Pompey

After Sulla retired as dictator in 79 BCE, two of his followers tried to seize power. ❸ Gnaeus Pompeius Magnus (Pompey the Great), as a general under Sulla, had liberated Italy's coasts from pirates. Now his political ambition awoke and in 70 BCE he shared the consulship with Marcus Licinius

5

Caesar crossing the Rubicon River, 49 BCE

6

Caesar's triumphal procession

Crassus, the wealthiest man in Rome. Together they repealed the major part of Sulla's constitution and re-established the tribunate, which made them very popular in Rome.

After Pompey brought eastern Europe up to Asia Minor under Roman control, everyone expected him to claim the dictatorship, but the opposition of the Senate caused him to delay. Instead, Pompey and Crassus sought an ally from within Marius's powerful party of the people. This ally was the general ❼ Gaius Julius Caesar. He was Marius's nephew and was married to Cinna's daughter. In order to get the plebeians on his side, Caesar forced the Senate to pass land reforms and purchase state lands for settlers and war veterans.

As the First Triumvirate, Pompey, Crassus, and Caesar shared power in 60–59 BCE and effectively repealed the republican constitution. They also divided the provinces among themselves: Pompey took Spain, Crassus took Syria, and Caesar took Illyria and ❷ Gaul.

When Crassus fell against the Parthians in 53 BCE, Pompey (the only consul for 52 BCE) and Caesar faced each other in a bid for sole power. Both depended on their loyal armies and financial strength. When Pompey's followers attempted to keep Caesar away from Rome so he couldn't campaign for the consulship in 49, Caesar marched out of Gaul with his troops and crossed the ❺ Rubicon River to Rome. Civil war broke out once more, and Pompey was soon forced to flee. Caesar occupied Spain and won the decisive Battle at Pharsalus (Thessaly) against Pompey. Pompey fled to Egypt, where he was

❹ assassinated when he arrived on orders of the Egyptian King Ptolemy. Caesar then ❻ entered Rome in 47 BCE as its undisputed ruler, popular and pardoning most of his rivals.

7

Gaius Julius Caesar

63 BCE | Siege of Jerusalem   53 BCE | Death of Crassus

70 BCE | Consulship of Pompey and Crassus   60–59 BCE | First Triumvirate of Caesar, Pompey, and Crassus   49 BCE | Civil war between Caesar and Pompey

The Rule of Caesar to the Victory of Augustus

Caesar's dictatorship was ended by his assassination. In alliance, Antony and Octavian, Caesar's grand-nephew and heir, forcibly assumed power. Octavian eventually became sole ruler.

8 Antony and Cleopatra after the Battle at Actium

Cleopatra VII

Cleopatra VII, the last Greek ruler of Egypt from 51 BCE and blessed with legendary beauty, successfully opposed her co-regent and brother Ptolemy XIII with the help of Rome and her lover Julius Caesar. After a stay in Rome, she removed Ptolemy XIII and elevated her son by Caesar to co-regent as Ptolemy XV (Cesarion) in 44 BCE. In 41, she became the lover of Mark Antony, who then moved to Alexandria. Both of them took their lives when Octavian entered Alexandria in 30 BCE, she using the poison of a snake.

above: Cleopatra VII, painting by Alexandre Cabanel, 1887

9 Julius Caesar, supported by his clients and soldiers, solidified his power and defeated the last supporters of Pompey and the Republic in Africa, Spain, and at sea in 46–45 BCE. He then carried out wide-ranging social and legal reforms in the empire. Caesar rejected monarchical titles, but in 44 became dictator for life. However, some senators who still held republican ideals **13** stabbed Caesar to death while he was on his way to the Senate on March 15 (the "ides" of March), 44 BCE.

10 Marcus Antonius (Mark Antony), one of Caesar's generals, called for the banishment of the murderers, who fled from Rome. Then the 19-year-old grand-nephew of Caesar, **11** Octavian, made his claim for the inheritance, and signs of a power struggle appeared. As Brutus and Cassius, two of Caesar's assassins, had won the entire east of the empire over to their cause, Octavian and Mark Antony entered into an alliance of convenience. Together with the consul Marcus Aemilius Lepidus, they formed the Second Triumvirate, which lasted from 43 to 33 BCE. In 42 they defeated the republicans at Philippi and then divided the provinces among themselves, Antony receiving the East (and, at first, Gaul), Octavian Italy and the West (eventually in-

9 Coin from Caesar: "I came, saw and triumphed"

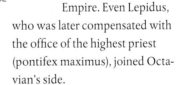

11 Bust of Octavian, ca. 40-50 CE

cluding Gaul), and Lepidus North Africa.

Antony's clashes with the Parthians gave Octavian the opportunity to build up his power in Rome. In 33 BCE, he was elected to the consulship, along with one of his followers. In the meantime, Antony had begun an affair with the Ptolemaic queen of Egypt, Cleopatra, to whose charms Caesar had also succumbed. This gave Octavian the excuse to fight Antony, who was married to Octavian's sister. He convinced the Senate that Antony was planning to separate the East from the rest of the Roman Empire. Even Lepidus, who was later compensated with the office of the highest priest (pontifex maximus), joined Octavian's side.

Using Caesar's money, Octavian armed an enormous fleet un-

10 Marcus Antonius

12 Marcus Vipsanius Agrippa

der the command of his friend **12** Agrippa, who destroyed the fleets of Antony and Cleopatra in 31 BCE at **8** Actium. The next year, Octavian occupied Egypt. With this he unified, for the first time, the empire under one man.

13 Murder of Julius Caesar on March 15, 44 CE, painting, 1815

48 BCE | Victory of Caesar against Pompey   **Mar 15, 44 BCE** | Murder of Caesar   **30 BCE** | Victory of Octavian over Antony and Cleopatra

47 BCE | Caesar becomes sole ruler   **43–33 BCE** | Second Triumvirate of Octavian, Antony, and Lepidus

The Empire under Augustus and His Family

Emperor Augustus reorganized the political structure of the Roman state. His reforms were successful and the modernized state proved stable under the rule of his successors.

In 27 BCE, the Senate bestowed upon the victorious Octavian the title ❶ augustus ("the exalted") and the office of princeps ("first citizen"). He was ultimately promoted via a number of intermediary offices to the position of imperator ("emperor") Caesar Augustus. He was seen as the emperor of peace, a savior who was ultimately venerated as a deity. Augustus carried out a reorganization of the empire's administration, its provinces, and the tax system. He implemented strict moral and marriage laws with the aim of revitalizing the ancient civic virtues of Rome. "Pax Augusta"— peace in the empire and an end to all party conflicts—was declared as the highest state goal and integrated into the state religion. Augustus recognized the increasing professionalization of the military and thus set up a standing army of 28 legions. He continued Marius's and Caesar's policy of rewarding veterans with state lands.

The emperor shrewdly avoided the excessive adulation of his person. He reinforced his position as the focus of centralized power, yet always maintained good relations with the Senate. Rome's economy rapidly recovered from the decline that had resulted from the civil war. The Age of Augustus was not only one of increasing wealth but also of abundance in art and literature. After Augustus's death in August, 14 CE, his stepson ❷ Tiberius continued his policies. His attempts at including the Senate in the administration of the government failed, however, and he withdrew, embittered, to Capri in 27. The Praetorian Guard, an elite detail of the emperor's personal bodyguards, which later became a "state within the state," then made its first attempt to seize power. Following the intermezzo of the megalomaniacal

1 Augustus

Caligula (37–41)—who terrorized the Senate and honored a horse with a consulship— Claudius (41–54), an idiosyncratic but capable regent, became emperor. Under his rule, the transition from republic to a state centered on the emperor was completed, and parts of the British Isles were conquered. His stepson ❸ Nero (54–68) ruled wisely and benignly at first, while still under the influence of his teacher, the philosopher Seneca. But gradually he lost his grip on reality, perhaps due to his inordinate admiration of the Greeks and the cult of his person. The administration of his empire was taken over by minions. ❹ Christians were persecuted and blamed

2 Tiberius

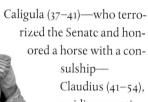

3 Nero

The peace realm of Augustus

Virgil, The Aeneid, book 1, foretelling the reign of Augustus: "Then dire debate and impious war shall cease, / And the stern age be soften'd into peace: / Then banish'd Faith shall once again return, / And Vestal fires in hallow'd temples burn; / And Remus with Quirinus shall sustain. / The righteous laws, and fraud and force restrain...."

above: Virgil and two muses, mosaic from the house of Virgil in Hadrumetum, Sousse, Tunisia

for the devastating fire in Rome in 64. With revolts in the provinces, Nero killed himself in 68, ending the Julio-Claudian dynasty.

4 Persecution of Christians after the fire in Rome in 64 CE

The Flavians and the Adopted Emperors

The Flavian dynasty consolidated the Roman Empire. The adopted emperors built on this reinforced empire and ushered in its golden age.

Domitian, marble bust

Colosseum in Rome, construction begun under Vespasian, 72 CE

Trajan gives a speech before soldiers, Trajan column in Rome

8
Marcus Aurelius

In 69 CE, in the vacuum left by Nero, four emperors claimed Rome. ❾ Vespasian, the governor of Judea and founder of the Flavian dynasty, prevailed. He balanced the treasury deficit through better economic administration and increased taxation—his sewer tax became known by the motto "Pecunia non olet" ("Money doesn't stink"). He began the construction of the ❻ Colosseum in Rome, reorganized the army, and tied the provinces closer by extending the right to citizenship. Under his successor ⓫ Titus (79–81), the cities of Pompeii and Herculaneum were destroyed by

❾ Portrait of Vespasian on coin

the ⓬ eruption of Mount Vesuvius. The Flavian era ended with the murder of Titus's brother and successor ❺ Domitian (81–96).

The ensuing era was that of the "adopted emperors"—each emperor adopted his most capable successor—and is considered the most humane of the Roman Empire. The rule of law was guaranteed and charities and social institutions were founded. ❼ Trajan (98–117), who was proclaimed optimus princeps by the Senate, was victorious in wars

⓫ Titus

against the Dacians and Parthians and in North Africa, and the empire was at its most extensive.

The era of Hadrian (117–138)—a general and admirer of Greek culture—and the peace-loving Antoninus Pius (138–161) is considered to be the golden age of the Roman Empire. Influenced by Stoicism, both aimed for a multiethnic and multicultural empire and developed a defensive foreign policy, which led to securing the borders, for example, in the form of ❿ Hadrian's Wall in Britain.

❽ Marcus Aurelius (161–180), who was sometimes referred to as the "philosopher on the emperor's throne," wanted to dedicate himself to the preservation of peace, yet was forced to wage defensive wars on the empire's borders. These were primarily against the Marcomanni, in northern Italy, and the Quadi in the Danube region, Egypt and Spain. Marcus Aurelius broke with the tradition of adoption and named his son Commodus (180–192) as successor. With Commodus's murder, however, the system of adoption collapsed.

10
Protective wall between Solawaybusen and the mouth of the Tyne, built under emperor Hadrian, 122 CE

The Greek philosophy of Stoicism

The Greek philosophy of Stoicism became popular in Rome during the 2nd century CE. The Stoics' ethic was modesty and the conscientious performance of one's duty. Peace of mind—"stoic" calm—justice, rational self-control, and humanity were considered the highest goals. The Stoics' ideal state included the whole world and built on the equality of all men before the law of divine reason. Hadrian, Antoninus Pius, and Marcus Aurelius were all Stoics.

12
Eruption of Mount Vesuvius in 79 CE

68 CE — Nero's suicide	98–117 CE — Trajan	161–180 — Philosopher-emperor Marcus Aurelius
54–68 CE — Nero; persecution of Christians	69 CE — "Year of the Four Emperors"	117–611 — Golden age under Hadrian and Antoninus Pius

The Severan Dynasty

Lucius Septimius Severus consolidated the power of the military within the state and thereby laid the foundations for the reign of the military emperors in the third century CE. Under the rule of his dynasty, Eastern influences increasingly shaped Rome.

1
Caracalla

Five generals competed for the throne after Commodus's death. The North African ❸ Septimius Severus triumphed in 193. He consolidated the empire, reorganized its finances, and equalized the status of the inhabitants of Italy and the provinces. Septimius Severus transformed the empire into a military monarchy by ignoring the Senate, replacing the Praetorian Guard with his own troops, and appointing loyal military men to increasingly power-

ful civil offices. He thus led the way for the military emperors that would follow.

His son ❶ Caracalla murdered his co-regent and brother Geta in 212 and encouraged a fusion of Roman and Eastern cults. Supported by the army and the Praetorian Guard, his was a reign of terror. When he failed in his campaign against the Parthians, he was assassinated by the commander of the Praetorians, Macrinus, who himself became emperor in 217–218.

The rule of Caracalla's Syrian cousin ❷ Elagabalus (Heliogabalus, 218–222), a priest of the sun god of Emesa (Elah-Gabal), was a new low point for the Roman emperors. He held extravagant nocturnal celebrations and founded secret cults. His attempt to make the Syrian sun cult the

2 Elagabalus

official state cult undermined the identity of the Roman Empire.

His cousin Alexander Severus (222–235) who was born in Palestine tried another course. He strengthened the Senate and, advised by the lawyer Ulpian, governed strictly in accordance with old Roman law. However, it became clear that the emperor could no longer rule against the will of the military and the Praetorian Guard. After the Praetorians ❹ murdered Ulpian in 228, Alexander Severus and his mother, who had great influence over her young son, fell victim to an assassination plot of his officers after his luckless expeditions to Mesopotamia and Egypt and against the Germanic Marcomanni. The army finally achieved total control of the Roman Empire.

The Severan Women

The Severan women consistently played an important role in the reigns of their male relatives. The wife of Septimius Severus, Julia Domna, daughter of the sun-priest Bassianus of Emesa, was highly respected and established a circle of scholars around her. Her sister Julia Maesa was the grandmother of the emperors Elagabalus and Alexander Severus and energetically campaigned for their coronation. Her daughters Julia Soaemias and Julia Mamaea, both mothers of Roman emperors, exercised great influence on the rule of their sons, with whom they were both murdered.

above: Julia Domna, marble bust, ca. 210 CE

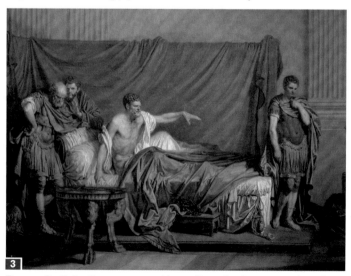

3
Emperor Septimius Severus accuses his son Caracalla of an attempted murder

4
Ulpian's murder before Emperor Severus and his mother, wood engraving, 1876

211–217 | Caracalla rules   222–235 | Revitalization under Alexander Severus

193 | Septimus Severus founds the Severan dynasty   **218–222** | Cultural decline under Emperor Elagabalus   **235** | Beginning of rule of the military emperors

The Military Emperors 235–284

The period of military emperors (235–284 CE), with its unclear succession rules and rapid changes of emperors and usurpers, was extremely unsettled. Only the last of the military emperors were able to achieve stability within the empire.

The 50 years that constituted the rule of the military emperors is also called the "crisis of the third century." It was an extremely turbulent era: 26 emperors and 40 usurpers were crowned—and murdered. Many of the emperors were officers of Illyrian-Pannonian origin; most were at war throughout their reigns. Often, competing emperors appeared and the empire fell apart. Rome was being forced into the defensive; from the beginning of the third century Germanic tribes, primarily the Goths, threatened the empire from the west. By the

6 Marcus Aurelius Probus

middle of the century, the Danube region, Asia Minor, and Greece had all been lost. In the Middle East, the newly founded Persian Empire of the Sassanids forced the Romans into retreat there. Emperor Valerian (253–260) was captured by the Persians after a crushing **5** defeat in 260. In 258 the usurper Postumus separated Gaul from the empire and founded a Gallo-Roman Empire that survived him. The Syrian governor of **11** Palmyra, Odaenathus, declared himself independent and forced Rome to recognize him as "governor of all the East." After his death, his widow **8** Zenobia took the title of empress.

It was the last of the soldier-emperors that finally restored stability to the empire. **9** Claudius II Gothicus (268–270) held off an invasion of the Alemanni in northern Italy and triumphed over the Goths on the Danube. Aurelian (270–75), the most significant military emperor, had the **10** Aurelian Wall built around Rome and drove the Goths out of upper Italy for good in 270–271. He then marched into the Orient and destroyed the Kingdom of

Palmyra (273) and reincorporated Egypt into the Roman Empire. Aurelian reorganized the economy and administration and installed the cult of the Syrian god *Sol Invictus* ("Unconquered Sun") as the unifying cult of the empire; the festival for this god on December 25 was later adopted by the Christians as Christmas. After Aurelian, **6** Probus (276–282) pacified the recently reclaimed Gaul and pushed the Franks back across the Rhine, which was once again defended as the empire's border. He also settled Germanic tribes as colonists or took them into the ranks of his army. After his **7** murder, conditions once again became unstable until Diocletian—building on the achievements of Aurelian and Probus—gave the empire a new character.

5 Triumph of Shapir I, king of the Sassanids, over the Roman Emperors Philippus and Valerian in the battle near Edessa in 260

7 Aurelian is murdered near Byzantium in 275

9 Claudius II Gothicus

8 Zenobia, Queen of Palmyra, after her arrest by Emperor Aurelian, painting, 1878

10 The Aurelian Wall

11 View of Palmyra in Syria

The Dominate: Diocletian and the System of the Tetrarchy

Diocletian restored the strength of Rome. His dual reign with Maximian and eventually the system of the imperial tetrarchy effectively dealt with an empire that was gradually pulling itself apart.

In November 284, ❶, ❷, ❹ Diocletian, a guard commander of humble origins, seized power and imbued the empire with a new order, thus ending the "crisis of the third century." As war broke out again in Gaul, he made his comrade-in-arms Maximian his co-regent (caesar) in 285 and, after he had successfully suppressed the rebellion in Gaul in 286, co-emperor (*augustus*). His rule was initially precarious; he had to simultaneously fight attacks on the Roman borders while stamping out civil unrest within the state. The two emperors divided their duties. Diocletian's main interests lay in an overall reform of the administration and the army. The tax system, the salaries of public officials, and the courts were all completely reorganized, and the provinces were granted greater authority, which contributed to the decentralization of the empire that began to emerge. In the meantime, Maximian rushed from one war to another.

1 Portrait of the Emperor Diocletian, coin

When Britain separated itself from the empire under local usurpers in 286–287 and revolts broke out in the Near East, Diocletian recognized that the empire was no longer capable of being centrally governed and in 293 installed the system of ❸ tetrarchy ("rule of four"). Both regents adopted successors, who were to reign as caesars (junior emperors) and, when the emperors retired, would take their place. Diocletian and Maximian chose, respectively, ❼ Galerius and Constantius I Chlorus as caesars, and the tetrarchs divided their authority regionally. Diocletian, as augustus of the East, ruled from Thrace to the Near East and Egypt, with his capital at Salona (modern Split); Galerius was given the Danube provinces and Greece; Maximian, as augustus of the West, controlled Italy, Spain, and North Africa from his capital in Milan; and Constantius received Gaul and Britain. In conflicts of interest, Diocletian as "senior augustus" had the final word. For 20 years, the system demonstrated an astounding stability, until Diocletian decided that he and Maximian would retire on May 1, 305, and Galerius and Constantius would move up to the position of augusti.

The emperors held to the old Roman deity cult as state ideology and demanded veneration as divine rulers. The Christians' refusal to obey this demand led to their persecution in 299, which intensified between 303 and 305. The Christians were forced to hide in the ❺ catacombs of Rome, and ❻ Diocletian's memory was thereafter reviled in Christian historiography. Nevertheless, he had restored the power of Rome.

2 Diocletian

4 **above left:** Portrait of Diocletian
above: Jupiter with eagle and small goddess of victory on the reverse side of the same golden coin

3 "The Tetrarchs," relief at San Marco, Venice, interpreted as Diocletian, Valerius, Maximian and Constantinus

5 Depiction of the Apostle Paul in a mural found in one of the Roman catacombs in which Christians hid

6 Reconstruction of Diocletian's palace, which he built around 300 for his retirement in Split near Salona, Dalmatia

286–287 | Britain secedes from the empire
303–305 | Intense persecution of Christians
284–305 | Rule of the two emperors by Diocletian and Maximian
293 | New system of succession ("tetrarchy")

▪ Collapse of the Tetrarchy and the Victory of Constantine and Licinius

The power struggle between the contenders resulted in the collapse of the tetrarchy after 306. With the victory of Constantine the Great and Licinius, the Christians gained their first recognition by the state, and the process by which Christianity became the religion of the Roman Empire began.

8 Portrait of Constantine the Great on a coin

7
Galerius convincing Diocletian to make him caesar

From Galerius's Edict of Toleration of 311:

"Wherefore, for this our indulgence, they ought to pray to their god for our safety, for that of the republic, and for their own, that the republic may continue uninjured on every side, and that they may be able to live securely in their homes."

The tetrarchy was already teetering by 305 because Maximian, in contrast to Diocletian, was reluctant to give up power; furthermore, in addition to his adopted son Constantius, Maximian had a biological son, the ambitious Maxentius, who sought power. While the change of rule ran smoothly in the East and Galerius raised Maximinus Daia to caesar, in the West it came to bitter conflicts. When Constantius, who had stopped the persecution of Christians in his realm, died in 306, his biological son **8** Constantine, supported by his father's army, seized the imperial throne. Maxentius protested and had himself declared emperor by the Praetorians in Rome. The senior augustus Galerius sent his troops against him but **9** Maxentius was victorious, and thus a five-year struggle for control of the western Roman Empire began between Constantine and Maxentius.

The situation intensified in 308 when Galerius declared **9** Licinius augustus of the West. Licinius recognized Constantine as his caesar and convinced Galerius, who had been a persecutor of Christians, to issue an edict of religious tolerance in 311 to bring the Christians to support him—the first official recognition of the Christians by a Roman emperor. Together, Licinius and Constantine were able to prevail against

9 **above:** Maxentius on a coin; **left:** Licinius on a coin

their enemies. In 312 Constantine, who openly favored the Christians, moved with his legions against Rome and defeated Maxentius's troops at the **10** Milvian Bridge, although his troops were outnumbered by Maxentius's by at least two to one. The next year, Licinius triumphed in the east against Maximinus Daia, also with the aid of Christian soldiers. The victors divided the empire among themselves, Constantine ruling the West and Licinius the East. A new era had begun in the Roman Empire; one which was much more favorable for the Christians.

The Victory at the Milvian Bridge in 312

Constantine's politically calculated move to send his troops into battle wearing the Christogram XP—the initials of Christ—was glorified by the early Christian authors Lactanz and Eusebius of Caesarea. Eusebius in his Vita Constantini reported that Constantine, whose troops were significantly outnumbered by those of Maxentius, dreamed before the battle that the sign of the cross appeared in the heavens before him and a voice called, "In hoc signo vincis!" ("In this sign thou shalt triumph").

10
The Battle at the Milvian Bridge, 312 CE

306–337 | Constantine I   313 | Victory of Licinius over Maximinus Daia

May 1, 305 | Resignation of Diocletian and Maximian   311 | Official recognition of Christianity   313–324 | Joint rule of Constantine (West) and Licinius (East)

FROM CONSTANTINE TO THE RISE OF BYZANTIUM 312–867

In 313 CE, ❶ Constantine and Licinius issued an edict of tolerance in Milan, putting the Christian religion on equal footing with existing Roman cults. Less than a century later, Christianity would become the state religion of Rome. Constantine was the first to use it as an instrument to strengthen his rule, subjecting the Church to strict political control, a practice followed by his successors. The de facto division of the empire into a Western (Roman) and Eastern (Byzantine) became permanent in 395. While the Roman Empire declined, Byzantium rose as a new power in its own right.

Marble bust of Constantine I, the Great

2 The Christian symbol of the fish, early Christian mosaic, fourth c.

Constantine the Great

In 324 Constantine was able to establish sole rule and reorganize the empire. He encouraged Christianity in all areas.

Following the ❺ victory over their opponents in 313, Constantine and Licinius divided the empire between them and issued the Edict of Milan, which guaranteed ❷ Christians the right to practice their religion. Cooperation between the two did not last long, however. From 316 on, military clashes between the adversaries took place. Constantine ultimately triumphed and exiled Licinius.

Constantine increasingly saw himself as the representative of the Christian god and protector of Christianity. He clearly recognized the potential of the new religion and wanted to tie it into the Roman ideology of the state. He reimbursed the Church for confiscated property and financed the construction of ❹, ❻ churches. However, the ❸ "Donation of Constantine" of state-owned land to the church is a myth resulting from a document forged around 850.

Constantine implemented many new laws that were influenced by Christian standards. He repealed punishment such as gladiatorial service, maiming, and limited slavery and passed relatively progressive marriage and family laws. By emphasizing the divine right of kings, he reinforced the role of religious legitimacy in imperial rule. Any offense against

3 *The Donation of Constantine*, fresco, 1246

The Constantine basilica in Rome, christened by Constantine in 330

a Christian emperor became sacrilege toward God and God's order. The emperor not only intervened in Church politics, but also had the final say concerning matters of faith. Many Christians began to identify with the empire that had previously persecuted them and sought to participate in its affairs. The Church adopted many organizations and state offices into its own structures.

Constantine arc, 315 CE, christened after Constantine's victory over Maxentius at the Milvian Bridge

Excerpt from a Eulogy from the "*Panegyrici Latini*"

"You have, Constantine, indeed some secret with the godly spirit, who, after He has left to the lower gods all concern about us, only you He has dignified by showing himself to you directly. Otherwise, bravest Emperor, give account of how you have triumphed."

6 The Grave Church in Jerusalem, christened in 326

Constantine's Successors

A fratricidal war destabilized the empire after Constantine's death. Ultimately Constantius II was able to continue his father's policies successfully. The attempt of Julian the Apostate to revert to paganism remained an aberration.

7
Baptism of Constantine the Great by Pope Sylvester I, fresco, 1246

In 330 Constantine renamed the city of Byzantium ⓫ Constantinople as the new capital of the Roman-Christian empire. By 335 he had instituted a system of imperial succession influenced by Diocletian's tetrarchy: His oldest and second sons, Constantine II and Constantius II, were to be augusti, while his youngest son Constans and his nephew Dalmatius would be caesars. However, when Constantine died in

337 in the initial stages of a planned military excursion to Persia, a few days after he had accepted a Christian ❼ baptism, all three of his sons assumed the title of augustus.

A murderous fratricidal war flared up, during which ❿ Constantius II, son of his father's first wife Fausta, had all his relatives by his father's second marriage killed. Out of the struggle for power he emerged triumphant. After he had repulsed the attacking Persians, he actively continued his father's

8
Emperor Julian the Apostate, fresco, ca. 1320/25

9　Julian Apostata, coin portrait

10　Constantius II

church policies. Because the quarrel over Arianism and other early splinter groups of Christianity threatened to destabilize the empire, Constantius attempted to foster politico-religious unity by particularly emphasizing the overarching position of the Christian emperor. His court ceremonies already bore the features of the ruler's religious zeal that were later characteristic of the Byzantine Empire.

Constantius's successor in 361 was his cousin ❽, ❾ Julian, who had held the office of caesar of the West since 355 and had assumed the title of augustus against Constantius in 360. The philosophical and highly educated Julian is one of the tragic figures of late antiquity. Due to his enthusiasm for Greek philosophy and the greatness of ancient Rome, he lost his faith, reverted to paganism and attempted to suppress Christianity and install a neo-Platonic sun cult. He did not persecute the Christians, but his attempt to turn back time led to unrest in the empire. When he fell in battle against the Persians in June 363, his new sun cult broke up and the Christian historians damned him as "the Apostate." His death marked the end of rule by Constantine's dynasty.

Arianism

Arianism, as formulated by the Alexandrian priest Arius, taught that Jesus Christ was divine, but only of like substance to God and

there had been a time when he was not of divine substance. The teachings that were finally accepted at the council at Nicaea in 325 were formulated by Athanasius, who stated that Christ "was consubstantial ["of one substance"] and uncreated and co-eternal with the Father." Nonetheless, the "Arian heresy" continued and split Christianity between the 4th and 7th centuries, as some emperors and many of the Germanic peoples were adherents of Arianism.

above: The council at Nicaea 325 in Iznik, fresco, ca. 1600

11
Constantine founds Byzantium's new capital under the name Constantinople in 330

CHRISTIANITY

Since its beginnings as a Jewish sect, Christianity became established as one of the five main world religions as a result of its interaction with Greco-Roman culture and philosophy. Christianity, particularly in its organized form as a church, has played an important role in world history since its inception, whether as a state religion or as a powerful competitor to secular authority. It wasn't until the separation of church and state in the modern era that the Church lost its direct influence on political events.

The Virgin Mary and John witness Christ's crucifixion, mural, ca. 740

The Central Message and the Early Church

The Christian image of God is based on that of Judaism; both believe in a benevolent creator and preserver of the world who also demands of man an accounting for his actions. Christianity's central message, however, is the belief in the incarnate son of God, Jesus Christ, who suffered and ❶ died on the cross for the salvation of mankind and was resurrected. His story and message are recorded in the four ❸ Gospels of

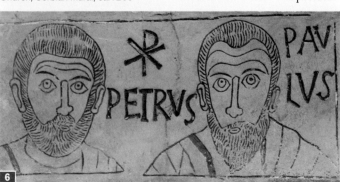

❸ Handwritten Gospel of John on papyrus, end of the second century

the New Testament, which is the basis of Christian belief.

Early Christianity engaged in an intensive spiritual debate with its Jewish and Greco-Roman rivals. Under the influence of the ❺ Apostle Paul, the Church decided upon an active mission to disseminate its message to the heathens and throughout the world. Up until the seventh century, the Church struggled with the definition of its image of God and its role in the world. Often this resulted in wars and persecu-

tion. Socio-politically, early Christianity wavered between the commandment of brotherly love, which required active engagement in the world, and the anticipation of the forthcoming Kingdom of God that is "not of this world." The claim of God and Jesus Christ to exclusive divine status kept the Christians, like the Jews, from participating in Roman cults that the Roman Empire mandated in order to maintain the loyalty of all peoples and cultures in the empire.

❷ The Good Shepherd, fresco in Catacomb of Calixtus, Rome, third c.

④ The Benedictine abbey Monte Cassino, Italy, founded in 529 by St. Benedict of Norcia

Christianity in the Roman Empire

The Christians proselytized in all of the larger cities of the empire, including Rome, so that by the end of the second century CE there were already numerous congregations. As they were suspected of disloyalty to the rulers, the Christians often experienced fierce persecution and took refuge in the ❷ catacombs of the cities; when discovered, they most often chose a ❼ martyr's death in keeping with the image of the suffering Jesus and apostles before them. At this time, however, a stable structure emerged that allowed the Church to survive. The "Constantinian Change" occurred

with the edicts of tolerance of 311 and 313 and the further policies of Constantine the Great. Christianity became the official religion of the Roman Empire. In the Eastern Roman Empire of Byzantium, the Christian doctrine of salvation was combined with the ancient cult of the ruler, and the emperor became the preordained advocate of the fate of man.

⑤ The Apostle Paul, founder of the Church, Serbian mural, ca.1265

⑥ The Apostles Peter and Paul, tombstone, after 313

⑦ Christians condemned to die as martyrs await their death in the arena

8

Charlemagne is crowned emperor by Pope Leo III on December 25, 800 in St Peter's Cathedral

The Middle Ages and the Rise of the Papacy

In the early Middle Ages, a surge in the development of European civilization and education was sparked by the work of Christian monastic orders. As a result of endowments, the ❹ monasteries also became powerful landowners. The conversion to Catholicism of the previously Arianist Germanic peoples in the fifth to seventh centuries strengthened the position of the bishop of Rome, the pope. Primarily through his alliance with France, the pope had won independence from Byzantium and built up a papal claim to jurisdictional primacy as the successor of the Apostle ❻ Peter. From the time of the ❽ imperial coronation of Charlemagne by the pope in 800, popes and the Holy Roman Emperors were closely tied. The estrangement from Byzantium led to a schism in 1054 between the papal Western church and the Eastern Orthodox Church, which endures to the present. The ❾ Crusades to the Holy Land initiated by the Western church between 1095 and the 13th century exemplified Christianity's most intolerant and violent side.

With the ⓫ Investiture Controversy in the eleventh and twelfth century, the Church won far-reaching independence from lay interference. Under Pope Innocent III (1198–1216), the papacy reached the zenith of its worldly power—until it went too far. The exile of the popes to Avignon from 1309 to 1377 and the Great Schism of 1378–1417 highlighted that reforms were necessary.

11

Emperor Henry IV, front, asks Mathilda of Tuscany to mediate in his conflict with Pope Gregory VII in the Investiture Controversy, book illustration

From the Reformation to the Enlightenment

The Reformation in the 16th century was a period of social as well as religious upheaval that can be considered the beginning of the Modern Era. In an attempt to return to the original message of the Gospels and prevent abuses of power by the Church, a number of Protestant churches sprang up. The most important among these were the Lutherans, followers of ❿ Martin Luther; the Reformists, followers of Huldrych Zwingli; and the Calvinists, followers of John Calvin. The first religious wars were ended by the laboriously negotiated Peace of Augsburg in 1555, but the religious disputes broke out violently again in the French Wars of Religion, and above all during the Thirty Years' War.

In the 17th and 18th centuries, Christianity and the churches in Europe found themselves on the defensive as a result of renewed self-awareness resulting from the Enlightenment and the start of the Industrial Revolution. In the

10

Martin Luther at the Imperial Diet of Worms, 1521

19th century, they allied themselves with the powers of political conservatism. It was only later that they recognized the necessity of reacting to labor issues and socialism. In the "battle for culture" in many countries, the churches lost the supervision of the educational institutions of modern society.

The Churches in the 20th Century and Beyond

In the 20th century, the Eastern Orthodox Church experienced a period of widespread suppression between 1917 and 1991—or an authoritarian binding into the system of "socialism as it was ac-

9

The conquest of Jerusalem by the First Crusade under the leadership of Godfrey of Bouillon on July 15, 1099, book illustration, 14th century

tually practiced." The churches in Western and Central Europe wavered between currying favor with authoritarian regimes and suppression at their hands. After 1945, the Catholic Church reconciled with the Western democracies and opened to the modern age with the ⓬ Second Vatican Council (1962–1965). Protestantism experienced an upswing, particularly in the United States.

Since the late 20th century, the Catholic Church has focused on the "young churches" of Latin America and Africa. In Central Europe the Church is largely limited to a role in community work and providing ethical cues. Whether there will be a return to the Church in post-communist Eastern Europe remains unclear.

12

Celebration following the end of the Second Vatican Council in Rome, 1965

| 1378–1417 | Great Schism | 1555 | Peace of Augsburg | 17th–18th century | Enlightenment |
| until 1122 | Investiture Controversy | 1517 | Beginning of the Reformation | 1618–1648 | Thirty Years' War | 1962–1965 | Second Vatican Council |

Portrait bust of a youth, believed to be Emperor Gratian or Valentinian II

Theodosius I (the Great)

The patriarch Ambrosius absolves Emperor Theodosius, painting, 18th century

The Roman Empire under Valentinian and Theodosius

The emperors Valentinian I and Theodosius the Great strengthened the Roman Empire for the last time. While Valentinian undertook an internal consolidation, Theodosius made Christianity the state religion.

The rise of Christianity was not greeted favorably everywhere in the empire, and the reaction of Julian the Apostate had met with some approval, above all in the circles of the old Roman elite. However, Christianity as the religion of the empire did not collapse, and the empire was able to withstand the onslaught of the Germanic tribes once more due to the policies of the emperors Valentinian and Theodosius.

In February 364, the officer ❹ Valentinian was declared emperor. At the request of his army, he made his younger brother, Valens, who resided in Constantinople, co-emperor in the East. Valentinian dedicated himself first to the urgently needed strengthening of the empire's borders. In Gaul he pushed the invading Alemanni back across the Rhine and erected border fortifications from the North Sea to Rhaetia. Then he initiated his financial policies, which demanded extreme austerity and economizing and found little favor with the Roman upper class.

His brother in the East had to contend with ❻ Goths and Persians. In 376 he settled the Visigoths in Thrace, but they pushed down to Greece. A military confrontation was unavoidable. His nephew Gratian hurried to his aid with imperial troops, but Valens did not wait and was defeated by the Visigoths

in 378 at the Battle of Adrianople. He was killed, and the Goths took Eastern Europe.

Valentinian's successor in the West was his son ❶ Gratian, but general ❸ Theodosius I (the Great) held political leadership, and Gratian selected him as augustus of the East in January 379. Theodosius then concluded a treaty with the Visigoths in 382,

❹ "The Colossus of Barletta," a statue of Valentinian I

granting them territory south of the lower Danube as "federates" of the empire. After Gratian's death, Theodosius dedicated himself to the complete Christianization of the empire, fought against

❷ Emperors Eugenius and Theodosius I holding a symbol of victory

heathen cults and in 392 confirmed the theology of the Nicaean council and Rome as the religion of the empire. Gratian and Theodosius were the first emperors to discard the traditional title of pontifex maximus, which the pope now assumed, and to ❺ subject themselves to the decisions of the Church. Theodosius was religiously and politically visionary and an honest ruler, but his decision to call upon Teutonic army commanders for aid against the usurper ❷ Eugenius left a difficult legacy for his successors.

❻ Peace agreement between the Goths and Emperor Valens, 369

The End of the Western Roman Empire

In 395 the empire was irrevocably divided into the Western and Eastern empires. Until the end of the Western Empire in 476, the emperors were dominated by Teutonic army commanders.

Arcadius, son of Theodosius the Great, marble bust, ca. 395

Tomb of the Empress Galla Placidia in Ravenna, finished ca. 450

When Theodosius died in January 395, he left the empire divided among his sons. The elder, ❼ Arcadius, received the eastern part with Constantinople; the younger, Honorius, received the western Roman half. The sons and grandsons of Theodosius were for the most part dependent on their Teutonic commanders. Honorius, who shifted the Western capital from Rome to Ravenna in 402, was dominated by his imperial general Flavius Stilicho, a Vandal who from 395 held back the Germanic tribes. The impending invasion of the Visigoth Alaric into Italy evoked an anti-German backlash in Rome and led to Stilicho's execution in 408. Shortly after this, Alaric sacked ❾ Rome in August 410.

Valentinian III, the last emperor of the Theodosian dynasty, was under the influence of his mother ❽ Galla Placidia, who served as his regent between 425 and 437. The Roman general Flavius Aetius, the "Patrician," was virtual ruler in the West from 433. In 437 he destroyed the Burgundian kingdom on the Rhine and allied with the Visigoths, with whose help he defeated Attila and the Huns at the Battle of Châlons in 451. Valentinian, who felt threatened by Aetius's power, stabbed him to death during an audience in 454 and was then himself assassinated in March, 455 by Aetius's followers.

Thereafter, the decline of the Western Empire took on a rapid pace, particularly as the relationship to the Eastern Empire, which was growing in strength, had been tense since 450. Finally, in 475 Romulus Augustulus ("Little Augustus") ascended the throne in Ravenna. When Odoacer, a Germanic prince, conquered Ravenna in 476, he ❿ dethroned the last emperor and exiled him. Odoacer became the first barbarian king of Italy, and with that the Latin Western Empire had come to an ignominious end; now the only Roman emperor was the emperor of Byzantium.

Odoacer

Odoacer of the Sciri entered the service of the Western Empire in 470 as a mercenary and, militarily victorious, was declared king by his followers. In 476 he deposed the last Western Roman emperor and gained from the Eastern Empire tacit recognition as ruler of Italy. By strengthening the Senate, he was able to shrewdly balance the Romans and the Germans in Italy. He also reconciled with Catholicism, although he was Arian, and fought off other Germanic tribes. Eventually, the Eastern Empire sent the Ostrogoths under Theodoric against him. At a banquet supposedly designed to celebrate a reconciliation in Ravenna on March 15, 493, he was assassinated by Theodoric.

above: Odoacer's murder in Ravenna on March 15, 493

The Germanic army commander Odoacer dethrones Romulus Augustulus in 476, wood engraving, ca. 1880

392 | Christianity becomes state religion　　395–423 | Honorius is West Roman emperor　　451 | Aetius defeats the Huns under Attila

395 | Empire divided in East and West　　395–408 | Arcadius is East Roman emperor　　476 | "Romulus Augustulus" dethroned

The Consolidation of the Byzantine Empire

After 450, the emperors of Byzantium were able to strengthen the empire and assert their claim to rule in Europe. As capital of the Eastern Empire, Constantinople assumed the legacy of fallen Rome.

The council at Chalcedon, 451 CE

Emperor Anastasius I, ivory diptych, beginning of the sixth century

Under Theodosius's weak heirs, the Eastern Empire was coming to ruin as a result of enormous tribute payments to the Huns and German princes and was heading for a fate similar to the Western Empire. This changed quite suddenly when a period of capable rule began with Marcian in 450. Marcian refused to pay tribute to the Huns and was able to force them off to the West. Through confederation pacts with the Visigoths and the Gepids, while fending off Arab tribes in Syria and Palestine, he was able to consolidate the empire. In 451 he convoked a ❶ council at Chalcedon in order to condemn Monophysitism, which was dividing the empire.

Marcian's successor Leo I strengthened Orthodoxy and took up the fight against Aspar, the German general who had been all-powerful in the empire since 424. He created the Isaurian Guard, an elite force made up of Isaurians—a warrior mountain tribe from his homeland—and defeated Aspar in 471, ending the dominance of Germanic generals in the Eastern Empire. His son-in-law Zeno, who was also Isaurian, developed ❸ Constantinople into a new "center of the world" after the fall of Rome. Zeno was more of a diplomat than a warrior and so sent Theodoric, his "son-in-arms," to Italy in 488, where he eventually deposed Odoacer and officially placed Italy under the sovereignty of the Eastern Empire.

Constantinople (Istanbul): View over the Bosporus

> ### Church historian Socrates (died ca. 450), describing the
>
> ### Wealth of Constantinople
>
> "*Many come to Constantinople; for the city, although she feeds tremendous masses, has good reserves: By sea she imports from everywhere necessary, but the Black Sea, which is very near, supplies her with an inexhaustible supply of cereal, if she needs this.*"

Now the militarily strengthened empire needed a new internal structure. For the first time, a high administrative official, ❷ Anastasius, assumed the throne in 491. First, he dismissed the Isaurians in favor of the traditional administrative elite and fortified the empire against the Persians and the Bulgarians. Anastasius stood out for his humane legislation and through economical administration was able to accumulate immense state reserves.

❹ Justinian I was able to build on these achievements and, as emperor from 527, led Byzantium to its first golden age. A well-educated Illyrian farmer's son, Justinian had held a leading position in state affairs under his uncle Emperor Justin I (518–527), and in 525 married the actress ❺ Theodora, who proved to be of vital support and virtually coreigned with him.

Emperor Justinian with entourage, mosaic, before 547

Empress Theodora with entourage, mosaic, ca. 547

The Empire under Justinian and Heraclius

Under Justinian I, Byzantium became the leading power in Europe both politically and culturally. Heraclius reorganized the empire and gave Byzantium a structure that endured to its end.

Mother of God of Vladimir, icon from Constantinople, 12th–13th century

In foreign affairs, Justinian pursued the establishment of Byzantine dominance in the West, repulsion of the Persians in the East, and above all the elimination of the restless Germanic tribes. The kingdoms of the Vandals in North Africa (533–534) and the Ostrogoths in Italy (551–553) came under Byzantine rule.

In keeping with the idea of ❽, ⓫ imperial divine rule, Justinian elaborated Byzantine court ceremonies in a strongly religious vein ("caesaropapism") and subjugated the patriarchs and popes of Constantinople and Rome. Justinian's most significant work was the civil code of laws begun in 528. The Code of Justinian decisively set the pattern for the whole of European legal history. Under his rule, the empire experienced the first literary and artistic flowering of its own independent culture. He also invested the enormous state budget in buildings of extraordinary magnificence, such as the ❻, ❿ Hagia Sophia in Constantinople, and in the development of the cities.

Justinian's successors were occupied in wars against the Persians, Avars, and Bulgarians and embroiled in religio-political disputes. In 610 the general Heraclius rose to prominence and took the emperor's throne. He went on to mold the character of the Byzantine Empire. At first, however, he found himself on the defensive. In 614 Jerusalem fell to the Persians, and in 626 the Persians and Avars jointly laid siege to Constantinople. However, once the Persians were driven out of Anatolia, things changed. The Byzantines advanced into Persian territory and in 627 reclaimed Jerusalem. Heraclius now restructured the empire, reorganized the Orthodox Church, divided the empire into military districts, and crushed the power of big landowners. Above all, as the official state, administrative, and military language, he replaced Latin with the Greek used by the church and the people. The imperial title of *augustus* was replaced with *basileios*. Heraclius thereby achieved the final stage of development in the Greco-Byzantine character of the empire.

The Heraclian dynasty that ruled until 711, as well as the following rulers, had to contend with ❾ Arab and Bulgarian invasions in the seventh through ninth centuries, which were a mortal threat to the empire. Internally, the empire was shaken from 711 to 843 by violent religious controversy regarding the ❼ veneration of icons. The emperor and patriarchs fell

The Hagia Sophia, completed 360; rebuilt under Emperor Justinian 532–537

Mary with Jesus between Constantine and Justinian, mosaic, Hagia Sophia

The siege of Constantinople by the Arabs in 717, book painting, 13th c.

victim to the icon disputes, and several provinces were able to gain their independence by civil war. Despite this, Byzantium's structures and borders remained largely intact.

11 Crucifixion scene with Constantine and Helena under the cross

Interior of Hagia Sophia

ARMENIA AND ASIA MINOR FROM THE DIADOCHOI TO THE ROMANS 550 BCE–CA. 200 CE

Armenia and the kingdoms of Asia Minor were the point of intersection between the Orient and the Greco-Hellenic—and later Roman—world. Stubbornly protective of their independence, these states were constantly under threat from the great powers, particularly Rome in the first century BCE. Under Mithradates VI, however, Pontus proved to be an opponent the Roman rulers could not easily dismiss.

Relief on the Armenian Church of the Holy Cross on the island Ahtamar, with a depiction of George the Dragonslayer

Armenia and Bithynia

Armenia first gained independence from the Seleucid Empire in the second century BCE. It became the first Christian nation around 300 CE. Bithynia maintained its independence at first, but later came under Roman control.

Armenia was heir to the ancient Kingdom of Urartu. Initially used only by the Scythians and Cimmerians as a passage to other regions, it became a province of the Achaemenid Empire of Persia about 550 BCE. After the conquest by Alexander the Great in 331 BCE, it was awarded to the Seleucids but then occupied by the Parthians. The defeat of Antiochus III of Syria led to a division of the country in 189 BCE.

King Tigranes I was able to unite the region again about 90 BCE. In addition, he enlarged the kingdom in the west, conquering Cappadocia and the remains of the Seleucid kingdom with Phoenicia and Cilicia. In 69 BCE, however, he was defeated by the Romans and lost the conquered territories. Armenia became a contested buffer state between the Romans and Parthians, and later the Sassanids.

Around 300 CE, Bishop ❸ Gregory the Illuminator converted Armenia to Christianity, creating the first Christian state even before the conversion of Rome. The head of the ❶, ❷ Armenian Church—also known as the Armenian Apostolic or Gregorian Church—is the supreme catholicos. The Armenian Church adheres to Monophysitic doctrine and has, up to the present day, maintained its independence from other Christian churches.

The Kingdom of Bithynia in the northwest of Asia Minor was ruled since the end of the fourth century CE by a local dynasty able to repel even Alexander the Great and the Diadochoi. In 264 BCE its most significant ruler, Nicomedes I, founded the capital of Nicomedia, becoming a center of Hellenistic culture. The last Bithynian king, Nicomedes IV (95–75 BCE), was expelled by Mithradates of Pontus, but returned to the throne in 84 with the help of Sulla. In return, he bequeathed his kingdom to Rome, who took possession in 74 BCE.

The Armenian Church of the Holy Cross on the island Ahtamar

Gregory the Illuminator baptizes King Tiridates III, 296 CE

Monophysitism

Monophysitism, a religious doctrine founded by Alexandrian theology, states that Jesus Christ, as the son of God, had only one nature (mono physis), the divine. He is seen as the incarnate word of God. In contrast, Catholicism and Orthodoxy teach that Jesus has two natures—divine and human. That "Christ is truly God and truly human" was confirmed by the Council of Chalcedon in 451, whereupon the Monophysite churches—those in Egypt (Coptic), Armenia, and Ethiopia—split away from the Catholic and Orthodox churches.

above: Cyril of Alexandria, icon painting, second half of 16th c.

ca. 550 BCE | Armenia becomes a Persian province	331 BCE | Armenia passes to the Seleucids	2nd century BCE | Independence of Armenia
late 4th century BCE | Independence of Bithynia	280–250 BCE | Nicomedes I king of Bithynia	189 BCE | Division of Armenia

Cappadocia and Pontus

Cappadocia allied itself with Rome, as did early Pontus. However, under Mithradates VI, Pontus became a dangerous enemy of the Roman Empire. After Mithradates was defeated, Rome controlled all of Asia Minor.

4

Mithras shrine in the minor church of San Clemente in Rome

6

Mosaic depicting the seven grades of consecration, Ostia Antica, second half of third century CE

Cappadocia, in the east of Asia Minor, was originally a Persian province, but gained independence after the death of Alexander the Great. It managed to assert itself against the Diadochoi but eagerly assimilated Hellenistic culture. After 190–189 BCE Cappadocia was allied with Rome. From 114–113 BCE it was threatened by Mithradates of Pontus, who styled himself the defender of the kings. About 100 BCE ❽ Mithradates murdered King Ariarathes VII and installed his own son as Ariarathes IX. After Rome's victory over Mithradates, Cappadocia came under direct Roman control. In 36 BCE, Mark Antony appointed the loyal Archelaus as king, and after Archelaus's death, Tiberius made Cappadocia a Roman province.

7   Mithradates VI Eupator

The Kingdom of Pontus on the north coast of Asia Minor was the last significant opponent of Rome. With its capital at Amaseia, the kingdom was politically separated into eparchies, each of which had its own administrative center. Starting in the third century BCE, Pontus brought the Greek cities of Asia Minor under its control. While Pontus had earlier been an ally of Rome, conflict between the two developed under Pontus's son ❼ Mithradates VI Eupator. In 112 BCE, when the Greek cities called for aid against Rome, Mithradates used it as an opportunity to occupy the Bosporus and the Chersonese, as well as to subjugate the Crimea and southern Russia up to Armenia Minor. Attempts to incorporate these territories into his kingdom ultimately led to war with Rome.

In the First Mithradatic War (89–84 BCE), Pontus occupied all of Asia Minor and Greece, but was forced to a settlement after its defeat by Sulla in 84. In 74–73 BCE Mithradates occupied Bithynia and thereby ignited the Second Mithradatic War. After initial successes, the "Hellenized

5

Mithras kills the bull, marble sculpture, second c.

barbarian" was defeated by Pompey in 63. His successor allied with Rome, which now controlled the whole region of Asia Minor. In 40 BCE, Rome appointed Darius, Mithradates's grandson, king. The kingdom was then dissolved in 64 CE and integrated into the Roman Empire as administrative provinces.

It was probably during wars with Mithradates that the ancient Indo-Iranian ❹, ❺, ❻, ❾ cult of Mithras spread through the Roman army. Mithras worship was prominent even in Rome, primarily through its mixing with the state cult Sol Invictus. Numerous Mithras shrines were built. Only with the expansion of Christianity did its influence fade.

8

Mithadates of Pontus stables his son Ariarathes

9

Ritual meal in a Mithras shrine

89–84 BCE | First Mithradatic War   **63 BCE** | Defeat of Mithradates VI by Pompey   **ca. 300 CE** | Conversion of Armenia to Christianity

74 BCE | Bithynia becomes a Roman province   **64 CE** | Pontus becomes a Roman province

PERSIA UNDER THE PARTHIANS AND THE SASSANIANS 250 BCE–651 CE

2 Parthian olive garland, gold, third century BCE

The Parthian dynasty, and the Sassanians who followed them, were for centuries the most dangerous opponents on Rome's eastern frontiers. The kings considered themselves heirs to the Achaemenid Empire. While the Pathians adopted much from Hellenic tradition, the Sassanians sought to revive Persian traditions such as Zoroastrianism. Rome was also influenced by Persian traditions, the Byzantine Empire inspired by Eastern "divine rule." Exhausted by its struggles with Rome, the Sassanid Empire ultimately succumbed to the Arab Muslim invasions of the seventh century CE.

1 **left:** Statue of a Parthian king, marble, second century BCE

■ The Parthian Empire 250 BCE–224 CE

The Parthians emerged as the successors to the Seleucid Empire. They extended their territories westward, which eventually brought them into conflict with the Roman Empire.

Beginning in the fourth century BCE, the Parni, a tribe of nomads, migrated from the southeastern shore of the Caspian Sea into the Iranian highlands. They were known as **❶,❷, ❹** Parthians after the province of Parthia, which they conquered in 250 BCE under their first ruler, Arsaces I. He and his successors, the Arsacids, drove the Seleucids out of Iran and under Mithradates I in the second century BCE, out of Mesopotamia. This then became the center of their empire, with its capital, **❻** Ctesiphon, located on the Tigris River. The Parthians adopted the **❸** Hellenistic culture of the Seleucids, as well as their administrative structure. The provinces were almost autonomously ruled by independent governors, who were often mem-

3 Parthian Temple in the Hellenistic style, Hatra, Iraq

bers of the ruling royal dynasty.

The Parthian Empire reached its greatest extent under Mithradates II "the Great" in the first century BCE, when it stretched from the Euphrates to the Indus. There were clashes with the Roman Empire over the control of Armenia, but neither side was able to gain the upper hand. The Parthians defeated the Roman consul Crassus in the Battle of **❺** Carrhae in 53 BCE. However, during the reign of Augustus the Romans were able to take advantage of the Parthian provincial governors' desire for independence and dynastic disputes over the throne. The Romans thus pursued a policy of divide and rule

by supporting different pretenders to the Parthian throne.

Emperor Trajan conquered Mesopotamia in 114 but it was lost again under Hadrian. Further Roman campaigns against the Parthians followed at the beginning of the third century. The Parthians were forced to make peace with the Romans in 218, as their empire was starting to collapse from within. Finally, Ardashir, who as a Parthian governor had run Fars (Persis), the ancient Achaemenid home

4 Parthian soldier, color lithograph

province, ended Arsacid rule in 224 and replaced it with the Sassanid dynasty.

5 Crassus's defeat at Carrhae

6 Palace of the King in the Parthian capital, Ctesiphon

| 2nd century BCE | Defeat of the Seleucids by Mithradates I | | 53 BCE | Triumph over Rome in the Battle of Carrhae | 218 | Peace with Rome |

| 1st century BCE | Greatest extent of the Parthian Empire | 114 CE | Conquest of Mesopotamia by Trajan |

The Empire of the Sassanians 224–651 CE

The Sassanians saw themselves as heirs to the Achaemenids and sought to revive their culture. War with the Romans drained the kingdom and it succumbed to the Arab invasions.

The Sassanid **⑩** Ardashir I overthrew the last of the Parthian rulers in 224. To a much greater extent than the Arsacids, the Sassanians identified with the ancient Persian traditions and sought to revive this culture, particularly Zoroastrianism. This became the official state religion. The Sassanians attempted to revoke the autonomy of the provinces—which would ultimately result in the downfall of the Parthian Empire—and centralized all authority. The Sassanians continued to pursue the conflict with the Romans and the Byzantine Empire. Shapur I defeated the Romans with ease at Edessa in 260 and even took **❾** Emperor Valerian prisoner. Under Shapur's successors in the fourth century, Christians were seen as politically suspect and persecuted as potential suppor-

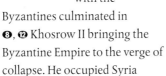

7 The gold and crystal "Khosru Bowl," decorated with an enthroned Khosrow I

ters of Rome. Once the conflict ended, in the fifth century, they were granted freedom to practice their religion.

The Sassanid Empire reached the height of its power under **❼** Khosrow I, who had destroyed the Hephthalite Empire by 560 and conquered southern Arabia by 570. War with the Byzantines culminated in **❽**, **❶** Khosrow II bringing the Byzantine Empire to the verge of collapse. He occupied Syria and Egypt, before capturing Jerusalem in 614, and stealing holy relics. The Emperor Heraclius, however, halted the Persian advance, and won a decisive victory in the Battle of Nineveh in 627. Khosrow II was

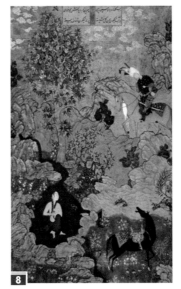

8 Khosrow II and the Christian Shirin, illustrated book, 15th century

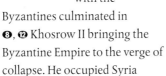

9 Shapur I takes the Roman Emperor Valerian prisoner, engraving, third century

deposed and **⓫** murdered, while his successor had no choice but to make peace with Heraclius.

Persia had been so militarily exhausted by the conflict that it was unable to defend itself effectively against the onslaught of the Arab invaders spreading Islam. The last Sassanid, Yazdegerd III, fled eastwards and was murdered in 651. However, the language and refined culture of the Persians fused with the new faith, and marked out the elite.

Manichaeism

In the third century CE, a Persian thinker, Manichaeus, propagated a dualistic doctrine that integrated elements of Zoroastrianism, Christianity, and Buddhism, and to which he gave his name. He identified God with the kingdom of light that opposed a kingdom of darkness and taught that man must constantly defend himself against the darkness, which threatens him. Mankind is helped in this by redeemers sent by God. Manichaeism strongly influenced both Gnosticism and Christianity. He was persecuted as a heretic and flayed to death in 276 CE.

above: Manichaeus, third century

10 Ahura Mazda passes the ring of power to the Sassanian Ardashir I, rock relief in Persepolis, third century

11 Khosrow is executed by his own son after his defeat, engraving, 17th century

12 Khosrow II and the Christian Shirin, book illustration, 15th century

224 | Sassanid rule begins   **560** | Khosrow I destroys the Hephthalite Empire   **627** | Sassanids defeated by Heraclius at Nineveh

260 | Victory of Shapur I over the Romans at Edessa   **614** | Conquest of Jerusalem by Khosrow II

Celts, Slavs, and Germanic Tribes

6TH CENTURY BCE–7TH CENTURY CE

During antiquity, much of Europe was inhabited by the ❶ Celts, Slavs, and ancient Germanic tribes. They were considered uncivilized barbarians by the Mediterranean peoples, although some Greek and Roman writers expressed more favorable opinions. These ancient accounts, medieval epics, and archaeological finds provide what little information there is about these peoples, while elements of their culture and language have survived to this day.

Celtic bronze helmet, first century BCE

The Migrations of the Celts

The Celts moved out from their original homeland in western France and southern Germany and into western and southeastern Europe. They also settled in northern Italy and the plains of central Anatolia.

The name "Celt" dates from the sixth century BCE when Greek sources used the term to denote tribes living around the Danube and Rhone rivers. Evidence of the migratory movements of the Celts is found where they ❸ encountered the Etruscans, Romans, and Greeks. In the sixth century they began to

A Celt kills his wife and himself after losing a battle, marble statue, third c. BCE

settle the plains of the Po River, which had previously been controlled by the Etruscans. In the fourth century BCE, they began to send raiding parties south, even sacking Rome about 390 BCE. In the third century, the Celts pushed through southern Europe and the Balkans into Greece and plundered Delphi. The ❺ Celtic Galli reached Asia Minor as mercenaries of Nicomedes I of Bithynia in 278 BCE. They were defeated in the ❻ "Battle of the Elephants" in 275–274 by Antiochus I of Syria. He then settled them permanently in central Anatolia (Galatia), where they were still living in the first century CE.

There is no evidence of a mass Celtic migration into either the Iberian Peninsula or the ❹ British Isles. It is more likely that the in-

digenous societies adopted aspects of Celtic culture. The bearers of Celtic culture began to spread south from northern Spain in the fifth century BCE and are referred to as Celtiberes. The inhabitants of the British Isles in pre-Roman times were seen as Celts due to their culture and language.

In the early first century BCE, Germanic tribes advancing out of the north drove the Celts of Central Europe out of the valleys north of the Rhine and Danube, until they eventually came under Roman rule.

Under Roman influence, an independent ❷ Gallo-Roman culture developed in Celtic Gaul. The Celts on the British Isles, who were never part of the Roman Empire, maintained their independence in ❼ Ireland, Scotland, and Wales. From these regions, tribal groups who spoke

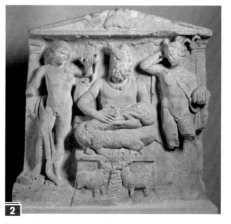

The Celtic horned god, Cernunnos, associated with nature and fertility, seated between Apollo and Mercury, stone relief, first century CE

Celtic despite having been Romanized migrated into Brittany in the fifth and sixth centuries CE. The Celtic language and culture has been preserved in these areas up to the present.

The remains of a Celtic ceremonial complex built of stone, consisting of a round room, two galleries, and a tunnel, in Cornwall, southwestern England

Remains of a Celtic fort in Dun Aengus, Ireland, ca. first century BCE

Celtic warrior on horseback

Celtic warrior trampled by an elephant, terra-cotta statuette, second century BCE

The Celts and the Romans

Between 200 BCE and 100 CE, the Romans conquered almost all of the Celtic territories.

The first great clash between the Romans and the "Gauls"—as the ❽, ❾ Celts were called—ended in 390 BCE with the sacking of Rome by the Celtic Senones, under Brennus. The Celts, bribed by the Romans to leave, then withdrew to the north and settled on the Po River plain. The Romans subjugated the region between 225 and 190 BCE.

The conquest of Celtic regions beyond the Alps began in 125 BCE and occurred in several stages. The tribes living there frequently quarreled with each other and were incapable of offering collective resistance. Sometimes they even sought help from the Romans against other enemies. Julius Caesar was therefore able to intervene in Celtic affairs when he assisted the Gauls against the Germanic warlord Ariovistus in 58 BCE. By 51 BCE he had subjugated all of Gaul—present-day France and Belgium—often forming alliances with individual Celtic tribes. The Romans' most stubborn and serious opponent was prince ❸ Vercingetorix, who in 52 BCE was proclaimed king by a number of tribes. He was finally captured and became Caesar's prisoner in Alesia. After being paraded through Rome in 46 BCE, Vercingetorix was executed.

Under Caesar's successors, the boundaries of the empire expanded to the Rhine and Danube so that all of the Celt-occupied areas in central Europe came under Roman control. The Celts on the Iberian Peninsula and in present-day Eng-

9 Tombstone showing the Pannonian Umma in Celtic garb, first c. CE

land also succumbed to Roman rule. In 60 CE, the British Celtic queen Boudicca rebelled against the Romans. After initial success, the rebellion was defeated and Boudicca committed suicide.

The Romanization of Gaul led to the development of a mixed ❿ Gallo-Roman culture. The Gauls rapidly adopted Latin, Roman law and administration. They assimilated the civilization and culture of Rome. The Celtic nobility adapted to Roman ways, gained citizenship, and could even be admitted to the Senate, although they continued to prefer life in the country.

Celtic settlements, such as Paris and ❷ Trier, became flourishing Gallo-Roman cities. Gaul was one of Rome's most important provinces as a result of the revenues generated from the ⓫ export of grains, wine, and finished textile products.

10 Gallic warriors, stone sculpture, second century BCE

The sacking of Rome by Brennus

The Roman writer Livy described the sacking of Rome by Brennus in his History of Rome. According to Livy, Brennus was unable to take the Capitoline Hill because the defenders were alerted to the attack by the cries of geese. Since then, geese have been particularly honored there. Brennus made a deal, accepting 1,000 pounds of gold in exchange for his withdrawal. When the Romans complained that the weights on the scales were too heavy, Brennus threw his sword on top with the words: "Vae victis!" ("Woe to the vanquished!").

above: Brennus throws his sword onto the scales, steel engraving, 19th century

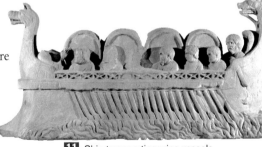

8 Gallic warrior with tattoos (left) and Senone chief in full armor, artist's reconstruction

11 Ship transporting wine vessels, detail from a wine merchant's tomb, second–third century CE

12 The Porta Nigra, Trier, in Germany, second century CE

13 Vercingetorix surrenders to Caesar, wood engraving, 19th century

52 BCE | Vercingetorix is appointed Celtic king   60 CE | Queen Boudicca's rebellion against the Romans

58–51 BCE | Conquest of Gaul by Caesar   46 BCE | Execution of Vercingetorix in Rome   5th and 6th centuries | Immigration of Celtic tribes into Brittany

Celtic Culture and Society

The Celtic culture is differentiated from other ancient cultures primarily by its lack of writing. In all other respects, it achieved a very high level in social differentiation, material culture, economy, and trade.

1 Reconstruction of the defensive walls of a Celtic settlement

The Celts had no unified national identity, but were instead subdivided into many tribes and clans who alternately formed alliances and fought with one another, according to political necessity. In early times the tribes were led by kings, who were later replaced by assemblies of the nobility. The ❷ princes stood out among the nobles, distinguishing themselves through exceptional wealth and influence. They also led the armies into battle in times of war. They were buried in large ❺ burial chambers with valuable funerary objects. Below the nobility was the broad mass of the ❼ populace, and subordinate to them were the serfs. The rigid system of allegiances and personal loyalties was of great importance. The princes held extensive properties, exacted tolls and taxes, and even minted their own ❸ coins.

Agriculture and animal husbandry formed the basis of the Celtic economy. In addition, ❻ metalworking and ceramic production reached a high level of sophistication under the distinct influence of the Etruscans, Romans, and Greeks. The Celts lived on individual farms or in ❽ villages, with larger settlements growing up around important seats of the nobility. In the second century BCE, ❶ fortified cities were also built.

The ❹ Druids, who formed a priestly caste, enjoyed particular esteem. They performed religious rites and made prophecies, as well as passing legal judgments. ❾ Deities and ancestors were worshiped—occasionally with human sacrifices—in man-made ⓬, ⓭ shrines as well as at springs, rivers, or trees. The Druids imparted their knowledge through an exclusively oral tradition. The history of the Celts was also passed on orally through the poems of the bards, in which—as in the legend

2 Celtic warrior nobility, sandstone statue, fifth century BCE

5 Celtic burial mound in southern Germany, ninth–fifth century BCE

7 Celtic woman and her warrior husband, chalk drawing, 19th century

3 Celtic gold coin, second century BCE

6 The Gundestrup Cauldron, made of silver, discovered in 1891 in a bog in Denmark, 1st c. BCE

of King Arthur—historical events were interwoven with mythical tales.

4 Druidic meeting in a stone circle, still from a film

The Legend of King Arthur

The epic tale of King Arthur reflects the clashes between the Celtic Britons and the Germanic Anglo-Saxons. Some elements reoccur repeatedly in its numerous literary versions. Among these are Arthur's triumph over the Anglo-Saxons, his famous round table, and the unfaithfulness of his wife Guinevere. He has been identified with a number of historical figures, including a Roman named Lucius Castus and the Celtic King Riothamus.

8 Reconstruction of a Celtic village in Ireland

ca. 8th–7th centuries BCE | First Celtic tribes   2nd century BCE | First fortified cities   ca. 550 | Slavs besiege Constantinople

from 6th century BCE | Hierarchic class society   from the 5th century CE | Slavic migration to the west and south

The god Cernunnos, detail on the Cauldron of Gundestrup, first c. BCE

Excavation of a Slavic fortification, in Mecklenburg, northern Germany

Under the Yoke of the Avars

"Each year the Avars came to the Slavs to spend the winter and slept with the wives and daughters of the Slavs: the Slavs tolerated other perfidies as well, and also paid tribute to the Avars. The sons, however, which the Avars had fathered with the women and daughters of the Slav menfolk, would not tolerate this brutal oppression and refused to subject themselves to the Avars."

From the Chronicles of Fredegarius

above: The Avars humiliate the Slavs, forcing them to draw their carts like packhorses, book illustration, 15th century

■ The Early Slavs

The advance of the Huns in the late fourth century CE, and the resulting migratory movements of the Germanic tribes, provided the stimulus for the movement of the Slavs. At first they settled in the regions deserted by the Germans, but then increasingly headed south into the Balkans.

The Slavs probably originated north of the Carpathian Mountains between the Vistula and Dnieper rivers. During the Great Migration of Peoples, they spread out and began following the withdrawing Germanic tribes in the fifth century CE. The Slavs went as far west as the Elbe River and the Baltic Sea and as far east as Kamchatka. In the south, they were at first halted at the Danube, on the border of the Byzantine Empire. However their raiding parties soon led them to Ragusa and up to the gates of Constantinople. The Slavs even-

11 Slavic urns, ninth-tenth century

tually crossed the Danube in great numbers and settled the Balkan region. Ancient writers refer to them as Sarmatians and Scythians.

The Slavs of the Danube region were dominated from the sixth to the eighth centuries by the Avars, an equestrian tribe. In the ninth century, the Magyars, who originated in the Eurasian steppes, settled in present-day Hungary. The region settled by the Slavs split between western, eastern, and southern Slavic groups, who developed separately from one another.

The basis of the communal life of the early Slavs was the clan, several of which would band together to form a tribe. Ancient descriptions picture them as industrious pastoral peoples. In the sixth century subsistence farming still prevailed and crafts were little developed. Articles such as drinking ⓫ vessels and tools were produced mainly for domestic needs. Only gradually did clan leaders become a distinct class—and only where the Slavs were not dominated by foreign powers. In the seventh century, the fortified ⓬ castles were built. Little is known of the religion of the early Slavs except that they worshiped nature deities. Christianity was introduced in the ninth century by Cyril and Methodius, the former giving his name to the Cyrillic alphabet.

12 Cape Arcona on the island of Rügen, a sacred site for pre-Christian Slavs

13 Celtic stone circle in Ireland created ca. 150 BCE

from the 7th century | First Slavic nobility appears
from 565 | Invasion of the Avars
9th century | Progression of the Magyars / Separation of Slavic regions
ca. 880 | First known writings about King Arthur

The Culture and Society of the Ancient Germans

The ancient Germans were described by Roman writers as an especially warlike people. They successfully defended themselves against Roman conquest and, despite the lack of a unified leadership, came to pose a serious threat to the Roman Empire.

By the first century BCE, the ancient Germans, whose exact origins are unclear, had spread from the northeast down to the plains of the Rhine and the river

3 Two warriors, one with a horned helmet, the other with a wolf mask, perform a war dance for Odin, bronze stamp used for the decoration of helmets, sixth century

Tacitus on the Religion of the Germanic Peoples

"At a stated time of the year, all the various peoples descended from the same stock, assemble with their deputies in a wood; consecrated by the idolatries of their forefathers, and by their superstitious awe as in times of old. There, by publicly performing a human sacrifice, they commence the horrible solemnity of their barbarous worship."

Above: Giant stones in the Teutoburg Forest, a pagan ritual site

Danube. German societies were split into various tribes, each dominated by a warrior aristocracy, which based its power on property and personal allegiances. In times of war, kings were also chosen to lead the armies. During the period of the great migrations, the office of king became permanent. The population practiced ❹ agriculture and animal husbandry and was divided into a noble elite, freemen, and slaves. They traded extensively with the Roman Empire. Elected judges officiated at the ❶ community assembly and also heard legal cases. Legal verdicts were aided by oaths and considered the judgment of God. Personal conflicts often resulted in bloody feuds.

Despite near continuous ❸ conflict with the Romans, in which Arminius was the greatest threat, from the first century CE on, Germans were increasingly recruited into the Roman army as mercenaries, eventually coming to dominate it. The Romans admired the physical size and fighting power of the Germans, as well as

2 Illustration of *Twilight of the Gods*, stone relief, tenth century

6 Rune engraving showing the arrival of a warrior in Walhall and the story of the blacksmith Wölund, limestone, eighth–ninth century

their sparse, simple life. The Roman historian Tacitus emphasized the frenzy into which the warriors transported themselves before battle and called it "Teutonic rage."

War and battle also played a large role in German religion and ❷ mythology, which was permeated with the fights of pugnacious gods against giants and demons. The ❺ war god Wodan (Odin), who was most likely also the chief of the Germanic deities, received fallen soldiers in his castle, Valhalla. The gods were worshiped in holy sites or at natural monuments. These rituals apparently included animal, and even ❼ human, sacrifice.

The Germanic world of fantasy is known primarily through medieval epics and myths such as the *Edda*, based on early Icelandic poems. The earliest written first-hand accounts— oracles, magic formulas, and curses—were written in runes and date from the second century CE. Only in Scandinavia were texts of significant length written in runes, most notably on ❻ gravestones.

1 A tribal assembly, known as a "Thing," attended by all freemen

4 Germanic tribal village

5 Germanic gods Odin, Thor, and Frei, tapestry, twelfth century

7 Head of a strangled male, human sacrifice, found in a peatbog in Denmark

2nd century BCE | Migration of the Cimbri and Teutons southward   101 BCE | Marius's victory over the Cimbri and Teutons   12 BCE | Roman occupation up to the Elbe

58 BCE | Victory of Caesar over Ariovistus

The Ancient Germans and the Romans

Beginning in the first century BCE, there were constant clashes along the Rhine and Danube rivers between the Germanic tribes and the Roman Empire.

8 Cimbrian women in battle against the Romans, engraving, 19th century

From as early as the first century BCE, there were regular clashes along the Rhine and Danube rivers between the Germanic tribes and the Roman Empire.

9 A legionnaire apprehends a fleeing German woman with her child, plaster mold of a second century CE relief

Even before the Great Migration of Peoples that began in the third century CE, the Romans came into conflict with nomadic Germanic tribes such as the Cimbri and Teutoni, who had moved south during the second century BCE. The defeats inflicted on several Roman armies sent to the aid of threatened Celtic tribes triggered a panic in Rome in 113 BCE, as residents feared another sacking of the city like that of the Celts under Brennus. Under Marius, however, the army turned the tide and **8**, **9** annihilated the Cimbri and Teutoni around 102–101 BCE. The next great challenge was an invasion of Gaul by the Germanic warlord Ariovistus. Again, the Celts were dependent on Roman aid. Caesar repelled the Germans in 58 BCE and went on to conquer all of Gaul. From this point on, the Rhine and Danube marked the boundaries of the Roman Empire, but the Germans continued to send small raiding parties into the empire.

From 12 BCE, the Romans sought to eradicate the problem by occupying all the lands up to the Elbe. It was only after the defeat of the Roman governor Varus, in the 9 CE **10** Battle of Teutoburg Forest, that the Romans abandoned these plans of conquest. On the north side of the Rhine and Danube, only the Agri Decumates, in the area between the two rivers, stayed in Roman hands; it was protected by a **11** fortified border (a "limes"), reinforced with palisades, trenches, and watchtowers.

Despite the regular incursions, the Romans were able to keep the divided Germanic tribes in check until the second half of the second century, when larger tribes, such as the Alemanni and Franks, began to emerge. It was only with great effort that Marcus Aurelius was able to repel the Marcomanni and Quadi, who had settled between the Elbe and Danube, around 170. The occupation of the Agri Decumates by the Alemanni and the Suebi in 260, along with the settlement of Frankish allies on the empire's territory, foreshadowed the changes that finally led to the fall of the Western Roman Empire.

Armin of the Cherusci

The Cherusci prince Arminius —later Germanized to "Hermann"—was originally an ally of Rome. He trained in the Roman army, was a citizen of Rome, and fought for the Romans against other Germanic tribes. It was only when the governor Varus tried to introduce the Roman tax and legal systems in Germania that he rebelled and defeated the Roman forces. He was murdered by relatives who feared his growing power around 21. In the 19th century, with a total disregard for history, he was pronounced the "defender of the Germans."

above: Colossal statue of Armin (Hermann) of the Cherusci, built in the Teutoburg Forest, 19th c.

11 The Saalburg, a Roman stone fort, on the limes of the Danubian frontier

10 The Battle of Teutoburg Forest, painting, 19th century

THE GREAT MIGRATION OF PEOPLES 375–568 CE

The formation of great tribes on the Rhine and Danube rivers put immense pressure on the Roman Empire in the third century. At first it was possible to hold the ❶ Germans back, and when necessary they were included in the empire, where they were welcomed as soldiers. The appearance of the Huns in 375 changed the situation. They triggered a massive migratory movement that the Roman Empire, which officially divided into Western and Eastern parts in 395, was unable to oppose. The Romans were forced to accept the founding of Germanic kingdoms on imperial territory until finally, in 476, the last Western Roman emperor was deposed by the Germans. Only the Eastern Empire, later Byzantium, survived the upheavals during the mass migrations.

1 Warrior's helmet, seventh century

◼ The Migrations of the Germanic Peoples

The Huns stormed out of the Eurasian steppes in 375, driving some of the Ostrogoths and the Visigoths out of their settled regions north of the Danube and the Black Sea. Other Germanic tribes were also on the move.

3 General Stilicho with his wife and son, ivory carving, ca. 400

Even before the Hun invasion of 375, the Romans were forced to cede territory to the Germanic tribes. The Romans were unable to repel the incursion of the ❷ Franks across the lower Rhine in 350, and were forced to accept a settlement. The Franks were granted the status of allies and pacified with payments of money. Some of their leaders were appointed to posts in the Roman army and, after the fall of the empire, gained independence in Gaul. Some Germanic leaders rose to become imperial generals—even commanders of the Roman army—and, like ❸ Stilicho at the time of the division of the Roman empire in 395, were the power behind weak emperors. The German Odoacer deposed the last Roman emperor in 476.

The ❺ migration of peoples began with the Huns driving the Goths out of their homeland in 375. The Goths, who most likely originated in Scandinavia, settled the area south of the Baltic Sea along the Vistula River during the first and second centuries CE and had reached the Black Sea and the Danube by the third century. From there, they raided both Greece and Asia Minor. During the second half of the third century, the Goths divided into the Ostrogoths and the Visigoths.

After the Huns attacked in 375, many Visigoths fled south over the Danube border, and their victory over the ❻ Romans at Adrianople in 378 led to an alliance. After the Roman Empire's division in 395, the Visigoths effectively used the rivalry between East and West Rome to their advantage. The Visigoth king Alaric fought many battles against the Western Roman general

2 Frankish stone carving, seventh c.

Stilicho, invading Italy in 401 and then ❹ plundering Rome in 410. When the Visigoths moved on in 418, the emperor offered them the south of France. There they esta-

4 The conquest of Rome by the Visigoths under Alaric, wood engraving, 19th century

6 Romans battle the Goths, wood engraving, 19th c.

5 Germanic caravan, wood engraving, 19th century

7

Nicasius, Bishop of Reims, kneels before the Vandals, sculpture, 13th century

blished a kingdom that later stretched on into Spain.

The majority of the ❾ Ostrogoths initially joined forces with the Huns. After the death of the Hun king Attila, they settled in Eastern Roman territory as allies. The Ostrogoth king, ❽ Theodoric, who was raised in Constantinople, marched into Italy in 488 in the name of the Eastern Roman emperor Zeno, defeated the Western Roman regent Odoacer in 493, and founded his own realm.

In the meantime, at the turn of the fifth century, another wave of Germanic peoples pushed out of their former settlements in Central and Eastern Europe towards the West. In 406–407 the Vandals and Burgundians crossed the Rhine and moved into Gaul. The ❼ Vandals continued over the Pyrenees, settling in Spain by 409, while the Burgundians established their own kingdom on the Rhine. Under increasing pressure from

8   Theodoric the Great, king of the Ostrogoths, image on a coin, ca. 500

Visigoth attacks encouraged by the Western Roman emperor, the Vandals under King Gaiseric crossed over to North Africa in 429. There they founded an empire with its capital at Carthage, depriving Rome of lands valuable for growing grain.

From the Baltic Sea coast, groups of Angles, Saxons, and Jutes, under the leadership of ❿ Hengist and Horsa, set off in the middle of the fifth century for Britain, which had been abandoned by the

9   Ostrogothic eagle clasp, ca. 500

Romans around 400. The Germans drove the Celtic Britons into Scotland, Wales, and Cornwall. The Saxons who had remained on the continent were able to fend off the Franks, and Christianization was not widespread until the end of the eighth century.

The last of the important Germanic tribes to join the migration were the Lombards, who until the fifth century had lived between the Elbe and the Danube. Driven out by the equestrian nomadic Avars, under ⓫ King Alboin they left their homeland and occupied a region in northern Italy that came to be named after them—Lombardy—in 568. This is considered the end of the Great Migration.

The widespread migration of peoples led to the fall of the Roman Empire and a westward shift of the areas settled by the Germans and the Slavs who followed. The union of late antiquity and Germanic tradition in the culture of the Visigoths, Franks, Angles, Saxons, and Lombards characterized the culture of Europe in the early Middle Ages.

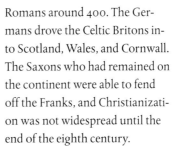

Ulfilas

During the Great Migration of Peoples, Ulfilas (or Wulfila) was an influential leader of the Germans. In 341 he was ordained "bishop of the Goths" and about 370 he translated the Bible into Gothic. Because he was an adherent of Arius, the Goths and most of the other Germanic tribes came to be called Arians. This led to conflicts with the Romans in the territories conquered by the Germans and hindered an integration of the two groups of peoples. The acceptance of Catholicism by the Franks, and later by the Visigoths and Lombards, eased their acceptance by the native inhabitants and lent their empires greater stability.

above: Ulfilas explains the gospel to the Goths, engraving, 1890

10

Hengist and Horsa land on the British coast, wood engraving, 19th century

11

King Alboin entering Pavia, wood engraving, 19th century

THE NOMAD EMPIRES OF THE EURASIAN STEPPES 3RD CENTURY BCE– 7TH CENTURY CE

The Eurasian belt of steppes that stretches eastward from the Black Sea in the west to the Yellow Sea in China has always been inhabited by nomads. Clashes with the Scythians, Sarmatians, or Sakas who lived there played a role in the history of the ancient empires of the Persians, Greeks, and Indians, but these peoples never became organized as a nation. One of the oldest groups was the Xiongnu, who established a great nomad empire at the end of the third century BCE on the northern borders of China. Their defeat and displacement by the Han dynasty triggered a chain reaction of migratory movements whose western ripples in the fourth century CE pushed the ❶ Huns into the Goths and set off the Great Migration of Peoples that altered the makeup of Europe.

Huns in Europe, steel engraving, 19th century

Xiongnu, Kushana, and Hephthalites

Even before the rise of the Huns, great nomad empires were formed on the basis of moving confederations of tribes.

The empires of the ❷ equestrian nomads of the Xiongnu, Huns, and Turkic people, as well as the ❸ Mongolian empire of Genghis Khan in the 13th century, were all based on coalitions of different tribes and peoples. Because the founders of the empires did not define themselves by ethnicity, every group that identified with the interests of the empire—even former enemies—was taken in. Of course, this confederal style easily led to fragmentation of the nomad empires, and most of them were very short lived.

The tribal federation of the Xiongnu, which formed at the end of the third century BCE, presented a serious threat to Han dynasty China, which went to great lengths—from the construction of the Great Wall to offensive military strikes—to rid itself of this opponent. During the course of the second and third centuries, the Chinese succeeded in gradually dividing and driving off the Xiongnu. Parts of the confederation then became dependent on the Chinese and were assimilated; other groups were

defeated by the Chinese and driven westward. It seems likely that the Xiongnu, as they withdrew, forced out other peoples and tribes living further west—the Kushana, who then invaded Central Asia and India, for example. Today it is considered doubtful that the Huns who appeared in the fourth century were directly related to the Xiongnu, although it is possible that some remains of the Xiongnu merged into the tribal confederation of the Huns.

Two horse-riders, clay figurines, 2nd–1st c. BCE

In the fifth century, the powerful Sassanians of Persia came into conflict with the nomad empire of the Hephthalites, who were also known as the "white Huns." After the Hephthalites swept south to destroy the remains of the great Gupta empire in northern India, they were themselves annihilated in 567 by the Sassanians under Khosrow I.

Nomad yurts in the Gobi Desert, present-day Mongolia

The Huns under Attila invade Europe, wood engraving, 19th century

from the 3rd century BCE | Tribal confederation of the Xiongnu   **375 CE** | Defeat of the Goths by the Huns   **451** | Attila's defeat at the Catalaunian Plains

2nd century BCE–3rd century CE | Expulsion of the Xiongnu from China   **445** | Attila as single ruler over the Huns

The Huns

The military expeditions of the Huns, particularly under King Attila, the "scourge of God," were so devastating that many in Europe believed that they were experiencing the end of the world.

The Huns pour across the steppes north of the Caspian Sea, wood engraving, 19th century

Looting of a Gallo-Roman villa by the Huns, wood engraving, 19th century

The Battle of the Catalaunian Plains, color print, 20th century

The Meeting between Leo the Great and Attila, fresco by Raphael, 16th century

The Huns overran the Ostrogoths and the Visigoths in 375, destroying everything in their path. Due to their custom of strapping their children's noses flat from an early age, in order to widen their faces, they were described by early chroniclers as "animal-like creatures"—which only increased the terror they instilled. The Huns were not set on totally exterminating the Germans, though, since they needed them for their army.

East Rome tried to hold off the Huns from its borders with payments of up to 1,500 pounds of gold annually. But despite this, the ❹ Huns under Attila—who had earlier killed his brother and co-regent Bleda in 445—pushed deep into East Roman territory ❻, ❼ devastated the Balkan provinces, and extorted ever greater tribute payments. Attila then turned towards the West, leading his immense, and growing, army of Huns and Germanic tribesmen. Along the way many cities, such as Trier and Metz, were burned to the ground. In June 451, the Franks,

Visigoths, and Romans, led by the imperial commander Aetius, brought the Huns' advance to a halt. The resulting ❽ Battle of the Catalaunian Plains, near Chalons-sur-Marne, lasted several days and cost around 90,000 lives.

The Huns and their allies were forced to withdraw toward Eastern Europe, but Attila was still not completely defeated. In 452 he invaded northern Italy and threatened Rome. However, Pope ❾ Leo I managed to persuade the Huns, who were afflicted by starvation and epidemics, to turn back. Attila ❺ died suddenly in 453, just after his wedding celebrations. The Huns split apart in the battles that followed, and were ultimately defeated and dispersed almost as quickly as they had conquered.

Following in the footsteps of the Huns, new equestrian nomads began to move into Europe from the east, among them the ❿ Avars and Magyars. The Avars are credited with introducing the stirrup to Europe, which gave their mounted warriors a major advantage in battle. In Central Asia, the Turkic people took up

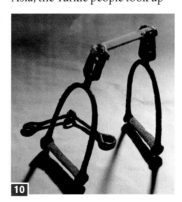

A pair of stirrups, an innovation imported into Europe by the equestrian nomads, particularly the Avar nomads

Attila dies on his wedding night, wood engraving, 19th century

the legacy of the Huns and from the sixth to seventh century established a great nomad empire that stretched all the way from China to the Caspian Sea.

The Appearance of the Huns

"For by the terror of their features they inspired great fear in those whom perhaps they did not really surpass in war....Their swarthy aspect was fearful, and they had...pinholes rather than eyes. Their audacity is evident in their threatening appearance, and they are beings who are cruel to their children on the very day they are born. For they cut the cheeks of the males with a sword, so that before they receive the nourishment of milk they must learn to endure wounds."

Jordanes, Getica (History of the Goths, ch.XXIII) 551 CE

above: Artificially deformed skull of a noblewoman, fifth century CE

ANCIENT INDIA   321 BCE–CA. 500 CE

Since the time of Alexander the Great, India had been in touch with Hellenic culture. The rulers of the Maurya Empire in particular maintained contact with the West. The most significant among them was Asoka, who promoted Buddhism. After the fall of the Maurya, local dynasties continually fought against the invading nomads from the Central Asian steppes. Only the Gupta Empire was able to once again unite large parts of India. In the meantime, Hinduism experienced a renaissance and eventually pushed Buddhism out of the subcontinent.

1 The lion capital of the Asoka Column, model for the Indian state crest, third century BCE

◼ The Mauryan Dynasty ca. 321–185 BCE

After 321 BCE, the Mauryan dynasty became the leading power in India. Emperor Asoka made Buddhism the state religion and gave the teaching and missionary efforts decisive impetus.

Alexander the Great marched with his army into the Indus Valley in 327 BCE and despite great resistance from the hill tribes, he reduced most of their fortresses and defeated King Poros, as well as other local rulers, with his 2,000 war elephants. Alexander's successors in the east, the Seleucids, came into conflict with what had become the dominant power on the Indian subcontinent—the Maurya Empire, which had been founded around 321 by Chandragupta Maurya, in the area of Magadha on the Ganges. Chandragupta defeated Seleucus but eventually reached an agreement with the Seleucids about their common borders. He and his suc-

3 Depiction of the female earth spirit Yakshi, recognized as a symbol of fertility by Hindus, Buddhists, and Jains, sandstone, third century BCE

cessors maintained close contact with the Greeks, ensuring the continued influence of Hellenic culture in India.

Asoka, grandson of Chandragupta, came to the throne between 273 and 265 BCE, and is considered the most significant ruler of the Maurya Empire and of an-

cient India as a whole. During his reign, the empire included nearly all of the Indian subcontinent and reached present-day Afghanistan. His experiences during a brutal military campaign led to his conversion to **❷**, **❸** Buddhism. Accounts and edicts on **❶**, **❹** pillars and rock faces testify to Asoka's goals and achievements. While tolerant of other religions, he promoted the spread of Buddhism, even sending missionaries abroad. Around 250 he called a Buddhist council in his capital, Pataliputra, to establish the textual canon of early Buddhism. After his conversion, he refused to wage war. Instead, he sought to extend the social support within his empire. Soon after Asoka's death in ca. 232 BCE, the Mauryan dynasty began to decline and in 185 BCE the last Maurya was killed.

2 Buddha, old Indic

From an Edict of Asoka

"All men are my children. What I desire for my own children, and I desire their welfare and happiness both in this world and the next, that I desire for all men.... Your aim should be to act with impartiality."

Fragment of an inscription of an edict by emperor Asoka on a column in a Buddhist column, third century BCE

4 Asoka Column, third century BCE

The Gupta Dynasty ca. 320–550 CE

Foreign conquerors and tribes continually pushed out of the northwest into the Indian subcontinent and founded kingdoms, though they tended to be short-lived. The last great Indian empire of antiquity was that of the Guptas.

After the fall of the Mauryan dynasty in 184 BCE, several forms of states with strong Hellenistic traits established themselves independently in the northwest, stretching from ❺ Bactria (Afghanistan) to the Punjab, whose western part became for some time part of the Parthian empire. They were overrun in the first century CE by the nomadic Sakas, who swept down from Central Asia into India and established several kingdoms that survived into the second century under the domination of the Parthians and Kushana. The empire of the Kushana in the northwest of India, then disintegrated in the third century under pressure from the intruding Sassanians.

At first, orders of Buddhist ❻ monks exercised great po-

9 The *Bhagavad Gita*, part of the *Mahabharata*, excerpt from a script scroll

6 Buddhist cave monasteries and temples, second century BCE–sixth century CE

7 Illustration of the *Ramayana*, the life story of Rama, miniature painting, 18th century

wer in the numerous Indian states. The princes then promoted the ancient Indian cults and priest castes as a counterweight, which brought about a renaissance of ❽ Hinduism. In this period, the great Indian hero epics ❾ *Mahabharata* and ❼ *Ramayana*, in which the political events of the times are reflected, were written. In the long run, the revitalization of Hinduism pushed Buddhism out of India.

In the fourth century Magadha once again became the foundation of a great empire. The local princes of the Gupta Dynasty (320-500 CE), which reigned during the golden age of Hindu culture, under Chandragupta II and his son Samudragupta, were able to make vassals of the neighboring rulers in quick succession. Under Chandra-

gupta II, who also stood out as an ⓫ architect, the empire stood at the pinnacle of its power at the beginning of the fifth century, stretching over all of North India. But then it was destroyed by invading Hephthalites. The last Guptas in the sixth century reigned only in Magadha, while in the rest of northern India a number of warring powers emerged. Among them only the powerful Hindu dynasty of the ⓾ Gurjara-Pratiharas stood out, as they were able for some time to withstand the onslaught of Islamic conquerors, who had been invading India repeatedly since the eighth century.

Several states existed in central and southern India, among which the central Indian Andhra of the first and second centuries is of note. The Tamils were able to

5 Ruins of the city Bactra, present-day Balkh, Afghanistan, former capital of Bactria

8 The god Vishnu shows sympathy for the animal world, fifth century

maintain their independence and the characteristic features of their southern Indian culture in the great plain of the Carnatic and northern Ceylon even in the times of the Maurya and Gupta empires.

10 Shiva as Nataraja, lord of the dance, sandstone from Pratihara, ninth century

11 Vishnu Temple in Deogarh, fifth century

| 3rd century CE | Destruction of Kushana empire by Sassanians | ca. 380–414 | Chandragupta II | 750–ca. 1000 | Hindu dynasty of Gurjara-Pratiharasharas |
| 320–500 CE | North Indian dynasty of the Guptas | | | ca. 500 | Hephthalites destroy Guptas Empire |

CHINA'S FIRST EMPERORS OF THE QIN AND HAN DYNASTIES 221 BCE–220 CE

In the "Period of the Warring States," China was split into seven individual states that were eventually conquered by the Qin Empire. The "first sovereign emperor" of China, Emperor Qin Shi Huang Di, brought about the political and cultural unification of the country. The succeeding Han dynasty built upon this unification, expanded the area of Chinese rule, and successfully defended itself against the nomadic tribes in the north. In addition, Confucianism became the state ideology during the Han period. Under these first two imperial dynasties, developments that would characterize the history of China for more than 2,000 years were initiated.

1 Armor protection, shown in a third century BCE clay figure

The Qin Dynasty 221–206 BCE

China's first emperor created a unified state within a few years and began outwardly fortifying his empire. He ruled the land with an iron fist and in accordance with the state philosophy of Legalism.

Qin Shi Huangdi, former Zheng, king of Qin, wood carving, ca. 1640

2 The grave of Qin Shi Huangdi, with 6,000 life-size men and horses, third century BCE

Archaeologists at the excavation of Qin dynasty clay figures

The unification of China into a state in the third century BCE was accomplished by the western state of Qin, which gave the country its name. Its frontier position opposite Tibet and the territories of the mounted nomads required it to have a powerful army and a tight administration. Its newly conquered territories were not given over to nobles as fiefs but were directly administrated by the ruler, which impeded the development of an aristocratic opposition. From this power base, King **3** Zheng of Qin was able to conquer the other seven Chinese feudal states by 221 BCE. This ended the "Period of the Warring States" and a unified state with a divine emperor (Shi Huang Di: first august emperor) at its head was created.

The emperor then extended Qin's centralized administrative system over all of China. Disregarding old boundaries, the empire was reapportioned into provinces and districts that were run by imperial administrators. The government was based on

the philosophy of the Legalists, who declared that the central laws should supersede all else and instituted the regulation of all areas of life by strict laws and taxes. Within a few years, language, measurements, weights, and coinage had been standardized in the empire. Even the gauge and length of wagons were standardized to accommodate uniform road networks. The people were forced to extend the walls against mounted nomads, which is the first section of the **5** Great Wall.

After his death in 210 BCE, China's first emperor was laid to rest in an enormous burial monument with thousands of individually crafted **1**, **2** terra-cotta figures. Its **4** discovery in 1974 was an archaeological sensation. The Qin dynasty ended shortly thereafter in 206 BCE with an uprising of the people that brought the Hans to power.

5 The Great Wall of China in the hills near Beijing

The Han Dynasty 206 BCE–220 CE

In the power struggle at the end of the Qin era, a peasant rebel leader, Liu Bang, triumphed and took the emperor's throne in 206 BCE as Emperor Gaozu.

The most important task of the first Han emperor, Kao Ti (206 BCE), was defending against the ❻ mounted nomads, above all the Xiongnu. Emperor ❾ Han Wu Ti, the most illustrious of the Han emperors, took the offensive, and his search for allies led the Chinese to their first contact with the West. The Xiongnu were finally defeated and forced westward, displacing Eurasian steppe peoples and ultimately triggering the Great Migration of Peoples in Europe of the fourth and fifth centuries. China conquered eastern Turkistan to the borders of today's Afghanistan, where a trade link to the west— the ❿ Silk Road—developed. Domestically, Han Wu Ti carried out several reforms that were to have a longlasting effect. He tried to repair the

7 Generals in their armor, clay figures, Han period

educational vandalism of Shi-Hwang-ti. He divided the central administration into departmental ministries for the first time. The system of training of ⓬ officials through schooling and examinations was perfected and remained in effect until the 20th century. The basis of this training was a synthesis of Legalism, Confucianism, which stressed the relationship between father and ⓫ son, and the yin–yang nature philosophy. The veneration of Confucius in a state cult began under the Hans. In 174 BCE, Emperor Han Wu Ti made a sacrifice on the philosopher's grave in ❽ Chu Fu, which survives to this day. The Han period was one of the greatest epochs of Chinese prosperity.

Han Wu Di's successor increasingly came under the influence of the family of the empress. In 9 CE, the

Hans were even temporarily deposed by the nephew of an empress until in 25 CE a distant relative of the Hans, Liu Hsiu, restored the dynasty as Emperor Guang Wu Di. He moved his capital from Xi'an to Luoyang in the east, and his dynasty is therefore called the "Eastern Han" in contrast to the former "Western Han." The empire was stabilized—and even grew— into the first century. However the empress clan began to regain its influence, while palace intrigues were

9 Burial mound of emperor Han Wu Ti, first century BCE

aggravated by the intervention of the eunuchs. The ❼ generals formed a third power factor so that the epoch became known as that of the Three Kingdoms. In 184, the religiously motivated revolt of the Yellow Turbans erupted. The generals involved in crushing the revolt gained a level of autonomy, but then grew in their ambitions and ended up fighting each other in a civil war. In 220, the last Han emperor was forced to abdicate. From that time until the end of the sixth century, China remained divided into many competing kingdoms.

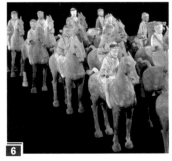

6 Horses and riders, terra-cotta figures, second–first century BCE

8 Statue of Confucius in his commemoration temple in Chu Fu

The Invention of Paper

One of the most important developments of mankind—the invention of paper—was made in China during the Han period. Plant fibers were worked into a mash through soaking in water, boiling, and pulping. The mash was spread into flat forms, and it settled as a thin, cohesive layer. In the 13th century, paper came to Europe by way of Arabia.

Paper manufacture in China, ink drawing, 18th century

10 A Buddhist shrine on the Silk Road in western China

11 Depiction of model sons, varnish painting on a woven basket, Han period

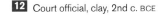

12 Court official, clay, 2nd c. BCE

THE FIRST KINGDOMS IN NORTH AND NORTHEAST AFRICA CA. 1000 BCE–8TH CENTURY CE

More or less on the periphery of the ancient Mediterranean world, the kingdoms of the ❶ Berbers, Nubians, and Ethiopians developed in north and northeast Africa as early as 1000 BCE. Despite their geographically marginal position, these states and peoples played a significant role in the history of the Egyptians, Carthaginians, and Romans. Intensive trade relations led to a lively cultural exchange. These areas also came into contact with Christianity, where, primarily in Ethiopia, it has maintained a form of its own since ancient times.

A fortified Berber village called Ksour, and a citadel, in Tansikht, Morocco

North Africa

While the Phoenicians and the Greeks settled on the coast, the hinterland of North Africa remained in the hands of the Berbers.

North Africa has been inhabited since early times by the Berber peoples, who were partly settled and partly ❹ nomadic. The ❺ Libyans in the east began invading Egypt on a massive scale during the 13th century BCE, but some were also employed by Egypt as mercenaries. Eventually, in the early tenth century, several Egyptian pharaohs were Libyan.

From the ninth century, Phoenician colonies, and in the seventh century ❻ Greek colonies, developed on the North African coasts and would later come under the rule of either Carthage or Egypt. The ❷ Numidians, who were allies of Rome, used the fall of Carthage in the Punic Wars to found a kingdom in present-day Algeria and Tunisia. When battles of succession broke out there in 118 BCE, ❸ King Jugurtha bought the support of Roman senators and so provoked a bribery scandal in Rome. In 112 he resorted to violence and ordered a massacre of his opponents, whereupon Rome felt forced to intervene. The Jugurthine Wars ended in 105 BCE, and the king was executed the following year. But it wasn't until 46 BCE that Julius Caesar deposed the last of the Numidian kings, who had supported Pompey in the civil war. Another ally of Rome, Mauretania profited from Numidia's fall following this event.

After the ruling dynasty had died out there in 25 BCE, Emperor Augustus installed the Numidian Prince Juba II as king. Mauretania remained independent until 40 CE when Caligula had King Ptolemy, a grandson of Antony and Cleopatra, killed.

Under Roman rule, North Africa flourished and became rich through its agriculture and trans-Saharan trade, particularly under Emperor Septimius Severus, who originated from the area and had many of the cities magnificently improved. Christianity also spread early through this area. In Hippo Regius (today's northeastern Algeria), the great church father Augustine acted as bishop and must have seen firsthand the invasion of the Vandals around 430. In the seventh century, Muslim Arabs conquered North Africa and revitalized the region.

Roman and Numidian riders going into battle, copper engraving, 18th century

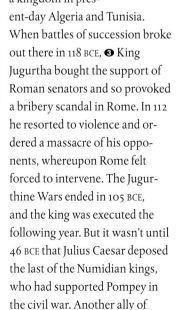

❸ King Jugurtha of Numidia, coin, ca. 110 BCE

Farmers herding cattle, rock painting, Sahara, second c. BCE

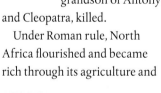

A Libyan and a Syrian are captured by Pharaoh Ramses II, relief, twelfth century BCE

Temple of Zeus in Cyrene, Libya, sixth century BCE

Northeast Africa

From the beginning, Nubia was under the strong influence of Egypt. The roots of the Kingdom of Aksum in Ethiopia lay, however, in local legend.

7 Nubians pay tribute to Pharaoh Tutankhamun, wall painting, Thebes, ca. 1340 BCE

8 Colonnade of the Kushite Pharaoh Taharka in the Amun Temple of Karnak, Eastern Thebes, seventh c. BCE

Early on, the Egyptian pharaohs began to undertake expeditions south into Nubia (present-day Sudan), which was rich in gold. It was **7** annexed in the 15th century BCE as the vice-kingdom Kush (or Cush) and colonized. Kush regained its independence in 1070 BCE and was ruled by native princes, who initially resided in Napata. The Kushites used the internal collapse of Egypt in the eighth and seventh centuries BCE to extend their **8** rule over Egypt, where they reigned as the 25th dynasty. The intensive contact resulted in the Nubian culture becoming strongly influenced by the **9** Egyptian culture. The Kushites built pyramid-shaped temples and burial complexes after the Egyptian model and

used the title of pharaoh, demonstrating the extent of this influence. About 530 BCE the capital was moved from Napata further south to **10** Meroe, which became an important shipping hub for Nubian precious metals. In the fourth century CE, Christianity reached Egypt by way of Nubia, but by that time, the kingdom of the Kushites was already in decline. Small Christian kingdoms existed

9 Pharaoh Taharka kneels in front of the falcon god Hemen, seventh c. BCE

in Nubia, however, into the 1500s.

Ethiopians trace their ancestry back to Menelik, the legendary son of the biblical King Solomon

and the Queen of Sheba in today's Yemen. Menelik is believed to have brought the Ark of the Covenant to Ethiopia, and it is said to be, until this day, in the town of Aksum.

In the fourth century, King Ezana Meroe, who had inherited the throne when still a child, destroyed the capital of the Kushites and also established Christianity as the state religion. To protect the southern Arabian Christians, Aksum conquered Yemen in the sixth century, marking the kingdom's greatest territorial expansion. The spread of Islam in the surrounding countries beginning in the seventh century, as well as the loss of direct access to the ocean, eventually led to cultural and economic isolation. Aksum's importance diminished after the eighth century, while Ethiopia's political focus shifted to the south, where the protected highlands lie. As a holy city, however, **11** Aksum remained the coronation site of the Ethiopian emperors into the 19th century.

The Ethiopian Church

The Ethiopian Church dates back to the missionary work of the Alexandrian brothers Frumentius and Aedesius in the early fourth century. Their opinions conflicted with those of the Catholic Church, particularly on the issue of Christology and on the biblical canon. The head of the church was the Coptic patriarch of Alexandria until 1959, after which the Ethiopian Church installed its own patriarch in Addis Ababa.

Passion scenes in a Coptic church in Ethiopia, mural, 18th century

10 Pyramids of Meroe, lithograph, ca. 1800

11 Church in Aksum, copper engraving, 19th century

40 CE | Murder of King Ptolemy of Mauretania · · · · · · · · · · · **from the 4th century CE** | Christianity reaches Ethiopia and Egypt

4th century CE | Decline of the Kushite Empire · · · · · · · · · · · **from the 7th century** | Spread of Islam in Ethiopia

Glossary

animal husbandry The agricultural science involving the breeding and rearing of farm animals.

antiquity Ancient history, especially during the ancient Greek and Roman civilizations.

capricious Describing someone or something that's prone to sudden changes.

Christianity The religion based on the teachings of Jesus Christ.

cuneiform A writing system of Southwest Asia involving wedge-shaped impressions made in soft clay.

Fertile Crescent The area in Southwest Asia reaching from present-day Israel to the Persian Gulf where the ancient Babylonian, Sumerian, Assyrian, Phoenician, and Hebrew civilizations flourished.

Hellenistic Relating to ancient Greek civilization from the late 4th century BCE to the 1st century BCE.

hierarchy An organizational structure characterized by ranking members based on power or other attributes.

historiography The recording of history based on the study of source material.

ideology A system of beliefs, morals, and ideas that forms the basis of a societal plan.

Individualism The focus on the pursuit of the individual's, rather than the group's, interests.

metropolis A large, complex, and thriving city.

migration The journey of a population from one region to another, often for political or socioeconomic reasons.

millennium A period of 1,000 years.

monarch An absolute ruler, usually a king or queen.

nomad A member of a group of people characterized by transience.

Paleolithic Referring to the early part of the Stone Age from 750,000 to 15,000 years ago.

pharaoh A ruler of ancient Egypt.

plebeian An ordinary citizen, or commoner (as opposed to the patricians), in ancient Rome.

polity A state, society, or institution that is in itself a political entity.

prehistory The time before events were first recorded for historical record.

rationalism The belief in the superiority of reason and that it should influence action.

Spartan Somebody who came from ancient Sparta, a civilization marked by stern discipline, frugality, simplicity, and courage.

syllabary A set of characters in which each character represents a single syllable.

Zionism A movement that sought to establish a Jewish nation in Palestine.

For More Information

The British Museum
Ancient China
38 Russell Square
London, WC1B 3QQ
+44 (0)20 7323 8000/8299
Web site: http://www.ancientchina.co.uk
The British museum is one of the most respected museums in the world, and its Ancient China exhibit features Chinese history, artifacts, and writings.

Brooklyn Museum
Egyptian, Classical, and Ancient Middle Eastern Art
200 Eastern Parkway
Brooklyn, NY 11238-6052
(718) 638-5000
Web site: http://www.brooklynmuseum.org/collections/egyptian_classical_middle_eastern/
The Brooklyn Museum's collection of ancient Egyptian art is one of the largest in the United States. The museum's Web site offers information about many artifacts and archaeological digs undertaken by the curatorial staff.

Carnegie Museum of Natural History
4400 Forbes Avenue
Pittsburgh, PA 15213
(412) 622-3131
Web site: http://www.carnegiemnh.org/exhibits/egypt/
This museum's Walton Hall of Ancient Egypt includes rich examples of Egyptian culture and life.

China Institute
125 East 65th Street
New York, NY 10065
(212) 744-8181
Web site: http://www.chinainstitute.org
Founded in 1926, the China Institute educates visitors about the art, history, and culture of China.

The Perseus Digital Library
Tufts University
Medford, MA 02155
Web site: http://www.perseus.tufts.edu
This digital library provides information on the humanities and offers collections on history, literature, and culture of the Greco-Roman world.

Royal Ontario Museum
100 Queen's Park
Toronto, ON M5S 2C6
(416) 586-8000
Web site: http://www.rom.on.ca/schools/egypt/learn/
The Web site of this Canadian museum offers information about mummification, hieroglyphics, geography, religion, life, and culture in ancient Egypt.

WEB SITES

Due to the changing nature of Internet links, Rosen Publishing has developed an online list of Web sites related to the subject of this book. This site is updated regularly. Please use this link to access the list:

http://www.rosenlinks.com/wtoh/prehis

For Further Reading

Bard, K. *Introduction to the Archaeology of Ancient Egypt.* Malden, MA: Blackwell, 2007.

Barringer, J. M. *Art, Myth, and Ritual in Classical Greece.* Cambridge, England: Cambridge University Press, 2008.

Brewer, D., and E. Teeter. *Egypt and the Egyptians.* Cambridge, England: Cambridge University Press, 2007.

Erskine, A., ed. *A Companion to the Hellenistic World.* Oxford, England: Blackwell, 2005.

Fletcher, J. *The Egyptian Book of Living and Dying.* London, England: Duncan Baird Publishers, 2009.

Hall, J. M. *A History of the Archaic Greek World ca. 1200-479 BC.* Oxford, England: Oxford University Press, 2007.

Hill, M., ed. *Gifts for the Gods: Images from Egyptian Temples.* New Haven, CT: Yale University Press, 2007.

Lehner, M. *The Complete Pyramids.* London, England: Thames and Hudson, 2008.

Morales, H. *Classical Myth: A Very Short Introduction.* Oxford, England: Oxford University Press, 2007.

Morris, I., and B. B. Powell. *The Greeks: History, Culture, and Society.* Upper Saddle River, NJ: Pearson Prentice Hall, 2005.

Ogden, D., ed. *A Companion to Greek Religion.* Oxford, England: Blackwell, 2007.

Osborne, R. *Athens and Athenian Democracy.* Cambridge, England: Cambridge University Press, 2010.

Osborne, R. *Greece in the Making 1200–479 BC.* 2nd ed. London, England, and New York, NY: Routledge, 2008.

Raaflaub, K. A., and H. van Wees, eds. *A Companion to Archaic Greece.* Oxford, England: Wiley-Blackwell, 2007.

Ray, J. D. *The Rosetta Stone and the Rebirth of Ancient Egypt.* Cambridge, MA: Harvard University Press, 2007.

Reeves, N., and R. Wilkinson. *The Complete Valley of the Kings: Tombs and Treasures of Egypt's Greatest Pharaohs.* London, England: Thames and Hudson, 2008.

Romer, J. *The Great Pyramid: Ancient Egypt Revisited.* Cambridge, England: Cambridge University Press, 2007.

Samons, L. J., II, ed. *The Cambridge Companion to the Age of Pericles.* Cambridge, England: Cambridge University Press, 2007.

Shapiro, H. A., ed. *The Cambridge Companion to Archaic Greece.* Cambridge, England: Cambridge University Press, 2007.

Shaw, I., and P. Nicholson. *The Princeton Dictionary of Ancient Egypt.* Princeton, NJ: Princeton University Press, 2008.

Stewart, A. *Classical Art and the Birth of Western Art.* Cambridge, England: Cambridge University Press, 2008.

Wilkinson, T., ed. *The Egyptian World.* London, England: Routledge, 2007.

Wilkinson, T. *Lives of the Ancient Egyptians.* London, England: Thames and Hudson, 2007.

Index

A

All images from akg-images Berlin/London/Paris and from dpa Deutsche Presse Agentur, Hamburg. For detailed copyright information, please see *The Contemporary World: From 1945 to the 21st Century*.

The publishers would like to express their special gratitude to the team at akg-images Berlin/London/Paris who have made their incredible picture archive accessible and thus the extraordinary illustrations of this book possible.